POSITIVE SEXUALITY

This book focuses on an emerging, multidisciplinary, positive sexuality framework that guides sexuality research, education, and practice.

Using this positive sexuality framework, this book will provide helping professionals and others with current research and information on topics and populations that are often missed or misrepresented, including but not limited to: lesbian, gay, bisexual, asexual, and other orientations; transgender, nonbinary, and other non-cisgender identities; seniors; sex workers; racial minorities; and other marginalized peoples. This framework, based on the social and behavioral sciences, can be used in tandem with other theoretical frameworks, modalities, and methodologies to better support a growing, multifaceted, and unique human population. Chapters are authored by topic experts and utilize the most recent scholarship pertaining to positive sexuality. Readers will come to understand diverse sexuality more completely and inextricably linked to other parts of one's identity and learn to address diverse sexual topics and issues more openly and with a spirit of compassion and human connectedness.

This edited volume is a must-read for sexuality researchers, clinicians, helping professionals, policymakers, and students from diverse educational backgrounds who are interested in human sexuality.

Emily E. Prior, **M.A.** (she/her) is the Founder and Executive Director for the Center for Positive Sexuality. She is a queer femme, an interdisciplinary social scientist, and adjunct professor.

D J Williams, **Ph.D.**, is a professor at Idaho State University and a Research Affiliate and Executive Board Member for the Center for Positive Sexuality. His work is known worldwide and focuses primarily on sex as leisure experience and also violent crime as leisure.

POSITIVE SEXUALITY

A Promising Future for Sex Research, Education, and Practice

Edited by Emily E. Prior and D J Williams

Routledge
Taylor & Francis Group

NEW YORK AND LONDON

Designed cover image: MUHAMMAD ASIM © Getty Images

First published 2025
by Routledge
605 Third Avenue, New York, NY 10158

and by Routledge
4 Park Square, Milton Park, Abingdon, Oxon, OX14 4RN

Routledge is an imprint of the Taylor & Francis Group, an informa business

ISBN: 978-1-032-63179-0 (hbk)
ISBN: 978-1-032-63132-5 (pbk)
ISBN: 978-1-032-63182-0 (ebk)

DOI: 10.4324/9781032631820

Typeset in Joanna
by Apex CoVantage, LLC

This collection is dedicated to the many people across the globe who, in whatever capacity, continue to promote and support a positive sexuality approach to research, education, and practice. Indeed, many people's lives are better because of such efforts. Gratitude is particularly extended to each of the many volunteers – past, present, and future – who willingly contribute their time, energy, and talents to the Center for Positive Sexuality.

CONTENTS

PREFACE

This collection includes cutting-edge scholarship on diverse topics that clearly reflect a stance of sex-positivity or positive sexuality, in stark contrast to the common, traditional assumptions of sex-negativity that are saturated in discourses of problems and risk. Consistent with a contemporary positive sexuality emphasis on welcoming diverse scholarship from multiple disciplines, epistemological orientations, and methodological and theoretical approaches, the book is comprised of original work by various experts, both scholars and practitioners, from multiple nations who are well-known and respected within their fields. Such a rich variety of sexuality topics – and the human diversity represented by these topics, ways of knowing, and authors' voices and social/cultural positionings thereby provides an excellent illustration of the breadth and importance of positive sexuality, and why such a positive sexuality is essential for future progress, across the world, in sexuality research, education, and practice.

This book is an essential read for any student, educator, practitioner, or researcher with an interest or training needs pertaining to sexuality, gender, relationships, human behavior, cultural diversity, and identity.

Emily E. Prior (she/her) is a Sociology and Psychology Professor and researcher in Los Angeles, as well as the founder and Executive Director of the Center for Positive Sexuality. Her work primarily focuses on the intersection of marginalized identities and social norms.

D J Williams is a Professor of Sociology, Social Work, and Criminology at Idaho State University. He is also a current Executive Board Member and former Director of Research at the Center for Positive Sexuality in Los Angeles.

ACKNOWLEDGMENTS

Our positive sexuality journey together began a decade-and-a-half ago, when we discovered that we were each engaged in alternative sexuality research. Very quickly, a lasting personal and professional relationship developed, which has continued to the present day. We have each been fortunate to have been mentored by some outstanding scholars, including the late Drs. James and Veronica Elias (Emily) and Drs. Billy Strean and Gordon Walker (D J). We continue to enjoy warm, productive collaborations with our friends at The Alternative Sexualities Health Research Alliance (TASHRA), the Community-Academic Consortium for Research on Alternative Sexualities (CARAS), and the National Coalition for Sexual Freedom (NCSF). In all of our various endeavors, we appreciate the love and support we receive from our families and friends. Of course, we are especially grateful to the chapter authors herein. Their diligent work is significant in lessening the grip of sex-negativity, with its fears and injustices, while moving positive sexuality forward.

INTRODUCTION

Toward Solutions: The Transition from
Sex-Negativity to Positive Sexuality

D J Williams and Emily E. Prior

In recent years, there has been an explosion in the academic usage of
the terms, *positive sexuality*, and especially *sex-positive* and *sex-positivity*. While
these terms may or may not be interchangeable, depending on the user
(we'll get to this issue shortly), they appear to have common underlying assumptions that are in stark contrast from traditional Western
approaches to sexuality. Sex is normal and can be rather interesting, like
many topics, to explore; and it's perfectly okay, perhaps even healthy, to
openly discuss it.

We illustrate the above point by sharing a favorite class activity at the
beginning of the semester for our university students in human sexuality
courses. For this activity, we write a list of words on the board, vertically,
such as "brunch," "tacos," "meatloaf," "quinoa," "bananas," "beet salad,"
etc. We divide the class into small groups, and each student in the group
picks a word and, one by one, uses their selected word in a sentence.
Very easy stuff. Sometimes students start to get creative and also incorporate prior words in their sentences, too. Next, we add another list to

DOI: 10.4324/9781032631820-1

the board, such as "mountains," "prairie," "North Sea," "high street," and so on, and each student selects a word and shares it in a new sentence as they had done before. Finally, we add a third list with new words, such as "threesome," "dildo," "nipple clamps," "vibrator," "butt plug," and so on. Predictably, there is often a prolonged hesitance, along with visible changes in students' facial reactions, to engage with the words in the third list. Students quickly realize, experientially, that there are powerful, unwritten rules regarding what sorts of things are culturally acceptable to talk about publicly, and sex is not one of them.

Commonplace of Sex-Negativity

The most common and prevalent perspectives of sex and sexuality come from a deficit approach that focuses exclusively on problems. Most U.S. sex education focuses on what not to do, how to avoid pregnancy and sexually transmitted infections, and the negative health and social consequences that occur if premarital sexual interests, or behaviors that are not widely accepted, are pursued (Santelli, et al., 2006; Shapiro & Brown, 2018). The fact that much sex education is also not inclusive, only focused on heteronormative, monogamous, sex after marriage, and with those within one's same socio-economic, racial, and religious groups also reflects a sex-negative perspective. From a medical/health perspective we see the historical prevalence of a deficit model (De Block & Adriaens, 2013), wherein the focus is primarily on preventing or curing injury and disease in young heterosexuals, rather than nurturing sexual wellbeing and pleasure across the life cycle, supporting LGBTQIA+ individuals, and accepting a wide range of diverse relationship styles. As we will see in some of the upcoming chapters, the lack of quality sex education may begin early in middle or high school; however, even professionals in medicine, social work, and other helping professions are offered little if any supportive and comprehensive education on sexuality more broadly, much less from a positive sexuality perspective.

Sex-negativity is hardly contained to sex education, or the lack thereof. We can see an overwhelming amount of sex-negativity being supported through U.S. and worldwide legislation against LGBTQIA+ individuals and communities, educators, physicians, and others (American Civil Liberties Union, 2024). These laws promote homophobia and antagonism, and do not support the health, safety, or wellbeing of those who are not cisgender and/or heteronormative. Legislation that specifically prevents discussions, healthcare, and education for and about specific groups of people is not humanizing and does not promote peacemaking. This level of sex-negativity only serves to further marginalize individuals and groups already at higher risk for violence and suicide (Burks, et al., 2018; Mongelli, et al., 2019)

These societal boundaries around sexuality contribute to a lack of education and support within the home and among peers and co-workers. LGBTQIA+ individuals are more likely to face discrimination within their own families (Parker, et al., 2018), at work (Levy & Levy, 2017), and in communities than those who are cisgender and heterosexual. Such negativity is further extended to people who may also be kinky and/or practice forms of consensual nonmonogamy.

Even individuals who may be cisgender and heteronormative are not excluded from sex-negative pressures, as we recognize the glaring lack of support for women's sexual health, especially for women of color, people who are disabled, and senior citizens. It seems that almost all people are harmed in some way by sex-negativity, and yet, historically, there has been very little focus on how this can be ameliorated.

The Emergence of "Sex-Positive" Thinking

The psychiatrist Wilhelm Reich is often credited for initially contrasting sex-positive societies from sex-negative ones, while Vern Bullough (1976) further expanded research on this topic. While anthropologists for quite some time had become well-aware of the extensive variation in sexual norms across cultures (i.e., Hayes & Carpenter, 2012; Popovic, 2006), it has taken much longer for more "medicalized" professions, such as psychology, counseling, and social work, to begin to recognize and subsequently challenge longstanding sex-negative assumptions that remain embedded to this day in both research and practice applications (De Block & Adriaens, 2013; Hammack et al., 2013).

Only in recent years have these professions begun to challenge seriously underlying sex-negativity. For example, it was less than two decades ago that psychologists began focusing extensive research on the potential health benefits of good sex (Diamond & Huebner, 2012); physicians and healthcare providers (at least in the U.S.) were advised to take a more sex-positive approach to patient care (Satcher et al., 2015); and a sex-positive approach in social work could help resolve a number of contemporary social issues (Williams et al., 2016). An impressive array of scholarship more recently has led to the recognition that a positive approach to sexuality is inextricably linked to sexual health, and that sexual health is an important aspect of overall health and wellbeing (Williams & Thomas, 2023; World Health Organization, 2024). Despite our current progress, the deep roots of sex-negativity are difficult to extricate. Thus, ignorance and misunderstanding, hesitance, and sometimes distrust and outright political hostility remain strong, even in academic and professional contexts.

"Sex-Positive" or "Positive Sexuality?"

The terms "sex-positive" and "positive sexuality" are often used interchangeably, including by contributing authors within this collection. While this may be generally okay, there may be some technical semantic differences in what each means, which draws us to prefer positive sexuality. "Sex-positive" was used first in research as early as 2000 (see Glickman, 2000), although one can see evidence of a sex-positive movement as far back as the Gay and Women's Rights movements of the 1960s and 1970s, and likely even earlier. Still, this term potentially can imply to some folks the promotion of sex and sexual activity (not that either is bad!), and thus might not fully support those who are not interested in, or capable of, sexual activity. As a term, sex-positive potentially, then, could be unintentionally marginalizing or restrictive in its use and conceptualization.

Specifically, positive sexuality as a term is offered to more broadly encompass a myriad of sexual identities, expressions, activities, and behaviors, and without focusing on whether or not an individual is interested in being directly sexually active. Positive sexuality, at least as we envision, opens a conversation about what this could mean on multiple levels, including for individuals, families, social groups, communities and organizations, and perhaps globally.

Recently, we conducted a brief exercise at an international sexuality conference, asking audience members to use their handheld devices to log into an interactive presentation where they could provide feedback on various questions about sexuality. Participation was anonymous and attendees could respond as frequently as they liked in the time allotted (just a few minutes for each question). The results were presented in real-time as the audience watched a word cloud develop with each response, providing an immediate visualization of what was important to them about the subject matter in question. In a few moments, the audience at the conference saw dozens of responses to questions asking them to define consent, communication, caring, and caution – all pillars of positive sexuality and healthy relationships.

These informal results found that the following terms are frequently used around healthy sexual interactions: *agreement, understanding, exchange, listening, empathy, safety, patience,* and *awareness*. Through this exercise we can see that core concepts of positive sexuality, particularly around interaction, are far more expansive than simply having "good" sex. Positive sexuality supports personal and social awareness, respect, open and honest communication, empathy for oneself and others, safety, support, and similar social values.

The Positive Sexuality Framework

Although there are some general commonalities regarding how individuals conceptualize sex-positivity and/or positive sexuality, we recognized years ago the need to create a more specific structure so that components of these terms can more readily be operationalized. We particularly focused on positive sexuality, given that scholarship increasingly recognized that sexuality is complex (and unique to each individual) and includes curiosities, interests, fantasies, preferences, behaviors, practices, identities, and communities (see van Anders, 2015; Williams & Thomas, 2023; World Health Organization, 2024). Furthermore, sexuality studies (sexology) is multidisciplinary, thus positive sexuality, as a term is similarly aligned as a noun, whereas sex-positive is usually an adjective.

By creating a basic framework of positive sexuality (Williams et al., 2015b, 2016, 2020), it was possible to incorporate essential features (and content) of existing relevant core disciplines, utilize new scholarship pertaining to sexuality directly, while also promoting a salient general sex-positive (as conceived by many) attitude. The fruit of our efforts was a broad framework, which includes eight interrelated dimensions, that happens to be, simultaneously, both old and new. We think this unique blend is a significant strength. Social scientists, helping professionals, community members, and students can quickly notice multiple dimensions that are very familiar and quite commonplace in practice (see also Chapter 2 by Allen and Williams, this volume), yet also gain new insights as to how, in contrast to sex-negativity, a new, much more holistic, way of approaching sexuality, can be conceived and implemented.

The dimensions of the positive sexuality framework were identified by carefully reviewing the social and behavioral sciences and the various helping professions, then distilling common, essential attributes. Thus, these dimensions can be found across diverse areas of research and practice. Along with then situating essential attributes in a sexuality context, we also summarized sexuality scholarship (multidisciplinary), specifically, for a specific dimension (individual sexuality is unique and multi-faceted). That being said, the eight dimensions of positive sexuality (for us) are:

1) **The "positive" refers to strengths, wellbeing and happiness.** In other words, similar to the approach of "positive" psychology, where psychologists are interested in what's happening when people are successful, happy, and thriving, positive sexuality focuses on how people can be successful, healthy and happy in their particular sexuality. Furthermore, people have specific strengths that potentially can contribute to sexual health and wellness, and they often have strengths in their sexualities that are transferrable to other areas of their lives.

2) **Individual sexuality is unique and multifaceted.** Rather than conceptualizing broad generalizations of sexual orientations, we recognize that there are as many sexual identities as there are people. Particulars matter. Each person, including their sexuality, is unique.

3) **Positive sexuality embraces multiple ways of knowing.** Sexuality knowledge has been generated from multiple disciplines, epistemologies, methodologies, methods, and orientations. A variety of both science-based approaches and arts-based methods are now utilized

across a wide-range of disciplines. While underlying assumptions may vary extensively (thus standards differ) each process of knowledge production has limitations but potentially can contribute to understanding, more fully, sexuality as a whole.

4) **Positive sexuality reflects professional ethics**. Most professions have codified standards that dictate professional conduct. These standards reflect common ethical values, such as self-determination, avoiding causing harm, integrity, and competence. Positive sexuality should prioritize and follow such standards regarding matters of sexuality.

5) **Positive sexuality promotes open, honest, communication**. Sex-negativity is characterized by the lack of open, honest communication. Sexual topics, unfortunately, are often taboo. The lack of open, honest communication directly impacts the quality of sex education and sexual and relationship satisfaction. A number of serious sexual problems might be avoided if open, honest communication could occur safely.

6) **Positive sexuality is humanizing.** Sex-negativity promotes stigmatization, marginalization, and social injustice. In worst cases, people can be demonized. Dehumanization, in any form, is a problem. Even when people make rather serious mistakes, dehumanization only contributes to more problems.

7) **Positive sexuality encourages peacemaking.** The peacemaking dimension is perhaps the most difficult for many to implement. Its inclusion is borrowed from peace studies, restorative justice, and tenets of critical criminology, which themselves are grounded in centuries of wisdom from indigenous cultures. At issue is how people can come together, to promote responsibility and accountability, so that all people can best heal. Peacemaking is in stark contrast with much of modern culture, wherein power and influence are largely hierarchical, some people win while others lose, and voices (and needs) of many are excluded. Even much of the language of modern culture, especially in the U.S., reflects a war-making stance, such as the war on drugs or fighting for sexual rights (or any number of causes). Peacemaking recognizes that an underlying cultural fighting mentality is a natural response to our fears, ignorance, and uncertainties, thus compassion and support are necessary.

8) Positive sexuality is applicable across all levels of social structure. Positive sexuality is applicable to individuals, couples and partnerships, families, friendships, organizations, and communities. It applies to people of all ages and demographic backgrounds; to lay people and professionals, academics and practitioners. While particular needs and issues often vary from person to person, group to group, and place to place; the framework has sufficient flexibility to accommodate substantial variation. People impact each other, directly or indirectly, at multiple levels, and this recognition is an important component of positive sexuality, overall.

Since the positive sexuality framework was introduced, it has been cited over 170 times at the time of this writing and is being utilized, in both research and practice, for diverse contexts and populations. Indeed, positive sexuality and sex-positive approaches are being used to guide research and/or practice for people living with disabilities (i.e., Benoit et al., 2022; Bonder et al., 2021; Parchomiuk, 2022); promoting healing for female survivors of sexual and intimate partner violence (i.e., Bagwell-Gray, 2019; Christensen & Hoover, 2015); educating youth, including young children, about sexuality at home and schools (i.e., Christensen et al., 2017; Helmich, 2009; Koepsel, 2016; Roach, 2024); preventing and resolving sexual violence issues (i.e., Williams, et al., 2015a; Wodda & Panfil, 2021a, 2021b); and many more issues that impact health and life satisfaction for diverse people. It is clear that positive sexuality is starting to gain significant momentum as we move into a new era of approaching human sexuality and the various social issues surrounding it.

Chapter Contributions

This unique collection includes a range of original, thoughtful essays on a variety of key topics that are particularly important regarding the current socio-cultural transition away from sex-negativity and into positive sexuality. Across research, practice, and education, a positive sexuality stance generally promotes health and wellbeing; supports personal responsibility and self-determination; values social justice and equality; requires open communication and knowledge development; acknowledges all people and welcomes all voices; recognizes peoples' fears and pain; promotes compassion and healing; and applies within multiple social levels and contexts. The chapters herein strongly reflect these themes and are authored by topic experts, including both scholars and practitioners. Chapters 1–5 address positive sexuality issues in specific fields, while Chapters 6–10 address specific sexuality topics.

We begin with something that seems quite basic on the surface and yet is at the core of everything we do – language and communication. Without a clear means of interacting with one another, we cannot hope to understand the importance of critical thinking and analysis. Chambers (2025) insightfully discusses how although both queer linguistics and critical discourse analysis methods are often used in the field of sociolinguistics, a clear connection to positive sexuality has not yet occurred. Chambers then explains how by directly connecting sociolinguistics and positive sexuality, valuable new contributions can occur for each. Queering the approach, the first chapter provides a discussion of how positive sexuality and linguistics can assist one another while also challenging social norms. Chambers' chapter creatively highlights how synergistic relationships involving positive sexuality can naturally occur.

In Chapter 2, Allen and Williams (2025) summarize the curious and often contradictory approach that the social work profession has had, historically, in addressing sexuality. They point out that the social work profession, having strong roots in Christianity and psychology, remains sex-negative. Allen and Williams note, however, that despite the reluctance of contemporary social work to embrace positive sexuality, the positive sexuality framework actually has strong components of generalist social work practice built into it. Despite the glaring absence of required human sexuality training in current social work education, the profession is very capable, even if not yet realized, in operationalizing positive sexuality in research, education, and practice.

Continuing with the theme, the third chapter focuses on healthcare more broadly and the need for an expansion of how we define "healthy" and "normal." Recognizing that discussion of sexual and gender identities has become more complex and nuanced, Randall and Sprott (2025) emphasize the need of healthcare professionals to be more skilled at communicating and supporting their patients and clients. They note the historical medicalization of sexuality, while then discussing the transition from understanding health, and especially sexual health, as dysfunction to a more holistic conceptualization. Randall and Sprott skillfully critique and expand notions of "normal" and "healthy" to arrive at a much more diverse and inclusive perspective of wellness. They wrap up their chapter by discussing how healthcare providers can talk effectively with patients/ clients by using a positive sexuality approach with specific provider communication tools, including PLISSIT.

The sex-positive Intuitive Sexuality Model is presented by Lewis (2025) in Chapter 4. Lewis, a sex-therapist, draws from recent scholarship to contrast "compulsive sexual behavior" from "sex addiction." Lewis then explains how the Intuitive Sexuality Model to treat compulsive sexual behavior was developed in response to both recent empirical research and limitations in other models to treat compulsive sexual behavior. Throughout the chapter, Lewis shows how a positive sexuality approach was integrated to promote client engagement, communication, and successful outcome. Rather than blaming and shaming, this model is supportive and provides practitioners and clients with a better chance of reaching their goals.

Moving on from the healthcare fields, the positive sexuality model is used in Chapter 5 as a basis for supportive and innovative criminology to reconstruct social policies and the criminal justice system. Wodda and Panfil (2025) discuss their sex-positive criminology model, which integrates positive sexuality, queer, feminist, and critical perspectives to theorize sexuality within the crimino-legal complex. They highlight several essentials of sex-positive criminology, including bodily autonomy and consent, quality sex education as a human right, having access to health/medical resources, and a harm reduction perspective. Wodda and Panfil then focus on the Marea Verde/The Green Wave in Latin America as a powerful example of how social movements can generate powerful momentum across geographic locations, which ultimately bring about policy changes that reduce injustice. Their chapter brilliantly illustrates the multiplied harms and injustices that accumulate from contemporary sex-negativity, while also offering a way out through positive sexuality and its complementary scholarship.

On a more light-hearted note, Chapter 6 examines "polygeezers," people over the age of 55 who have been practicing various forms of consensual nonmonogamy. Summarizing years of extensive research, Sheff and Labriola (2025) show how these seniors have used their skills to navigate aging, deal with social issues and stigma, and display resilience. Along with the common physical effects and social issues associated with aging, seniors in consensual non-monogamous relationships also face additional social issues and stigmas. Sheff and Labriola discuss these issues and offer sex-positive strategies for navigating them. They note that much more research in this area is needed, especially given the increasing numbers of people who are choosing to live in diverse relationship structures. The excellent work conducted by Sheff and Labriola is critical in supporting and promoting sex-positive education and training.

Chapter 7 takes us in a completely different direction, while still focusing on resilience and intersectionality. Using Photovoice, Capous-Desyllas, Loy, Ambartsumyan, and Chavez (2025) provide sex workers the opportunity to record and reflect on themselves and their lives. By applying this unique methodological approach, the authors include research participants throughout the research process, thus empowering them to create and interpret their own stories. People who are all too often marginalized and even sometimes criminalized are given space to explore and create, challenging stereotypes and providing a new, artistic, way of viewing sex workers and their particular occupation.

Also challenging stereotypes, Laureano, Kaufman, Thev, Tomás, and Young (2025) provide us with a fly-on-the-wall perspective during a conversation with these incredible sexuality educators as they discuss challenges faced in training, finding mentors, and with the not-always-as-inclusive-as-it-should-be application of positive sexuality. Their powerful narratives do not hold back and thereby provide an important critique of the state of professional sexuality education and the continued need for inclusion and representation within the field of sexology.

As we start to conclude the volume, Chapter 9 provides incredibly useful data and perspectives from a group that is often underrepresented and legitimized, 5th–12th graders. Using anonymous questions gathered over the years from middle and high school sex educators, Hughes (2025) analyzes students' questions primarily focused on BDSM and kink. Not only does this unique study demonstrate that pre-teens and teens are thinking about sex and sexuality, findings reveal that they have sexuality questions and concerns about much more than just heteronormative, penis-in-vagina sexual intercourse. Hughes' chapter continues to emphasize the need for educators to be fully prepared and ready to answer a myriad of student questions about sexuality.

Texting and social media have radically changed how people communicate about everything, including sex. In the final chapter, Wignall and McCormack (2025) discuss how technology, specifically texting and social media, are being used to help people define and negotiate safer safe needs and boundaries. While reminding us that communication around and about sexuality is historically, culturally, and sometimes geographically bound, people are attempting to engage in conversations about their sexual needs and desires using digital means. This study recognizes the need for everyone to have better access to accurate information about sexuality and sexual health in order for people to better and more clearly communicate their needs and desires.

Conclusion

Positive sexuality can be interpreted and utilized in many ways. Just as human beings and their sexualities are complex, multidimensional, and dynamic — our various methods for understanding are also fragmented, messy, and always incomplete. The rich diversity in voices, epistemologies, approaches, and methods together increases our overall understanding of what positive sexuality both is and may become. We hope that this text offers a glimpse into how the positive sexuality framework can be used across disciplines, methodologies, and subjects. And, we think that this is all, well, very positive!

References

Allen, P. D., & Williams, D J (2025). The crisis of sexuality training in social work: A need for positive sexuality. In E. E. Prior & D J Williams (Eds.), *Positive sexuality: A promising future for sex research, education, and practice*. Routledge.

American Civil Liberties Union (2024). Mapping attacks on LGBTQ rights in U.S. State Legislatures in 2024. https://www.aclu.org/legislative-attacks-on-lgbtq-rights-2024

Bagwell-Gray, M. E. (2019). Women's healing journey from intimate partner violence: Establishing positive sexuality. *Qualitative Health Research*, 29(6), 779–795.

Benoit, C., Mellor, A. & Premji, Z. (2022). Access to sexual rights for people living with disabilities: Assumptions, evidence, and policy outcomes. *Archives of Sexual Behavior*, 52(8), 3201–3255. https://doi.org/10.1007/s10508-022-02372-x

Bonder, R., Wincentak, J., Gan, C., Kingsnorth, S., Provvidenza, C. F., & MacPherson, A. C. (2021). "They assume you're not having sex": A qualitative exploration of how paediatric healthcare providers can have positive sexuality-related conversations with youth with disabilities. *Sexuality and Disability*, 39, 579–594.

Bullough, V. L. (1976). *Sexual variance in society and history*. University of Chicago Press.

Burks, A., Cramer, R., Henderson, C., Stroud, C., Crosby, J. & Graham, J. (2018). Frequency, nature, and correlates of hate crime victimization experiences in an urban sample of lesbian, gay, and bisexual community members. *Journal of Interpersonal Violence*, 33(3), 402–420. https://doi.org/10.1177/0886260515605298

Capous-Desyllas, M., Loy, V., Ambartsumyan, A., & Chavez, M. (2025). Sex work as a form of art: Using arts-based research to understand the profession. In E. E. Prior & D J Williams (Eds.), *Positive sexuality: A promising future for sex research, education, and practice*. Routledge.

Chambers, E. (2025). Positive sexuality and sociolinguistics: A conversation. In E. E. Prior & D J Williams (Eds.), *Positive sexuality: A promising future for sex research, education, and practice*. Routledge.

Christensen, M. C., & Hoover, S. M. (2015). Working with survivors of sexual violence from a sex-positive perspective. *Journal of Positive Sexuality*, 1, 31–36.

Christensen, M. C., Wright, R., & Dunn, J. (2017). "It's awkward stuff": Conversations about sexuality with young children. *Child and Family Clinical Social Work*, 22(2), 711–720.

De Block, A., & Adriaens, P. R. (2013). Pathologizing sexual deviance: A history. *Journal of Sex Research*, 50(3–4), 276–298. https://doi.org/10.1080/00224499.2012.738259

Diamond L. D., & Huebner, D. M. (2012). Is good sex good for you? Rethinking sexuality and health. *Social and Personality Psychology Compass*, 6(1), 54–69.

Glickman, C. (2000). The language of sex positivity. *Electronic Journal of Human Sexuality*, 3. http://ejhs.org/volume3/sexpositive.htm. Accessed May 22, 2024.

Hammack, P. L., Mayers, L., & Windell, E. P. (2013). Narrative, psychology and the politics of sexual identity in the United States: From "sickness" to "species" to "subject." *Psychology and Sexuality*, 4(3), 219–243.

Hayes, S., & Carpenter, B. (2012). Out of time: The moral temporality of sex, crime and taboo. *Critical Criminology*, 20(2), 141–152.

Helmich, J. (2009). What is comprehensive sex education? Going WAAAAAY beyond abstinence and condoms. *American Journal of Sexuality Education*, 4(1), 10–15.

Hughes, S. (2025). "Does it mean someone loves you if they call you Daddy?": Anonymous sex education questions about kink from 5th–12th grade students. In E. E. Prior & D J Williams (Eds.), *Positive sexuality: A promising future for sex research, education, and practice*. Routledge.

Koepsel, E. R. (2016). The power in pleasure: Practical implementation of pleasure in sex education classrooms. *American Journal of Sexuality Education*, 11(3), 205–265. https://doi.org/10.1080/15546128.2016.1209451

Laureano, B., kaufman, c., Thev, E., Tomás, L., & Young, S. (2025). Positivity sexuality as praxis: A collaborative and intergenerational discussion on the training and mentoring experiences of sexuality educators. In E. E. Prior & D J Williams (Eds.), *Positive sexuality: A promising future for sex research, education, and practice*. Routledge.

Levy, B. & Levy, D. (2017). When love meets hate: The relationship between state policies on gay and lesbian rights and hate crime incidence. *Social Science Research*, 61, 142–159. https://doi.org/10.1016/j.ssresearch.2016.06.008

Lewis, Y. A. (2025). Intuitive sexuality: A sex-positive model for understanding and treating compulsive sexual behavior. In E. E. Prior & D J Williams (Eds.), *Positive sexuality: A promising future for sex research, education, and practice*. Routledge.

Mongelli, F., Perrone, D., Balducci, J., Sacchetti, A., Ferrari, S., Mattei, G., & Galeazzi, G. (2019) Minority stress and mental health among LGBT populations: An update on the evidence. *Minerva Psichiatrica*, 60(1), 27–50. https://psycnet.apa.org/doi/10.23736/S0391-1772.18.01995-7

Parchomiuk, M. (2022). Sexuality of people with intellectual disabilities: A proposal to use the Positive Sexuality Model. *Sexuality and Culture*, 26(1), 418–448.

Parker, C., Hirsch, J., Philbin, M., & Parker, R. (2018). The urgent need for research and interventions to address family-based stigma and discrimination against lesbian, gay, bisexual, transgender, and queer youth. *Journal of Adolescent Health*, 63(4), 383–393. https://doi.org/10.1016/j.jadohealth.2018.05.018

Popovic, M. (2006). Psychosexual diversity as the best representation of human normality across cultures. *Sexual and Relationship Therapy*, 21(2), 171–186. https://doi.org/10.1080/14681990500358469

Randall, A., & Sprott, R. A. (2025). Sex-positivity and healthcare. In E. E. Prior & D J Williams (Eds.), *Positive sexuality: A promising future for sex research, education, and practice*. Routledge.

Roach, C. (2024). Teaching about good sex: Classroom reflections on a positive sexuality curriculum and the Good Sex Story. *Porn Studies*, 11(1), 12–17. https://doi.org/10.1080/23268743.2022.2139287

Santelli, J., Ott, M., Lyon, M., Rogers, J., Summers, D., & Schleifer, R. (2006). Abstinence and abstinence-only education: A review of U.S. policies and programs. *Journal of Adolescent Health*, 38(1), 72–81. https://doi.org/10.1016/j.jadohealth.2005.10.006

Satcher, D., Hook III, E. W., & Coleman, E. (2015). Sexual health in America: Improving patient care and public health. *Journal of the American Medical Association*, 314(8), 765–766. https://doi.org/10.1001/jama.2015.6831

Shapiro, S. & Brown, C. (2018). Sex education standards across the states. Report. May 9. *Center for American Progress*. Center for American Progress.

Sheff, E., & Labriola, K. (2025). Polyamorous elders: The "original gangsters" of sex-positivity. In E. E. Prior & D J Williams (Eds.), *Positive sexuality: A promising future for sex research, education, and practice*. Routledge.

van Anders, S. (2015). Beyond sexual orientation: Integrating gender/sex and diverse sexualities via Sexual Configurations Theory. *Archives of Sexual Behavior*, 44(5), 1177–1213. https://doi.org/10.1007/s10508-015-0490-8

Wignall, L. & McCormack, M. (2025). Communicating sex in digital spaces: From emojis to "What are you into?" In E. E. Prior & D J Williams (Eds.), *Positive sexuality: A promising future for sex research, education, and practice*. Routledge.

Williams, D J, Christensen, M. C., & Capous-Desyllas, M. (2016). Social work practice and sexuality: Applying a positive sexuality model to enhance diversity and resolve problems. *Families in Society*, 97(4), 287–294. https://doi.org/10.1606/1044-3894.2016.97.35

Williams, D J, Prior, E. E., & Vincent, J. (2020). Positive sexuality as a guide for leisure research and practice addressing sexual interests and behaviors. *Leisure Sciences, 42*(2–3), 275–288.

Williams, D J, & Thomas, J. N. (2023). Healthy sexuality. In H. S. Friedman & C. H. Markey (Eds.), *Encyclopedia of mental health* (3rd ed.). Academic Press.

Williams, D J, Thomas, J. N., & Prior, E. E. (2015a). Moving full-speed ahead in the wrong direction? A critical examination of U.S. sex offender policy from a positive sexuality perspective. *Critical Criminology, 23*, 277–294. https://doi.org/10.1007/s10612-015-9270-y

Williams, D J, Thomas, J. N., Prior, E. E., & Walters, W. (2015b). Introducing a multidisciplinary framework of positive sexuality. *Journal of Positive Sexuality, 1*, 6–11.

Wodda, A., & Panfil, V. R. (2021a). *Sex-positive criminology.* Routledge.

Wodda, A., & Panfil, V. R. (2021b). Sex-positive criminology: Possibilities for legal and social change. *Sociology Compass, 15*(11), e12929.

Wodda, A., & Panfil, V. R. (2025). "The term 'life' should be returned to us": Achieving a more just society through sex-positive criminology. In E. E. Prior & D J Williams (Eds.), *Positive sexuality: A promising future for sex research, education, and practice.* Routledge.

World Health Organization. (2024). *Sexual health.* https://www.who.int/health-topics/sexual-health#tab=tab_1

1

POSITIVE SEXUALITY AND SOCIOLINGUISTICS

A Conversation

Eric Chambers

Introduction

Positive sexuality,

> encapsulates notions of diversity, empowerment, and choice. Sex-negative perspectives tend to frame sexuality and sexual practices primarily as risky, difficult to manage, and perhaps adversarial; while variations of sex-positivity seem to acknowledge risks and concerns yet also emphasize the importance of sexual pleasure, freedom, and diversity.
>
> (Williams et al., 2015, p. 6)

A sex-negativity viewpoint assumes that certain sexualities are non-normative and therefore deviant and threatening – a standpoint that has permeated the history of sexuality as an object of study (Foucault, 1990). Any research that studies sexuality runs the risk of perpetuating sex-negative ideologies by taking for granted, or not challenging, beliefs and

DOI: 10.4324/9781032631820-2

values that continue to minoritize practitioners of some sexualities over others. Positive sexuality, on the other hand, focuses on the potential that one's sexuality can be a source of individual and sociopolitical power, freedom, and ultimately happiness and equity for all.

Williams et al. (2015) identify eight dimensions that comprise a positive sexuality framework, and that can be beneficial to researchers:

1. The term 'positive' focuses on the potential that one's sexuality has in developing strength, senses of well-being, and problem solving and resolution;
2. an individual's sexuality is unique and shaped by multiple factors on individual and social levels;
3. positive sexuality can be studied and experienced through multiple methodological and epistemological lenses;
4. positive sexuality supports professional ethical considerations, especially in terms of client self-expression;
5. positive sexuality promotes open and honest communication of one's needs and wants;
6. positive sexuality humanizes through avoiding language that objectifies and devalues people;
7. positive sexuality promotes conflict resolution through understanding, learning, and compassion;
8. positive sexuality can be enacted on micro-, mezzo-, and macro-social levels.

These tenets have informed much contemporary work done in mental health and therapy (e.g., Carlström & Andersson, 2019; Pitagora, 2017; Sprott et al., 2019) sexual health (Döring & Poeschl, 2020; Krüsi et al., 2018; Parchomiuk, 2022), sexual education (Christensen et al., 2017; Maes et al., 2023), social work (e.g., Williams et al., 2016), criminology (Williams, 2020), and numerous other disciplines. In 2015, the Center for Positive Sexuality, based in California, launched a peer-reviewed journal that focused on studies of positive sexuality, the *Journal of Positive Sexuality*, that focuses on the applications of positive sexuality within various fields.

One discipline that has not engaged directly with positive sexuality, however, is sociolinguistics – which is surprising, because many contemporary schools of thought within sociolinguistics share much in common with the above eight dimensions of positive sexuality. Disciplines such as Queer Linguistics and Critical Discourse Analysis share with positive sexuality a focus on critically engaging with dominant ideologies that Other and minoritize non-normative sexualities, and exploring how an individual's sexuality is informed on multiple levels by various ideologies, beliefs, and attitudes.

This chapter is therefore an attempt to start a direct conversation between sociolinguistics and positive sexuality, and to show what they can learn from each other. Sociolinguistics can give positive sexuality established frameworks that examines how language is used to reflect (or, in many cases, challenge) larger social ideologies and norms. Positive sexuality, in return, can give sociolinguistics a framework that moves beyond criticism, and suggests potential avenues towards action and greater equity for all.

This chapter is divided into two main parts. First, I will discuss two sub-disciplines within sociolinguistics that have as their goal the disruption of dominant ideologies: Queer Linguistics and Critical Discourse Analysis. I will give a brief overview of each and explore how their goals align with that of positive sexuality. Second, I will make an attempt to demonstrate what a union between sociolinguistics and positive sexuality might look like, by examining a corpus of texts that discuss whether or not people who identify as 'kinky' can also self-identify as queer. Exploring these texts in greater detail, I will look at how points of tension emerge between those who identify as kinky and those who identify as queer. Finally, I will use some of the insights gained in looking at those texts to make broader recommendations about how positive sexuality and sociolinguistics can work together meet the aims of positive sexuality.

Critical Discourse Analysis, Queer Linguistics, and Positive Sexuality

As a discipline, Critical Discourse Analysis (CDA) is best defined as a "form of linguistically-oriented, critical social research which is characterized by a deep interest in actual social issues and forms of inequality, such as racism, xenophobia, anti-Semitism, and sexism" (Esposito, 2023, 1–2).

CDA grew out of insights from the Frankfurt School, a group of theorists who understood such taken-for-granted foundations as 'truth' and 'knowledge' as both socially-constructed and able to be manipulated to meet the aims of dominant social groups. CDA analysts thus seek to uncover the roles that language plays in the construction and manipulation of these 'truths' and 'knowledges.'

CDA analysis begins from the starting point that *all* text, no matter how mundane or ordinary, reflect on some level ideologies of power. CDA explores how systems of text production serve to maintain or disrupt ideologies of who should have power within a society, and who shouldn't. All texts reflect the support, contestation, and/or resistance to these dominant ideologies.

In original conceptions of CDA (first formulated by Fairclough, 1992), texts are analyzed on three levels: a micro-level (an analysis of the text itself, including word choice, organization, and syntactic structures), a mid-level (how the medium of the text, and how it is presented and disseminated by others, contributes to how the text is meant to be interpreted), and a macro-level (how themes inherent within the text ties into larger ideologies of power). Taking a newspaper article about immigration as an example, a micro-level analysis would examine how the author of an article speaks about immigrants: if specific word choices, for example, are meant for the reader to evaluate the immigrants as 'good' or 'bad' through their actions or attitudes. A mid-level analysis would explore where the article is published (a liberal vs. conservative newspaper), and the appearance of the text itself (if the article is a news or opinion piece, which contributes to a reader's understanding of the article as 'fact' or not). A macro-level analysis would tie the specific claims made about immigrants within the article to larger ideologies that exist among readers about immigrants (whether we, as readers, should reinforce our stereotypes about immigrants because of the 'bad' things they're doing). For CDA analysts, looking at text simultaneously through these three levels provides a detailed understanding of how ideologies are created and maintained at each level, and how they can combine to provide avenues of sustaining or challenging those ideologies.

Fairclough's three-axis methodology has been expanded, in recent times, to include other methodologies, including social actor theories that analyze the role of subjects within a discourse (van Leeuwen, 2008), sociocognitive models that rely on the relationship between the mental and the spoken (van Dijk, 2008), and discourse-historical theories that advocate tracing histories and etymologies of words throughout a series of texts (Wodak & Meyer, 2016). In addition, many CDA analyses use tenets of Systemic Functional Grammar (Halliday & Matthiessen, 2004) to analyze relationships between power and resistance on a textual level.

Three important points about CDA are worth mentioning. First, Critical Discourse Analysis has been the subject of much criticism. Koller (2013) reminds us that discourses produced by marginalized groups are often under-represented in CDA, and there seems to be a disproportionate focus on texts created by individuals and social institutions that represent larger, hegemonic views of minority groups, although these texts are valuable for exposing ideologies that 'majority' groups have towards subordinate groups (and that have the potential to subjugate and disempower minority groups). This may be because, as Scott (1990) reminds us, many texts that are created and sustained by minority groups are often less available to the general public and to researchers: these 'hidden' transcripts are either more difficult to access or are more likely to be erased from general historical records (Bucholtz & Hall, 2004). Nevertheless, this bias in studying the texts of dominant groups has led critics to charge CDA with being *too* focused on exposing ideological difference, and not engaging enough with strategies for potential change (Breeze, 2022; Luke, 2002).

Second, CDA is not specific to linguistics. Although CDA does borrow much from linguistics, the primary object of study is the maintenance and resistance of power and dominance. In fact, many CDA analyses support an interdisciplinary approach that takes into account not only linguistic tools, but insights from other social science disciplines (such as sociology, anthropology, and psychology) to gain a fuller picture of the effects of power.

Third, unlike most social sciences that value objectivity and researcher distance, many CDA analysts espouse a specifically activist and political stance (Meyer, 2001; Martin, 2004; Chouliaraki & Fairclough, 2007). As Meyer (2001) states, CDA scholars "play an advocatory role for groups who suffer from social discrimination [and] endeavours to make explicit power relations which are frequently hidden" (p. 15). This 'explicitness' is built into the foundations of CDA analysis: the researchers who spend their time and energy unearthing power relations are necessarily being activists in their work, and should embrace their positions as such. This has even led some researchers (e.g., Hughes, 2018; Macgilchrist, 2011; Martin 2004) to specifically espouse what they term a 'positive discourse analysis that works to "amplify progressive discourses and better understand semiotic mechanisms of resistance and empowerment in order to increase their positive impact on society" (Hughes, 2018, p. 194).

Although not a direct offshoot of Critical Discourse Analysis, Queer Linguistics incorporates many of the same aims and paradigms as CDA. Queer Linguistics grew out of earlier sociolinguistic studies (Fishman, 1978; West & Zimmerman, 1987) that analyzed differences in the speech patterns of men and women. These earlier studies noticed quantitative differences in the ways men and women spoke around each other (women were more likely to use hedges such as "I think" when speaking to men, and men were more likely to interrupt women during periods of silence). Researchers tied these ways of speaking to larger sociocultural norms that posited men as dominant and women as submissive. In addition, in the 1980s researchers extended Judith Butler's (2006) conception of gender-as-performance to the realm of sexuality to claim that all forms of sexuality – including the cultural juggernaut known as heterosexuality – were also performances. Understanding that gendered and sexual performances were subject to the same essentialist and binary ways of thinking that placed one group (men, heterosexuals) in positions of dominance over another (women, non-heterosexuals), Queer Linguistics emerged to expose the ways in which binaries of sexuality are not only reproduced through language, but challenged and resisted.

As Queer Linguistics further developed, it extended its reach beyond sexuality categories: as Motschenbacher (2010) notes, within Queer Linguistics "all identity categories are problematic because they normatively regulate and exclude those who do not fully meet their normative requirements" (p. 10). This 'destabilization' of binaries has informed much work done on Queer Linguistics, whether it be through how speakers bypass linguistic requirements that control how adjectives and other parts of speech must agree in gender[1] with their nouns (Abbou, 2011; Knisely, 2020; Suwarno et al., 2021), how speakers innovate by creating non-gendered alternatives in both spoken and written language (Motschenbacher, 2014;

Scotto di Carlo, 2020), how race, class, and other markers of identity inter-act with discussions of sexuality (Bérubé, 2001; Brim, 2020; Valentine, 2003), and how transgender speakers use language to assert their own identities (Zimman, 2017b, 2017a; Zimman et al., 2014).

In perhaps a more extreme form of Queer Linguistics, Cameron & Kulick (2003) argue that underlying all linguistic discussions of sexuality is a deeper relationship between language and desire: "language *produces* the categories through which we organize our sexual desires, identities, and practices" (p. 19). Categories becomes linked to sexual identities and practices, in part, through their citationality: the ability to consistently associate a (linguistic) act with a specific desire or behavior (thus imbu-ing it with social meaning), and recognizing that the (linguistic) act can retain that meaning when transposed to other domains. An important object of study, then, becomes how speakers create those links, and use or challenge them to enact desire. Thus, a shoe fetishist who enacts desire towards a pair of high heels might do so by using a breathy voice to say the pick-up line "so baby, come here often?" thus using established cultural acts of desire in novel environments.

The above discussion highlights some of the tenets of CDA and Queer Linguistics. In many ways, the tenets are congruent with many of Williams et al.'s (2015) dimensions of positive sexuality. Positive sexuality, CDA, and Queer Linguistics both share a commitment in exposing language that objectifies and devalues people, and in promoting language use that both humanizes and encourages open and honest communication. Positive sex-uality, like CDA, welcomes multiple methodological and epistemological lenses within its fold, and explores the micro-, mezzo-, and macro-levels that shape an individual's unique sexual experience and personhood. In both using rigorous methodological tools and openly disclosing its activist stance, CDA can contribute to positive sexuality's focus on professional eth-ical considerations. And finally, through borrowing from Queer Linguistics, exposing the ways in which language use contributes to the development and expression of sexuality can lead to conflict resolution and the develop-ment of strength, well-being, and problem resolution.

Analysis of Texts

In order to more fully understand what positive sexuality and sociolin-guistics can offer each other, I analyzed a series of texts, written between

2018 and 2021 and published in various online contexts, that explore attitudes surrounding whether kink-identified individuals can use the label 'queer.' to describe themselves.[2] Some of these texts discuss the issue more generally, while others focus specifically on the 'appropriateness' of kink-identified individuals participating in Pride parades and events. I identified four articles that discussed why kink individuals should not call themselves queer (what I term 'no-kink' articles: Belinky, 2017; Cheves 2018; McGuire, 2019; Yates, 2021), and four articles that welcomed the expansion of 'queer' to include kink individuals (what I term 'yes-kink' articles: Nea, 2019; Rowello, 2021; Savage, 2019; Tiro, 2019). As an example of how to use particular frameworks of Critical Discourse Analysis, I am borrowing from van Dijk's (2008) difference model. Van Dijk posits a three-step process for how individuals are groups are differentiated and subordinated by dominant ideologies: (1) individual groups are constructed as an outside 'them' that is distinct from a unified us; (2) 'they' are acting in ways differently than 'us'; and (3) because of those differences, they should be seen as threatening to 'our' social order. In order to better understand where some of the tensions exist between queer- and kink-identified individuals, I read and re-read texts multiple times, keeping track of common themes that emerge within and among texts to discover tensions between queer- and kink-identified writers, and to find points of similarity that can be used to develop commonalities.

'No-Kink': Queerness as an Identity Antithetical to Straightness

One of the most important themes that seem to run throughout the texts under discussion is the 'meaning' of the terms queer and kink(y) themselves. A close analysis of the text suggests that the words queer and kink(y) are undergirded by tensions regarding the nature of community, and whether kinky individuals disrupt ideologies of a cohesive queer community that pits itself against dominant (hetero-)sexual and (cis-)gendered ideologies. These ideologies exist even when individuals identify as both queer and kinky, suggesting that these identities are still kept separate and distinct in the minds of some speakers.

Labels access cultural narratives: these cultural narratives can provide a sociocultural scaffold for individuals to base their identity on, identify themselves as part of a community based on shared values, beliefs, and activities, and contribute to who can be considered part of a community (and, conversely, what legitimates exclusion from the community, e.g. Bucholtz and Hall, 2004). Labels, in part, serve as a 'shorthand' for an entire community, encapsulating all of these identities, values, and beliefs within a word or phrase. This process seems especially salient for queer youth, whose sexual desire and presentation is an obvious mark of them as Other: as Jones (2020) notes in her study of coming-out stories, "one must at some point claim membership to a coherent cultural identity category in response to their own personal, intimate desires; *this assumption applies only to those who are not heterosexual*" (pp. 504–505, italics in original). For Jones, coming-out stories, and in particular the use of the word 'queer' as a self-identifier for now-public identities, are not just an affirmation of one's own sexuality: they align individuals with previously-existing labels (and, thus, cultural identity categories) that "underlie [. . .] normative and essentialist assumptions [. . .] which are associated with binary gender and innate sexual desire, employed in order to construct a culturally authentic sexual identity" (pp. 497–498). In essence, the declaration of oneself as 'queer' changes the world around them, not only orienting the user to a new identity (and allowing them to take on the cultural ideologies surrounding that new identity), but orients others around them to this new identity as well (Chirrey, 2003).

Queer as a term of community is implicit under all of the texts under consideration. However, some texts claim that the term *kinky* does not evoke the same ideologies of community as *queer*, and instead simply denotes actions that individuals engage in that do not amount to a cohesive community:

> being kinky and participating in alternative sex does not make you a part of the queer community.
>
> (Belinky, 2017)

> Homophobic people think my identity is a fetish – that my love amounts to a kink [. . .] Our identities aren't fetishes. Out fetishes are fetishes.
>
> (Cheves, 2018)

For both Belinky and Cheves, both of whom argue that kink-identified individuals should not fall under the queer umbrella, there is an implicit understanding that being queer encapsulates an identity: who I am, as it were. On the other hand, identifying as kinky (or in Belinky's words, *participating in alternative sex*), does not make one a part of the queer community because kink itself is idealized as simply an activity. Cheves seems to take the sentiment a step further, by directly opposing queerness as an identity with kink as a practice. By claiming that, in the minds of homophobic individuals *my love amounts to a kink*, Cheves acknowledges the objectification of their desires in the minds of those who wish to devalue them, but at the same time participates in the objectification of kink by contrasting what (queer) love *shouldn't* be: merely an action that belongs in the bedroom. Cheves solidifies this claim by stating that *our identities aren't fetishes [. . .] our fetishes are fetishes*. Here, Cheves draws a sharp distinction between what is part of their identity – who they love and, in essence, their 'queerness' – and what are considered fetishes (i.e., their kinks). The use of the word *fetish* is especially telling here, since it participates in a larger ideological conception of kink as something that is 'abnormal' and therefore subject to pathologization.

Placing the terms *queer* and *kink* within a brief historic and etymological context may be useful in understanding further how these terms have historically participated in community-building processes. *Queer*, as a descriptor, has its roots in the 1910s and 1920s to initially describe masculine-presenting men who were attracted to more effeminate men. Beginning in the 1940s, the word took on a derogatory term, but in the late 1980s and early 1990s organizations such as Queer Nation began to reclaim the term as an attempt, as Zosky and Alberts (2016) claim, to "disturb the discourse [around sexuality] with confrontation" (p. 600). Currently, the word has now become a more generalized term to describe those who identify primarily (but not necessarily exclusively) as lesbian, gay, bisexual, or transgender, but also retains an oppositional stance to cis-gendered and heteronormative ideologies that govern one's sexuality and gender presentations.

For writers that argue against incorporating kinkiness into conceptions of queer identity, one of the biggest threats is the incorporation of heterosexual, cis-gendered identities into a label that is expressly antithetical to what queerness should represent: "It's not that you're gay and/or trans, precisely; it's that you're not straight and/or cis" (Yates, 2021).

For Yates, what makes someone queer is not necessarily their sexuality or romantic attraction: rather, it is their opposition to straight, cis-normative cultures and ideologies. Yates further develops this idea:

> 'queer' already nods to false unity and erases differences of gender and race and class and ability and orientation. It masks inherent imbalances of privilege. It's easily co-opted [. . .] and when it's used to refer to straight cis people, whatever their additional sexual identities or practices, and when straight cis people want to make it theirs [. . .] the imbalances become greater. The gay becomes smaller. The unique challenges that queer people face are erased.
>
> (Yates, 2021)

Here, Yates astutely notes that the word *queer* has historically hid differences of class, race, gender, and others among groups. Indeed, this has often been the case: as Zosky and Alberts (2016) note, college-ages students tend to respond positively to the word 'queer' as a term for both gender and sexual orientation, and as a positive self-identifier. On the other hand, certain groups, such as urban LGBTQ youth of color and individuals of lower socioeconomic status, are less likely to use the term *queer* to describe themselves or others, and are more likely to perceive its use as an insult (Brim, 2020; Panfil, 2020).

However, Yates' use of that observation serves a larger, somewhat contradictory aim: by arguing that the word *queer* already hides class-, race-, and gender-based differences among community members, Yates points to the volatile nature of *queer* – one whose utility and power can be further co-opted by *straight*, *cis people*. The real danger in allowing kink-identified individuals to identify as queer is the allowance it would give for straight, cis-gendered individuals to appropriate the label, and therefore potentially dilute its political and social power. Queerness, thus, should be as 'pure' from the influences of heterosexuality as possible.

Other writers who argue against kink being part of the queer umbrella further claim that kinky individuals (who are conceptualized to be primarily straight and cis-gendered) are not subject to the same lack of social and legal safety that queer people face:

> A straight man who enjoys being spanked very, very hard and likes to wear leather [. . .] is not at risk of violence in the street for

his identity. He does not see people like him being murdered every day, neglected by a system that disrespects their gender identity even in death.

(Belinky, 2017)

In this quote, Belinky implies that what makes a person 'queer' is their social and legal vulnerability that they might face because of their sexuality or gender presentation, which includes increased rates of harassment, murder, and the specter of misgendering. For Belinky, kinky individuals (who Belinky personifies primarily as straight and presumably cis-gendered) do not have that worry, in part because of the social protections that are granted to them by their gender presentation. Thus, a kinky individual can be more open about their kinks without worrying about their safety in a way that a queer person cannot be so open about their own presentation.

What this (very) brief analysis of the text of arguments against incorporating kinky individuals into the queer umbrella shows is that, for many of these authors, queerness is defined in very strict terms. To be queer is to not be straight: to be queer is to share in an identity based on gender presentations and non-normative sexualities that is positioned as antithetical to straight and cis-gendered ideologies, and that is subject to social and legal vulnerabilities. Kinkiness does not belong as part of queerness because it is not an identity, but rather a practice that many straight- and cis-identified individuals engage in, and who are therefore seen as a threat to queerness.

'Yes-kink': Kink as Queer (and Queer as Not-So-Queer)

Much as queer emerged as a label of affirming identity against a heteronormative dominant culture, the etymology and history of the term kink also evokes community to its users. Speciale & Khambatta (2020) define kink as "an umbrella term signifying forms of sexual desire or expression that are viewed as atypical or unconventional, which incorporates a diverse range of practices that include power exchange, intense sensations, role-playing, and more" (p. 342). Both Sisson (2007) and Wignall (2022) locate the genesis of the term kink in the terms sadism and masochism, first used in 1886 in Krafft-Ebing's Psychopathia Sexualis and later appropriated within psychology as disorders. Although kink activity remained out of the public view for much of its history, gay leather groups and organizations such as New York's Eulenspiegel Society and San Francisco's Society of Janus provided support and community to kink and S/M practitioners.

Texts that support the integration of kink and queer identities challenge the notion that kinks are mere behaviors and activities that do not contribute to the notion of any identity, much less a queer one: "What do kinks mean to you that you [sic] that kinksters don't deserve to be represented when our identities are so intertwined with our kinks?" (Savage, 2019)

Savage challenges the narrative that queerness is more of a valid identity than kink by offering a (seemingly rhetorical) question to those who challenge the idea. For Savage, identities and kinks are not easily separable – just as, for many queer people, identities and gender/sexual presentation are not easily separable, if at all. By highlighting the futility of separating identity from kink (and ultimately, identity from activity), Savage is questioning the notion on which 'no-kink' authors have based a fundamental tenet of queer identity.

Other authors destabilize the very notion of queerness itself by claiming that non-heteronormative gender and sexual presentation are *not* sufficient markers of queerness. This attitude is best encapsulated in the below excerpt:

> Not all LGBT identified people are queer [. . .] queerness rejects homonormativity. Queer people say, we're not like you, we don't want to be like you, and we don't think you ought to want to be this way either. Queerness is a critique that many LGBT identified people want nothing to do with; they want the same things that cishet people want.
>
> (Tiro, 2019)

At first, Tiro accepts the premise that not all kink practitioners would identify themselves as queer, and that much kink is practiced by individuals who would otherwise readily identify as members of (and share the beliefs of) dominant straight and cis-gendered groups. But then Tiro states that *not all LGBT identified people are queer* [. . .] *queerness rejects homonormativity*. To Tiro, the distinction made between queerness and LGBT-ness reflects what Lisa Duggan (2002) has called 'new homonormativity': "a politics that does not contest dominant heteronormative assumptions and institutions but upholds and sustains them while promising the possibility of a demobilized gay constituency and a privatized, depoliticized gay culture anchored in domesticity and consumption" (Duggan, 2002, p. 179). Tiro argues that many LGBT-identified people do not identify as queer because, to them, 'queer' represents a specific social orientation and attitude that rejects dominant notions of capitalism, patriarchy, and assimilation. By comparing these 'non-queers' with *want[ing] the same things that cishet people want*, Tiro is arguing that queerness has very little to do with sexuality in and of itself, but is rather an orientation against dominant, hegemonic views of sexuality, which kink individuals fight back against just as much as (some) queer individuals. Thus, kinkiness shares with forms of queerness a strong sense of railing against dominant heterosexist and cis-gendered ideologies around sexuality – which some people who might otherwise identify as 'queer' don't share.

Texts that argue for kinkiness-as-queerness also invoke historical continuity that reaffirms their place under the umbrella of *queer*. As Nea (2019) notes,

> At the advent of the AIDS crisis, leathermen and leatherdykes were some of the first to take up the responsibility of caring for ailing LGBTQ+ people, throwing parties and BDSM events to raise funds for medical bills, acting as their nurses, and often being among the only people willing to provide human touch and affection to those the world at large treated as lepers.
>
> (Nea, 2019)

By noting that leather communities were among those who most supported other members of the queer community during the AIDS epidemic (especially those who became sick and were *treated as lepers*), Nea locates kinky individuals as part of a larger historical continuum of those deeply affected by AIDS – a time when queer communities began to mobilize for greater rights *en masse*. For Nea, this history demonstrates a 'right' for kinky individuals to consider themselves queer.

Conceptions of kinky identity, when espoused by those who believe that kink should fall under the queer umbrella, demonstrate fractures with conceptions of larger queer identities. By invoking kink as an integral part of one's identity, kinky individuals challenge larger understandings of kink by other queer communities as merely a practice. Through offering a definition of queerness that aligns with anti-homonormativity as opposed to gender/sexual orientation, kinky individuals bring to light the problematics of 'queerness' as a single, unified front that challenges the status quo. Finally, by placing kink within a larger history of the struggle for equity and rights, kinky individuals affirm their place among other queer communities.

Conclusion

So how can positive sexuality help us make sense of this messiness? If positive sexuality has as some of its goals the development of well-being, community-building, and conflict resolution, the first step is to illuminate some of the ways in which conflict among groups, even those who are similarly marginalized by dominant groups, manifests. But, as Martin (2004) reminds us, identifying these conflicts is only the first step to creating large-scale change: researchers must be able to move beyond objective viewpoints and actively advocate for alternatives. Positive sexuality, especially with its focus on such equity-building as humanization, open and honest communication, and peacemaking, can provide avenues through which to enact that change.

One way that this can be accomplished is by focusing on similarities between otherwise-divisive viewpoints: looking for commonalities within texts created by disparate and opposing groups that create opportunities for communication and goal-alignment. As an example, although both 'no-kink' and 'yes-kink' articles provide differing and conflicting definitions of queer and kink that largely exclude each other, writers within both groups share insights that supports the others' argument, and that can potentially lead to peacemaking and conflict resolution:

> [Kink labels are] more than sex roles, at least for most of us. They're integral parts of our identities. In this way, the words we use in kink are similar to words on the LGBT+ acronym.
>
> (Cheves, 2018)

> Not all BDSM is queer. Some of it is distinctively straight, done by cishet, monogamous people who believe that women ought to submit to men, that heterosexuality is natural, that there's nothing intrinsically suspicious about the way power is distributed in society or interpersonal relationships.
>
> (Tiro, 2019)

In the above excerpts, both Cheves (who advocates for kink identity as distinct from queer identity) and Tiro (who advocates for an integration of kink and queer identities) point out potential avenues for coalition building among both groups by legitimating (however inadvertently) each other's argument. Even though Cheves ultimately argues for kink to not be part of the queer umbrella, they still acknowledge the idea that kink can be an integral part of one's identity: the possibility is left open that kink *can* be an identity that can be validated, honored, and perhaps one day integrated into a larger conception of queerness. Tiro, for their part, acknowledges the potential of kink identity to be co-opted by otherwise-heteronormative individuals who have no desire to enact social change. This echoes a theme that many 'no-kink' espouse in their texts, and being aware of this aspect of fragility within kink identity can help kinky communities further strengthen by openly and honestly communicating these concerns.

On one level, the tensions between queer and kinky individuals these texts represent are visceral and easily-felt by members of both communities. However, frameworks and methods from Queer Linguistics and Critical Discourse Analysis can help elucidate how these tensions manifest on multiple social and textual levels, and in ways that may not even apparent to authors. Bringing these processes to light can help people realize where potential avenues for miscommunication and dehumanization lie, where avenues for honest communication and humanization exist, and how language can be changed to revolve around more equitable and ethical goals. Positive sexuality, for its part, gives Critical Discourse Analysis and Queer Linguistics a tangible goal: to help in creating that more just and moral world by moving beyond criticism and helping to enact social change.

Notes

1 In linguistics proper, the term 'gender' has a specialized meaning: gender refers to the linguistic requirement that some aspects of a sentence (such as adjectives or verbs) must agree with the subject of the sentence, through some sort of phonological or morphological congruence. While many languages do align linguistic gender with social gender, not all languages do. Some languages, such as Hungarian, demonstrate no

morphological gender, while others (such as Swahili) require nouns to agree with other aspects of a sentence based on animacy, material, and other qualities.

2 I would like to thank Philleshia Pershay-Spearman for helping me gather the texts under consideration.

References

Abbou, J. (2011). Double gender marking in French: A linguistic practice of antisexism. *Current Issues in Language Planning, 12*(1), 55–75. https://doi.org/10.1080/14664208.2010.541387

Belinky, B. (2017, March 23). No, being kinky is not the same as being queer. *Huck.* https://www.huckmag.com/article/kinky-queer. Accessed February 28, 2024.

Bérubé, A. (2001). How gay stays white and what kind of white it stays. In B. B. Rasmussen, E. Klinenberg, I. J. Nexica, & M. Wray (Eds.), *The making and unmaking of whiteness* (pp. 234–265). Duke University Press.

Breeze, R. (2022). Critical discourse analysis and its critics. *Pragmatics, 21*(4), 493–525. https://doi.org/10.1075/prag.21.4.01bre

Brim, M. (2020). *Poor queer studies: Confronting elitism in the university.* Duke University Press.

Bucholtz, M., & Hall, K. (2004). Language and identity. In A. Duranti (Ed.), *A companion to linguistic anthropology* (pp. 268–294). Basil Blackwell.

Butler, J. (2006). *Gender trouble: Feminism and the subversion of identity.* Routledge.

Cameron, D., & Kulick, D. (2003). *Language and sexuality.* Cambridge University Press.

Carlström, C., & Andersson, C. (2019). The queer spaces of BDSM and non-monogamy. *Journal of Positive Sexuality, 5*(1), 14–19.

Cheves, A. (2018, February 14). Kink is part of my identity – but don't call me LGBTK. *Advocate.* https://www.advocate.com/commentary/2018/2/14/kink-part-my-identity-dont-call-me-lgbtk. Accessed February 28, 2024.

Chirrey, D. A. (2003). 'I hereby come out': What sort of speech act is coming out? *Journal of Sociolinguistics, 7*(1), 24–37. https://doi.org/10.1111/1467-9481.00209

Chouliaraki, L., & Fairclough, N. (2007). *Discourse in late modernity: Rethinking critical discourse analysis.* Edinburgh University Press.

Christensen, M. C., Wright, R., & Dunn, J. (2017). 'It's awkward stuff': Conversations about sexuality with young children. *Child & Family Social Work, 22*(2), 711–720. https://doi.org/10.1111/cfs.12287

Döring, N., & Poeschl, S. (2020). Experiences with diverse sex toys among German heterosexual adults: Findings from a national online survey. *The Journal of Sex Research, 57*(7), 885–896. https://doi.org/10.1080/0022449 9.2019.1578329

Duggan, L. (2002). The new homonormativity: The sexual politics of neoliberalism. In R. Castronovo & D. D. Nelson (Eds.), *Materializing democracy: Toward a revitalized cultural politics.* Duke University Press. https://doi. org/10.1215/9780822383901-007

Esposito, E. (2023). Discourse, intersectionality, critique: Theory, methods and practice. *Critical Discourse Studies,* 1–17. https://doi.org/10.1080/1740 5904.2023.2230602

Fairclough, N. (1992). *Discourse and social change.* Polity Press.

Fishman, P. M. (1978). Interaction: The work women do. *Social Problems, 25*(4), 397–406. https://doi.org/10.2307/800492

Foucault, M. (1990). *The history of sexuality. 1: An introduction.* Vintage Books.

Halliday, M. A. K., & Matthiessen, C. (2004). *An introduction to functional grammar* (3rd Ed.). Hodder Education.

Hughes, J. M. F. (2018). Progressing positive discourse analysis and/in critical discourse sStudies: Reconstructing resistance through progressive discourse analysis. *Review of Communication, 18*(3), 193–211. https://doi. org/10.1080/15358593.2018.1479880

Jones, L. (2020). 'The fact they knew before I did upset me most': Essentialism and normativity in lesbian and gay youths' coming out stories. *Sexualities, 23*(4), 497–515. https://doi.org/10.1177/1363460719830343

Knisely, K. A. (2020). *Le français non-binaire*: Linguistic forms used by nonbinary speakers of French. *Foreign Language Annals, 53*(4), 850–876. https://doi.org/10.1111/flan.12500

Koller, V. (2013). Constructing (non-)normative identities in written lesbian discourse: A diachronic study. *Discourse & Society, 24*(5), 572–589. https://doi.org/10.1177/0957926513486166

Krüsi, A., Ranville, F., Gurney, L., Lyons, T., Shoveller, J., & Shannon, K. (2018). Positive sexuality: HIV disclosure, gender, violence and the law – A qualitative study. *PLOS ONE, 13*(8), e0202776. https://doi.org/10.1371/ journal.pone.0202776

Luke, A. (2002). 5. Beyond science and ideology critique: Developments in critical discourse analysis. *Annual Review of Applied Linguistics*, *22*, 96–110. https://doi.org/10.1017/S0267190502000053

Macgilchrist, F. (2011). *Journalism and the political: Discursive tensions in news coverage of Russia*. John Benjamins Publishing Company.

McGuire, L. (2019). Adding "K" to LGBTQIA: Is kink inherently queer? *Spectrum South – The Voice of the Queer South*, February 22. https://www.spectrumsouth.com/queer-kink/. Accessed February 28, 2024.

Maes, C., Trekels, J., Impett, E., & Vandenbosch, L. (2023). The development of the Positive Sexuality in Adolescence Scale (PSAS). *The Journal of Sex Research*, *60*(1), 45–61. https://doi.org/10.1080/00224499.2021.2011826

Martin, J. R. (2004). Positive discourse analysis: Solidarity and change. *Revista Canaria de Estudios Ingleses*, *49*, 179–200.

Meyer, M. (2001). Between theory, method, and politics: positioning the approaches to CDA. In R. Wodak & M. Meyer, *Methods of critical discourse analysis* (pp. 14–31). London: Sage Publishers.

Motschenbacher, H. (2010). *Language, gender and sexual identity: Poststructuralist perspectives*. John Benjamins Pub. Co.

Motschenbacher, H. (2014). Grammatical gender as a challenge for language policy: The (im)possibility of non-heteronormative language use in German versus English. *Language Policy*, *13*(3), 243–261. https://doi.org/10.1007/s10993-013-9300-0

Nea, C. (2019, June 17). Why kink, BDSM, and leather should be included at pride. *Them*. https://www.them.us/story/kink-bdsm-leather-pride. Accessed February 28, 2024.

Panfil, V. R. (2020). "Nobody don't really know what that mean": Understandings of "queer" among urban LGBTQ young people of color. *Journal of Homosexuality*, *67*(12), 1713–1735. https://doi.org/10.1080/00918369.2019.1613855

Parchomiuk, M. (2022). Sexuality of people with intellectual disabilities: A proposal to use the positive sexuality model. *Sexuality & Culture*, *26*(1), 418–448. https://doi.org/10.1007/s12119-021-09893-y

Pitagora, D. (2017). No pain, no gain? Therapeutic and relational benefits of subspace in BDSM contexts. *Journal of Positive Sexuality*, *3*(3), 44–54.

Rowello, L. (2021, June 29). Yes, kink belongs at pride. and I want my kids to see it. *Washington Post*. https://www.washingtonpost.com/outlook/2021/06/29/pride-month-kink-consent/. Accessed February 28, 2024.

Savage, D. (2019, June 25). Are straight kinksters queer? And does kink belong at pride? *The Stranger.* https://www.thestranger.com/savage-love/2019/06/25/40577856/are-straight-kinksters-queer-and-does-kink-belong-at-pride. Accessed February 28, 2024.

Scott, J. C. (1990). *Domination and the arts of resistance: Hidden transcripts.* Yale University Press.

Scotto di Carlo, G. (2020). An analysis of the use of inclusive language among Italian non-binary individuals: A survey transcending binary thinking. *I-LanD Journal: Identity, Language and Diversity, 2* https://doi.org/10.26379/IL2020002_005

Sisson, K. (2007). The cultural formation of S/M: History and analysis. In D. Langdridge & M. Barker (Eds.), *Safe, sane, and consensual: Contemporary practices on sadomasochism* (pp. 16–40). Palgrave Macmillan.

Speciale, M., & Khambatta, D. (2020). Kinky & queer: Exploring the experiences of LGBTQ + individuals who practice BDSM. *Journal of LGBTQ Issues in Counseling, 14*(4), 341–361. https://doi.org/10.1080/15538605.2020.1827476

Sprott, R., Meeker, C., & O'Brien, M. (2019). Kink community education: Experiential learning and communities of practice. *Journal of Positive Sexuality, 5*(2), 48–58.

Suwarno, Triyono, S., Ashadi, & Sahayu, W. (2021). Gender construction in the Indonesian government-distributed English textbook: Combining critical discourse analysis and corpus linguistics. *Sexuality & Culture, 25*(6), 2158–2175. https://doi.org/10.1007/s12119-021-09870-5

Tiro. (2019, September 8). Is BDSM queer? *Medium.* https://medium.com/@naraka.kalasutra/is-bdsm-queer-f6489815b063. Accessed February 28, 2024.

Valentine, D. (2003). "I went to bed with my own kind once": The erasure of desire in the name of identity. *Language & Communication, 23,* 121–138.

van Dijk, T. A. (2008). *Discourse and power.* Palgrave Macmillan.

van Leeuwen, T. (2008). *Discourse and practice: New tools for critical discourse analysis.* Oxford University Press.

West, C., & Zimmerman, D. H. (1987). Doing gender. *Gender and Society, 1*(2), 125–151. JSTOR.

Wignall, L. (2022). *Kinky in the digital age: Gay men's subcultures and social identities.* Oxford University Press.

Williams, D. J. (2020). Is serial sexual homicide a compulsion, deviant leisure, or both? Revisiting the case of Ted Bundy. *Leisure Sciences, 42*(2), 205–223. https://doi.org/10.1080/01490400.2019.1571967

Williams, D., Christensen, M. C., & Capous-Desyllas, M. (2016). Social work practice and sexuality: Applying a positive sexuality model to enhance diversity and resolve problems. *Families in Society: The Journal of Contemporary Social Services, 97*(4), 287–294. https://doi.org/10.1606/1044-3894.2016.97.35

Williams, D., Thomas, J., Prior, E., & Walters, W. (2015). Introducing a multidisciplinary framework of positive sexuality. *Journal of Positive Sexuality, 1*(1), 6–11. https://doi.org/10.51681/1.112

Wodak, R., & Meyer, M. (Eds.). (2016). *Methods of critical discourse studies* (3rd ed.). SAGE.

Yates, R. (2021, May 1). Being kinky doesn't make you queer. *Autostraddle.* https://www.autostraddle.com/kink-is-not-queer-374216/. Accessed February 28, 2024.

Zimman, L. (2017a). Gender as stylistic bricolage: Transmasculine voices and the relationship between fundamental frequency and /s/. *Language in Society, 46*(3), 339–370. https://doi.org/10.1017/S0047404517000070

Zimman, L. (2017b). Variability in /s/ among transgender speakers: Evidence for a socially grounded account of gender and sibilants. *Linguistics, 55*(5). https://doi.org/10.1515/ling-2017-0018

Zimman, L., Davis, J. L., & Raclaw, J. (Eds.). (2014). *Queer excursions: Retheorizing binaries in language, gender, and sexuality.* Oxford University Press.

Zosky, D. L., & Alberts, R. (2016). What's in a name? Exploring use of the word queer as a term of identification within the college-aged LGBT community. *Journal of Human Behavior in the Social Environment, 26*(7–8), 597–607. https://doi.org/10.1080/10911359.2016.1238803

2

THE CRISIS OF SEXUALITY TRAINING IN SOCIAL WORK

A Need for Positive Sexuality

Priscilla D. Allen and D J Williams

Introduction

Sexual health and the opportunity for consensual sexual fulfilment is essential to wellness and life satisfaction (World Health Organization, 2024). A host of physical and psychological rewards abound with embracing positive sexuality, yet social work, a profession deeply committed to nurturing human relationships, requires little, if any, focus on human sexuality in curricula, class, or practice, despite the urging of scholars to advance the field for the past 50+ years (Abramowitz, 1971; Berry, 2017; D'Adamo, 2022; Dodd & Katz, 2020; Dodd & Tolman, 2017; Valentich & Gripton, 1975). The mirror of reluctance reflects an internalized taboo of sexuality where Americans are highly sexualized but still fearful, hypocritical, and dishonest about investigating the basics of sex in the field of social work (Dodd & Katz, 2020; Ryan, 2010). Indeed, many persons' overtly expressed attitudes about sex are often in stark contrast with covert curiosities and behaviors pertaining to sexuality. Because social

DOI: 10.4324/9781032631820-3

workers are often effective in calling out various discrepancies that impact social justice and clinical practice, social work, as a profession, is fully capable of challenging this disconnect regarding sexuality more specifically (Abramowitz, 1971; Dodd & Tolman, 2017).

Generalist Practice: The Foundation of Social Work

In the United States, social workers comprise the majority of all mental health providers. According to the Substance Abuse and Mental Health Services Administration (SAMHSA), the collective number of social workers is higher than all psychiatrists, psychologists, and psychiatric nurses in the U.S. combined (cited by the National Association of Social Workers, n.d.). Social work espouses a generalist approach that considers the whole of the person in context to their environment across the life course, long known as a person-in-environment (PIE) perspective, which is borrowed from systems and ecology models. A generalist, versus an earlier model of specializations, has been used since the 1990s. Yet, with growing numbers of unmet mental health needs across the population, the social work profession is expected to do it all, and we do. Social workers are commonly found addressing diverse issues, such as mental health, school, homelessness, crisis and disaster work, suicide mitigation, medical needs, housing, social welfare, child welfare, counseling, advocacy, and substance abuse.

However, within the profession, the personal-internal world seems to have gotten lost in the vast expansion of a generalized education in a highly contextualized world. Much of what social work does is to navigate through a maze of limited health and mental health services, a post hoc practice vs. having the opportunity to work intimately with people, to explore their desires and hopes. The field has lost some of the key understanding of the person and internal behavior and has become more of a structural-functional force of social control – often against the profession's will. The generalist perspective in teaching works to expose students to the complexity of human relation and an array of conditions, vulnerabilities, and exploitations and has a higher reliance on supervised field education as well as the student themselves to round things out. The fixation on problems and maintaining social order distracts from the basis of life-quality and the potential of sexuality as healing and worthy of attention, particularly since social work deals with dimensions of human behavior, and sexuality is often at the fulcrum of behavior (Dodd & Katz, 2020; D'Adamo, 2022).

Sexuality Training in Contemporary Social Work Education: Where Is It?

The governing body of social work, the Council on Social Work Education (CSWE), certifies each social work program in the U.S. as following a range of principles that inform research and policy on evidence-informed practice. Nevertheless, there is a dearth of opportunity for students to learn and intellectually explore the most vital and natural of all functioning that people have – sexuality. Within social work curricula, human sexuality is assumed to be more of a responsibility fit for the medical than the social realm, but this assumption is, of course, highly problematic (Valentich & Gripton, 1975) and has been for decades (Dodd & Katz, 2020).

Educational preparation, especially concerning sexuality issues, is often a misfit with the actual practice skills that are needed after social work students graduate. In many respects, the real learning occurs once the social worker is launched from a college campus and finds their way in a professional practice setting. One may say this about many professions, but social work tends to deal regularly with the most vulnerable and oppressed people in society, which adds to the need for diversity exposure with an open-minded professional stance. Many social work students are driven to the field with a desire to engage in private practice; yet, most inevitably they will work to one degree or another in the public sphere and as leaders in organizations. It is important to note that the very roots of social work are based in justice and access to services, not therapy (Granger, 2022).

Being professionally competent in understanding and clinically navigating a wide range of sexuality issues is, of course, directly connected to matters of social justice and equality. Fifty years ago, Valentich and Gripton (1975) noted that graduated social work students were not equipped to assist clients with sexual issues. Unfortunately, this training problem still continues today, despite international recognition on the necessity of understanding sexuality and sexual relationships (Dodd & Tolman, 2017) and that that sexuality is central in the lives of many, if not most, clients (Dodd & Katz, 2020). Indeed, Foucault (1978) urged educators to consider sexuality as a fundamental part of who people are, using a discursive process rather than assigning ideas of sexuality as fixed personal attributes (Hicks, 2008). Where social workers commonly are trained to examine and address bias with respect to race, gender, age, ability, geography, class, and so on, the profession continues to fail to examine and address assumptions and biases about diverse sexuality. In so doing, social work lags behind many fields that address sexuality, including those that primarily focus on the brain/body connection to sex, such as psychology, kinesiology, and medicine (Berry, 2017).

In clinical/private practice, more than 50% of couples seeking therapy report sexual matters as concerns (Rubinsky, 2021). Despite sexuality issues being relatively common in clinical settings, Wineberg's (2015) study of the top 25 ranked social work schools in the U.S. found that none offered required courses on human sexuality. Wineberg (2015) found that over a third of top schools did offer one or more courses pertaining to sexuality as electives. Electives, however, are often based on the culture of the program and not CSWE accreditation criteria. Berry (2017) found that social workers said they were comfortable with the topic of sexuality, yet they had to seek additional training outside of the classroom in order to feel prepared in helping clients with sexuality issues. Clearly, the absence of sexuality training in standard social work education programs is a major problem that subsequently impacts the quality of clinical practice.

Sexuality and Social Work: Historical Roots and a Focus on Problems

The focus of social work has logically and historically been to address the darker sides of sexual behavior, such as sexual abuse and oppressive and/or violent acts against those who are most vulnerable and have little power (Foucault, 1978; Hicks, 2008). It is not surprising, then, that since a primary function of workers, since social work's beginnings, has been to address various socio-sexual problems, social work would be historically susceptible to, and reproduce, assumptions around sex-negativity.

Furthermore, social work has strong historical roots in Christianity, in particular, and psychology (and thus medicine), which have separate, yet similar (in terms of power), normalizing discourses around sexuality (Foucault, 1978).

Christian Influence

Christian religious ideals that sexuality is for reproduction – sex for pleasure is immoral and must be confessed – has caused an array of repressive repercussions that are both dangerous and exploitative (Foucault, 1978). We have seen the aftermath of such beliefs giving rise to abuse and secrecy, exploitation, and rape of children under the guise of paternalism and God's will. Religion and sex have a complex relationship that is neither clear or productive but, if mired in a projected perversion, clearly cause more harm than good, and systems based on denial and hypocrisy will eventually collapse (Ryan, 2010). Social work, with roots in Christianity, and sexuality thus have a complex and historically difficult relationship. Dodd and Tolman (2017) are working to "revive" discourse on sexuality within contemporary social work. However, social work classrooms reflect broader societal attitudes where moral culture wars prevail. Social work has deep roots in Christian beliefs of noblesse oblige – an obligation of nobility to aid those less fortunate – which reflects a definitive power imbalance that remains problematic.

The Mother of Social Work – Hiding in the Closet

Social work emphasizes that the personal is political. Nevertheless, Jane Addams, the first American woman to earn the Nobel Prize and widely recognized as the "mother of social work," was a closeted lesbian (Lynn, 2019). Addams was an incredible force of justice and opportunity for disadvantaged children and families through her establishment of the Settlement House Movement (SHM), which had a complicated lens on sexuality and sexual identity. She remained closeted for the entirety of her life, but has been controversially celebrated in recent years in the lesbian and queer literature. Addams met the love of her life, Mary Rozet Smith, but later destroyed her (Smith's) letters, perhaps to keep their relationship from the public domain. Hence, the voice of Smith is absent except for some of Addams' archival writings of longing and pain for her love (Lynn, 2019). Addams and Smith were together for more than 40 years until Smith died in February 1934. Addams died 15 months later. Addams once wrote that Mary could live without Jane, but Jane could not live without Mary (Lynn, 2019). Addams was said to have believed that sex was at the root of many social ills and exploits, and although she was asexual through her life, she maintained a deep and passionate love for Smith (Brown, 2004).

Recent Decades: DSM Changes, HIV/AIDS, and Legal Fears

Of course, the official removal of homosexuality from the *Diagnostic and Statistical Manual (DSM)* by the American Psychiatric Association in 1973 was a monumental milestone in advancing basic sexuality training across the helping professions. Some of the most adventurous and exciting teaching happened in the 1970s. Wineberg (2015) suggested that sex education rose in the late 1980s and early 1990s, but then fell with the HIV/AIDS epidemic. Discussions were carefully crafted not to blame sexual behavior for deadly outcomes, and the relationship between social work and sexuality became more complicated, and perhaps more paternalistic and guarded. At the same time, university environments became increasingly litigious, which continues to serve to restrict and omit opportunities for social work faculty and students to explore and investigate a broad range of practice implications associated with sexuality.

Current Focus: Categorization and LGBTQIA+ Identities

Social work has made significant strides in promoting anti-oppressive frameworks for vulnerable people categorized under the LGBTQIA+ umbrella, but Hicks (2008) cautions that a heteronormative view is still the dominant lens through which the other is viewed while working towards acceptance and inclusion. Indeed, the social work profession continues to approach sexuality, as a whole, through a pathological, problem-focused lens, thus a new approach to assessment is needed. Current assessment issues stem from viewing sexual identities as fixed, rather than taking a reflexive approach to understanding sexuality as flexible with health and wellness dimensions. From a contemporary social work perspective, the broad LGBTQIA+ designation can both help and hinder understanding as it still bases identity into particular categories. However, personal experiences across categories do not define the diversity of experiences and identity nuances within each respective category. The LGBTQIA+ grouping represents a huge array of diverse individuals lumped together under a growing acronym that, instead of advancing inclusion, often highlights differences. In no way is the intention to diminish the import that the inclusion of multiple allies and expressions from, as examples, self-love to intersex persons, to lesbian women and gay men, to people who identify as transgender, or asexual, or aromantic. However, in the social work classroom and sometimes even among many LGBTQIA+ people themselves, confusion abounds. Of course, people broadly categorized as LGBTQIA+ often do not put themselves in the designated boxes, and many have noted the acronym has become somewhat meaningless and problematic, rather than inclusive.

Categorical boxes, especially concerning sexual identities, do not reflect reality very well. Furthermore, although well-intentioned efforts to advance diversity are often appreciated, the vociferous opposition to accepting diversity has used sexual identity categorization as a weapon against social justice and inclusion. In short, the way categorization is utilized in social work is limiting and sometimes even stigmatizing, despite its good intention of inclusivity. Essentially, all social workers should be included in the LGBTQIA+ sphere if they truly are allies in addressing power imbalances associated with marginalized sexual identities. Indeed, social work education and training could use a large dose of queerification.

Problem-dominated approaches utilized in social work also have inherent process issues. Hicks (2008) cautions that the LGBTQIA+ content in social work is reductive, particularly if such content follows a theoretical practice framework. A basic understanding of the complexity and unending panoply of sexuality is lacking. Therefore, discussion on not only sexual minorities as groupings, but especially of all individuals as unique sexual beings, may be a good starting point. Additionally, social workers and many other clinical professionals also lack education on relationship diversity. For example, people who prefer alternative relationship arrangements, such as consensual non-monogamy, swinging, or BDSM/ kink relationships – irrespective of the sexual identities of the people in such relationships (see Hammack et al., 2019) – may not be familiar to social workers (Williams, 2015). This problem may reflect the historical deferral to heteronormativity and the tendency to normalize, through medicalization, the other.

Catching up on Competence: From Focusing on Problems to Facilitating Pleasure

Weiss and Westerhof (2020) have suggested a happiness outcome versus a problem-focused lens in the helping professions. Contemporary problem-focused interventions are typically based on addressing a problem or ill, crafting a treatment plan, and helping clients work toward change. However, traditional problem-focused approaches do not seriously consider intimacy needs and the wide array of potential sexual curiosities, interests, and practices within the internal and external landscapes of clients.

Social work generalist practice, as currently operationalized, misses key dimensions, such as sexual and relationship diversity. Educators and workers unfamiliar with current scholarship on those topics may commonly view these dimensions as largely perpetuating problems, rather than being capable of creating pathways for human connection, intimacy, and pleasure – whether expressed solely or shared with a partner(s)/ others. However, sexual satisfaction remains an important part of overall health and wellbeing for people everywhere (World Health Organization, 2024; Williams & Thomas, 2023). The lack of sexual satisfaction among one or more partners in a relationship may be a symptom of other problems and a source of frustration (Rubinsky, 2021). In inquiring about sexuality during client assessment, Dodd and Katz (2020) propose the following basic questions:

- Are you engaged in any sexual relationships? If yes, how would you describe the quality of those sexual relationships?
- Have you experienced any changes in your level of sexual desire recently?
- Are you happy with your current level of desire?

Similar additional recommendations for basic clinical assessment of client sexuality are discussed by Randall and Sprott (see Chapter 3, this volume).

Helping professionals with high quality training on the diversity and complexity of sexuality, and how to identify pathways to sexual pleasure, surely will have an increased capacity for helping clients, regardless of setting, to utilize available strengths and fulfill basic needs that can improve overall functioning.

Working with Clients in Restricted Settings

Helping professionals who have direct exposure (often everyday) with clients in restricted settings, such as hospitals, nursing homes, and prisons – and these clients have normal sexual desires – commonly deal with private matters visibly overlapping with professional context and structure (see Allen, 2022; Hughes, 2020). It is essential that workers receive training to empower and advocate for such clients during difficult times when clients may be most anxious and vulnerable. Workers should recognize, especially during such times, the importance of helping clients maintain coherent identities, including their sexual selves, amidst such extreme challenges. Social workers in long-term care, for example, are required to be openminded and innovative where sexual desires can be safely and satisfactorily expressed. Some clients may have paralysis or compromised mobility, yet still have sexual needs and desires that are an important part of their health and wellbeing. Some may need assistance in order to be safe. Anecdotal information sharing with social service staff has resulted in innovative and creative ways to move mattresses on the floor, assist with set up, or to be present as may be needed. Social work often deals with situations and navigates a strengths-based way to provide older adults with pornographic material or facilitate conjugal visits with persons outside of their legal partnership.

Social workers are less likely than other settings to seek employment in long-term care settings, and the lack of education and training on sexuality, including that sexual desire and need for expression usually remains strong across the lifespan, may act as a barrier that prevents workers from seriously considering a career in such settings.

Alternative Sexuality as Normal

There is an extremely wide range of potential consensual activities that bring erotic pleasure to particular individuals. Prevalence studies across multiple geographic regions find that approximately half or more of the general population have fantasies or curiosities about BDSM/kink behaviors, and approximately 20 to 45% have engaged in such activities (for a review, see Williams & Sprott, 2022). Despite widespread beliefs among clinicians and the general public that such interests must be rooted in psychopathology (including childhood trauma), a growing body of literature refutes these sex-negative assumptions (Brown et al., 2020; Williams & Sprott, 2022). Instead, scholars find that BDSM/kink interests and motivations are extremely complex and seem to be associated with sensation-seeking traits, altered states of consciousness, positive emotions, and social and psychological benefits consistent with legitimate leisure experiences (Williams & Sprott, 2022). For many BDSM/kink enthusiasts, such practices are often pleasurable, of course, but also seem to support personal growth and healing more broadly (Sprott, 2020).

The Alternative Sexual Health Research Alliance (2023) found that although there are very few studies of BDSM/kink prior to 1980, there have since been well over 7,300 publications on this topic. Indeed, multidisciplinary research has accumulated rapidly and may be conceptualized as its own particular field, referred to as BDSM studies (Simula, 2019). Unfortunately, despite tremendous progress in understanding BDSM/kink that has occurred over the past two decades, particularly finding that such interests are not inherently pathological but rather normal, stigma and marginalization persist, including among healthcare professionals. Research shows that nearly half of BDSM/kink participants do not disclose their erotic interests to helping professionals, and many are reluctant to seek care due to stigma and past discrimination from providers (Williams & Sprott, 2022). Curiously, the social work profession continues to ignore BDSM/kink, and despite the rapid growth of BDSM/kink scholarship published in other disciplines, the editors of peer-reviewed social journals have been reluctant, if not rather oppositional, in publishing work on this topic (Williams, 2015). Given this issue, social workers are left to themselves to find outside information to increase their competence in working with BDSM/kink-oriented clients. Thus, resources for helping professionals, generally, such as the Kink Clinical Practice Guidelines Project (2019), are highly valuable.

Positive Sexuality and Social Work: Perfect Partners?

Earlier herein, we noted that social work utilizes a generalist practice approach with a strong emphasis on how people function in their social environments (PIE) and across the lifespan. Understanding and normalizing diverse sexuality; including fantasies, curiosities, interests, and behaviors; across the life course and that pertain to specific client systems; such as individuals, partnerships, and poly-ships; can more fully explain the particular ecology of clients and their relationships with themselves and the external world (Constantinides et al., 2019). Furthermore, social work is a field that is especially poised to advance the discussion of sex across the life course, given its emphasis on productive and healthy aging. For years, we have challenged myths about aging, including the silly idea that older people disengage from society, and certainly from sex. Assessment and simple questions with clients, consumers, and patients about sex itself are sparse and often avoided by workers, particularly with older adults, which can be damaging to the therapeutic alliance, particularly in healthcare settings.

While a current, and much needed, focus of social work (regarding sexuality) is on LGBTQIA+ identities, the incorporation of positive sexuality with the realization that each person's sexuality is unique, can help resolve systematic limitations that social workers have not yet addressed. Furthermore, when considering identities, including sexual identities, an intersectionality lens should be applied. For example, emerging research suggests that those with LGBTQIA+ identities may be statistically more likely to also be involved in BDSM/kink practices (Sprott, 2023). Social workers who incorporate a positive sexuality stance should be far more competent in addressing the identity intersectionality (of all types) that may be encountered when working with clients.

Social Work and Sex Work: A Curious Side Note on Similarities

D'Adamo (2022), an advocate of sex work being recognized as a skilled helping profession, makes parallels between social work and sex work. She observes that both provide a service, both require skills to practice safely and constructively, both can be profoundly personal and revolutionary, and both deal with deep internal landscapes of human experience. Perhaps somewhat surprising to some readers, the profession of social work has humanized sex work for decades and does seem to acknowledge the complex interplay of multiple factors in such work that is often viewed as immoral or illegitimate. Once again, this illustrates the curious and somewhat conflicted approach that social work has had, historically, toward sexuality.

Interestingly, an analysis of professional BDSM found that while the work of the professional dominatrix is its own, unique occupation, it overlaps in some important ways with both sex work and social work (Williams & Storm, 2012). In fact, decades ago Mistress Monique von Cleef operated a BDSM dungeon for many years in New Jersey, and referred to herself and fellow dominatrices as "leather social workers" (Williams & Storm, 2012). Because BDSM requires explicit consent from all participants, includes safewords, and is carefully scripted to play in desired ways with erotic power, it has the potential to re-narrate damaging past experiences and promote healing from trauma (D'Adamo, 2022; Thomas, 2020). While sex work focuses on pleasurable sexual experiences for clients, professional BDSM centers on playing, often but not always erotically, with power dynamics. Of course, the widespread cultural acceptance and perceived legitimacy of both sex work and professional BDSM largely depends on how sex-negative or sex-positive the broader culture is (Williams & Storm, 2012).

The Fingerprints of Social Work on Contemporary Positive Sexuality

The current positive sexuality framework by Williams and colleagues (2015, 2016; See also the Introduction, this volume) was derived by distilling consistent components from across multiple social and behavioral science disciplines. Perhaps no discipline is reflected as prominently in the eight dimensions of positive sexuality as social work. For example, while the "positive" in positive sexuality is consistent with "positive" psychology (focus on how people are happy, successful, and thrive), this dimension is also directly linked to the strengths approach (help clients identify and apply strengths to resolve problems) that is now common-place in generalist social work (Williams et al., 2016). Positive sexuality draws from multiple disciplines and methodological approaches, which is also consistent with the eclecticism of social work. Of course, humanization and application of professional ethics are formal aspects of positive sexuality, social work (see National Association of Social Work-ers, 2020), and other helping professions. Finally, the positive sexuality dimension of applicability across micro-, mezzo-, and macro- levels of social structure came directly from social work formal designation of levels of practice, though multiple levels also are salient in other dis-ciplines and helping professions. The bottom line here is that positive sexuality is not foreign to social work or any other profession, really. Rather, historical sex-negativity along with old paradigms of thinking about sexuality have been so engrained – partly combined with the fact that new scholarship (especially on sexuality, gender, relationships, etc.) now accumulates so rapidly – that perhaps we haven't been prepared to incorporate new knowledge and conceptualizations into our founda-tional educational and professional processes. Simply put, positive sexu-ality in social work, though largely absent to date, mostly boils down to "putting our money where our mouths are," or perhaps "practicing what we preach." Social work does this very well with many issues, but not so much – yet – with sexuality.

Conclusion

The social and sexual economics of sex alone should merit more inves-tigation in a field that is determined to understand the root cause of injustice (Baumeister & Vohs, 2004). As an applied profession, social work can be gritty and dangerous, cluttered with paperwork, and pre-occupied with bureaucratic issues associated with compliance. Work-ers are spread thin, yet at its core, social work is life affirming and change-oriented. Practitioners are admonished to "begin where the cli-ent is," and explore various avenues and mechanisms to help clients improve their lives.

Both the National Association of Social Workers (NASW) and and the Council on Social Work Education (CSWE) are currently emphasizing the necessity of social workers becoming more attuned to the effects of personal bias and social injustice pertaining to race and ethnicity, gender, class, and age, but the profession has not seriously focused on sexuality, despite sexuality being a fundamental aspect of both identity and overall health and wellbeing (World Health Organization, 2024; Williams & Thomas, 2023). Unfortunately, this lack of attention can translate into unintentional, and potentially serious, harm to clients in the therapeutic process, which could rather easily be remedied via the embracement of positive sexuality. To echo a previous observation of the profession a decade ago, concerning sexuality training (Williams, 2015, p. 37), "Social work (*still*) needs a good spanking!"

References

Abramowitz, N. R. (1971). Human sexuality in the social work curriculum. *Family Coordinator*, 20(4), 349–354.

Allen, P. D. (2022). Close the door and open your mind: Advancing sexual openness in the nursing home. *Journal of Positive Sexuality*, 8(1), 12–19.

Baumeister, R. F., & Vohs, K. D. (2004). Sexual economics: Sex as female resource for sexual exchange in heterosexual Interactions. *Personality and Social Psychology Review*, 8(4), 339–363.

Berry, J. (2017). *Social workers' perspectives on sexuality in social work practice*. University of Calgary, Alberta. Unpublished thesis.

Brown, V. B. (2004). *The education of Jane Addams*. University of Pennsylvania Press.

Brown, A., Barker, E.D., & Rahman, Q. (2020). A systematic scoping review of the prevalence, etiological, psychological, and interpersonal factors associated with BDSM. *Journal of Sex Research*, 57, 781–811.

Constantinides, D., Sennott, S., & Chandler, D. (2019). *Sex therapy with erotically marginalized clients. Nine principles of clinical support*. Routledge.

D'Adamo, K. (2022). Kink as healing professional. *Ethics and Social Welfare*, 16(2), 206–213.

Dodd, S. J., & Katz, C. C. (2020). Sex positive social work education: Integrating content into HBSE courses and beyond. *Journal of Teaching in Social Work*, 40(1), 48–57.

Dodd, S. J., & Tolman, D. (2017). Reviving a positive discourse on sexuality within social work. *Social Work*, 62, 227–234.

Foucault, M. (1978). *The history of sexuality*. Pantheon.

Granger, T. B. (2022). *Understanding the effects of socioeconomic variables, career motivation, and MSW education on practice preferences: A quantitative national survey of MSW students.* Louisiana State University. Unpublished dissertation.

Hammack, P., Frost, D., & Hughes, S. (2019). Queer intimacies: A new paradigm for the study of relationship diversity. *Journal of Sex Research, 56,* 556–592.

Hicks, S. (2008). Thinking through sexuality. *Journal of Social Work, 8*(1), 65–82.

Hughes, S. D. (2020). Release within confinement: An alternative proposal for managing the masturbation of incarcerated men in U.S. prisons. *Journal of Positive Sexuality, 6,* 4–22.

Kink Clinical Practice Guidelines Project. (2019). *Kink clinical practice guidelines.* Retrieved May 1, 2024, from https://www.kinkguidelines.com/

Lynn, S. (2019). Jane Addams, Mary Rozet Smith, and the disappointments of one-sided correspondence. *The Jane Addams Papers Project* (online). Retrieved March 16, 2024 from https://janeaddams.ramapo.edu/2019/07/jane-addams-mary-rozet-smith-and-the-disappointments-of-one-sided-correspondence/

National Association of Social Workers (n.d.). *About social workers.* Retrieved May 3, 2024, from https://www.socialworkers.org/News/Facts/Social-Workers

National Association of Social Workers (2020). *Code of ethics.* Retrieved January 12, 2024, from https://www.socialworkers.org/About/Ethics/Code-of-Ethics/Code-of-Ethics-English

Rubinsky, V. (2021). Sources and strategies for managing sexual conflict in diverse relationships. *Sexuality and Culture, 25,* 904–924.

Ryan, C. (January 2010). On sexual hypocrisy: Truth, not hypocrisy, will set you free. *Psychology Today (online).* Retrieved April 15, 2024, from https://www.psychologytoday.com/us/blog/sex-at-dawn/201001/on-sexual-hypocrisy

Simula, B. L. (2019). Pleasure, power, and pain: A review of the literature on the experiences of BDSM participants. *Sociology Compass, 13,* e12668.

Sprott, R. A. (2020). Reimagining kink: Transformation, growth, and health through BDSM. *Journal of Humanistic Psychology (online first).*

Sprott, R. A. (2023). The intersection of LGBTQ+ and kink sexualities: A review of the literature with a focus on empowering/positive aspects of kink involvement for LGBTQ+ individuals. *Current Sexual Health Reports, 15,* 107–112.

The Alternative Sexualities Health Research Alliance (TASHRA) (2023). *TASHRA impact report.*

Thomas, J. N. (2020). BDSM as trauma play: An autoethnographic investigation. *Sexualities, 23,* 917–933.

Valentich, M., & Gripton, J. (1975). Teaching human sexuality to social work students. *Family Coordinator, 24*(3), 273–280.

Weiss, L. A., & Westerhof, G. J. (2020). The happiness route: Finding alternatives to the problem-based approach in social work for vulnerable groups. *Journal of Positive Psychology, 15*(5), 666–669.

Williams, D J (2015). Does social work need a good spanking? The refusal to embrace BDSM scholarship and implications for sexually diverse clients. *Journal of Positive Sexuality, 1,* 37–40.

Williams, D J, Christensen, M. C., & Capous-Desyllas, M. (2016). Social work practice and sexuality: Applying a positive sexuality model to enhance diversity and resolve problems. *Families in Society: The Journal of Contemporary Social Services, 97*(4), 287–294.

Williams, D J, & Sprott, R. A. (2022). Current biopsychosocial science on understanding kink. *Current Opinion in Psychology, 48,* 101473.

Williams, D J, & Storm, L. E. (2012). Unconventional leisure and career: Insights into the work of professional dominatrices. *Electronic Journal of Human Sexuality, 15.*

Williams, D J, & Thomas, J. N. (2023). Healthy sexuality. In H. S. Friedman & C. H. Markey (Eds.), *Encyclopedia of mental health* (3rd ed.). Academic Press.

Williams, D J, Thomas, J. N., Prior, E. E., & Walters, W. (2015). Introducing a multidisciplinary framework of positive sexuality. *Journal of Positive Sexuality, 1,* 6–11.

Wineberg, H. R. (2015). *Social work and human sexuality: An examination of the country's top 25-CWSE ranked MSW curricula.* Smith College. Unpublished thesis.

World Health Organization (WHO). (2024). *Sexual health.* Geneva, Switzerland. Retrieved April 28, 2024, from https://www.who.int/health-topics/sexual-health#tab=tab_1

3

SEX POSITIVITY AND HEALTHCARE

Anna Randall and Richard Sprott

Introduction

If there is a domain of life where the promise of sex positivity can make a significant impact on the well-being of people, it is in the area of healthcare. It is also an area where the distance between the promise of sex positivity and what actually occurs in healthcare interactions can be incredibly wide. How can healthcare professionals enact a framework of sex positivity in their interactions with patients and clients, and in their collaborative work with other healthcare professionals?

Sex Positivity as a Framework

While there is a growing affirmation of the importance of sexual health in healthcare settings, which includes some elements of a sex positive framework, there is also some criticism concerning the primary focus on problems, disease and dysfunctions in Western healthcare systems

DOI: 10.4324/9781032631820-4

(Wakefield, 2007; Wakefield, 2016). The focus on dysfunction does not facilitate a positive affirmation of many aspects of a sex *positive* framework, such as open and clear communication and a sense of empowerment, authenticity, and agency directly. The focus on dysfunction and treatment of disease in healthcare can frustrate attempts to prioritize the prevention of sexual health problems in the first place, or to address the social determinants of health in a comprehensive way. The focus on dysfunction and disease can facilitate the stigmatization of people and inadvertently support negative stereotypes of sexually diverse people, exacerbating health disparities.

The sex positive framework can be seen as an approach to human sexuality that is part of the biopsychosocial model (BPS), (Berry & Berry, 2013). Drawn in part from the interdisciplinary field of developmental science, BPS approaches health and illness as a complex interplay of biological (genetics, physiology, and pathology), psychological (including emotionally influenced, subconscious, conditioned, and behavioral), and social factors (e.g., environmental, cultural, relational, socio-economical). Jannini et al. (2010) discussed how health care, and in particular, sexology, have used the BPS approach to provide treatment approaches that emphasize personal satisfaction and quality of life. The assessment of sexual problems through the BPS lens combines current and historical factors, physical and laboratory testing, and insight and knowledge gleaned through patient/partner interviews. A focus on the interdisciplinary collaboration between a variety of healthcare professionals and their patients allows for more integrated, tailored, and personal care. "Collaborative practice happens when multiple health workers from different professional backgrounds work together with patients, families, carers and communities to deliver the highest quality of care across settings" (Gilbert, et al., 2010).

One of the roots of a sex positive framework in healthcare can be found in the work of Wilhelm Reich, an Austrian psychoanalyst who made significant contributions to psychoanalytic theory in the area of sexuality in the 1920s and 1930s (Corrington, 2003). He argued that psychological and physical ailments could arise from sexual repression, and argued that sexual freedom and equality would improve psychological and physical health (Reich, 1973). A sex positive framework also owes much to Alfred Kinsey and his groundbreaking research on human sexuality in the late 1940s and early 1950s (Kinsey et al., 1948; Kinsey et al., 1953). These scientific studies challenged the trend in our Western culture to repress and ignore sexual diversity in behavior and desire, and helped to establish the part of the sex positive framework that values holding a nonjudgmental attitude towards all forms of consensual sexual behavior. A significant moment in the development of a sex positive framework in healthcare came in 1994, at the International Conference on Population and Development, when the conference officially promulgated clear statements that sexual health is an essential component of people's health and well-being (Roseman & Reichenbach, 2010). Since then, other global health efforts, including policies from the World Health Organization, have prioritized sexual health as a significant part of the agenda for addressing all people's health and well-being.

Since the beginning of the 2000s, this approach has become more inclusive, pro-social and straightforward towards discussions of consent and the breadth of sexual expression. The sex positive approach has incorporated an emphasis on a reduction on stigma, bias, and personal autonomy, in both healthcare and personal sexual choice.

Question the Idea of "normal"

Given the centrality of respect for sexual diversity in a sex positive framework, healthcare workers can become aware of, and question, the idea of "normal" that permeates traditional Western approaches to medicine and health. In fact, the concepts of dysfunction or disease often involve criteria of what is "normal" in terms of average, or "normal" in terms of past medical knowledge and expert agreement. This includes the very commonly used term of sexual minority, as the term rests on a concept of majority/minority which can lend itself to ideas of what is normal. Even using the meaning of *statistically* normal or average, meant to refrain from making normative judgments, can still activate ideas and attitudes about what is acceptable or appropriate from a moral framework that might clash with the nonjudgmental approach valued in this framework. Hence, it is more helpful at this time to emphasize the term *sexual diversity* over the term *sexual minority* to describe the range of sexual behaviors, desires, identities and communities.

The highlighting of diversity in a sex positive framework over what is "normal", or over the majority/minority dichotomy can support an effort to "queer" healthcare (Manthey et al., 2022). By challenging traditional norms and assumptions, and highlighting the complexity of actual experience and how experience doesn't match clearcut categories or the culturally constructed boundaries dividing kinds of experience, a healthcare professional can be more inclusive and responsive to a wider range of sexual expression, identity, and desire. A positive sexuality focus on authenticity would mean that "normal" is not the goal for an individual client or patient. And approaching clients and patients with a more inclusive and responsive perspective will highlight the need to address health disparities and address stigma and a lack of cultural competence in the field of healthcare.

Reproductive Justice as an Example Area to Apply Frameworks

Reproductive Justice is a term meant to capture the idea that society should support individuals' bodily autonomy, which includes an individual's or family's decisions concerning all aspects and stages of sexual reproduction (Ross, 2020). A sex positive approach to healthcare would include this value. Since accurate knowledge is a key component of a person's ability to exercise bodily autonomy, a sex positive approach to healthcare would include an emphasis on medically accurate sex education. Access to medically necessary services would be an important component of this approach, including assisted reproductive services like in vitro fertilization (IVF) to treat infertility. This medical procedure is being indirectly discouraged and limited in the state of Alabama at the time of writing, due to a decision by the Alabama Supreme Court to legally classify embryos as children, with the serious implications that healthcare professionals and patients might be charged with homicide if embryos are destroyed, or be criminally investigated if miscarriages occur during pregnancy. Reproductive justice would also include proactive efforts to prevent sexual abuse; given the key values emphasized by a sex positive approach on consent and communication, the prevention of sexual violence and abuse would be a central goal for healthcare providers.

Talking About Sex with Patients

While many healthcare providers agree to the importance of a multidisciplinary and interdisciplinary approach to sexual health, providers are more likely to utilize this in assessment and diagnosis but find treatment to fall into more unimodal practices (Goldstein, 2012). Many studies indicate that patients and clients prefer to talk with healthcare professionals regarding their sexual health, but at the same time are often anxious about initiating these conversations, and healthcare providers often experience doubts and anxieties about initiating these conversations as well (Kelder et al., 2022). This is especially true of people who are sexually diverse in their behavior or identities; for example, many people who identify as LGBTQ+ or people involved in kink/BDSM alternative sexualities are especially likely to experience anticipated stigma in regards to healthcare encounters, to such a degree that they don't disclose their sexuality (Fikar & Keith, 2004; Rose & Friedman, 2013; Sprott et al., 2021). In light of this, it is important that healthcare providers who work from a sex positive framework are familiar with the PLISSIT Model.

The PLISSIT Model

The PLISSIT Model was created by Jack S. Annon (1976) and expanded into the Ex-PLISSIT Model (the extended-PLISSIT model) in 2006 by Sally Davis and Bridget Taylor (Taylor & Davis, 2006). The PLISSIT model assists healthcare providers in how to intervene more effectively with their patients/clients about their sexual health. PLISSIT approaches patients' sexual concerns through four expanding levels of intervention: (P) Permission, (LI) Limited Information, (SS) Specific Suggestions, and (IT) Intensive Therapy. Permission entails creating an atmosphere where open discussion of sexual experiences and concerns is encouraged, and this often includes reassuring patents and clients that their concerns are valid. Limited information means providing basic information about sexual response, anatomy, and sexuality with the goal of addressing any misconceptions. The level of specific suggestions includes providers offering recommendations and strategies to address concerns. The final level, intensive therapy, involves situations where providing a strategy for action is not enough because the situations involve more complex or deep-seated issues. Taylor & Davis (2006) suggested that providers recognize how permission-giving is essential to the healthcare provider's role, and how this permission-giving needs to be explicit and direct, and not assuming that a nurse asking, "do you have any other questions?" is enough to give permission to discuss sexuality in a frank and direct manner.

Strategies for Intake

The National Coalition for Sexual Health (NCSH) recommends asking essential health questions of patients during intake, or at least, annually. They suggest the following script to start: "I'm going to ask you a few questions about your sexual health. Since sexual health is very important to overall health, I ask all my adult patients these questions. Before I begin, do you have any questions or sexual concerns you'd like to discuss?" (Altarum Institute, 2022). At The Alternative Sexualities Health Research Alliance, co-founded by the authors, the following is recommended after the introductory script outlined by NCSH and after any discussion that ensues from that prompt: "My clients participate in a wide variety of sexual practices, including oral, anal, or vaginal intercourse, using sex toys, as well as role play, bondage, rough sex, or other activities. Different activities have different risks and different implications for how I can best care for you. What types of sexual activity do you participate in?"

Conducting a Sexual History Assessment

A sex positive approach to taking a sexual history assessment will highlight questions around consent and agency, the wide range of sexual expression, and reducing shame and stigma. We will briefly compare this approach to a standard approach to taking a sexual history assessment in healthcare.

The Centers for Disease Control and Prevention, National Center for HIV/AIDS, Viral Hepatitis, STD, and TB Prevention offers a tool for guiding healthcare providers in taking a sexual history. The major aspects of a sexual history assessment include the five "Ps": Partners, Practices, Protection from STIs, Past History of STIs, and Pregnancy Intention (CDC,

2022). The design of the tool exemplifies the standard approach in healthcare, with its focus on disease and dysfunction. The discussion of the patient's sex partners contains some guidance that is sex positive: never make assumptions of a patient's sexual orientation or the gender identity of their partners. The rest of the guidance is focused on assessing risk factors for STIs that are related to the sex partners of the patient, and to specific sexual practices related to genital, oral and anal sex. Questions concerning STI prevention tools, including the frequency of using prevention tools and discussion of times when they do not use a prevention tool, are included in the guidance. Discussion of past STI occurrence, and intentions around having children, round out the guidance.

A sex positive approach to a sexual history assessment would include several aspects not contained in the CDC guidance. Naming different relational configurations when discussing sex partners would simultaneously address a wide range of sexual expression and reduce shame and stigma around relational diversity. Asking about consensual non-monogamies, like polyamory, open marriages, or swinging, and not assuming monogamy, would add to the CDC's recommendation not to assume the sexual orientation of the patient or the gender identity of partners. Asking about relational diversity would also enable a healthcare provider to have a fuller context for the types of sexual behaviors a patient might engage in, including those that might elevate some types of risk. This approach to sexual history would also discuss the purposes of sex, which would include experiencing pleasure, doing it for recreation or procreation, enhancing intimacy and emotional bonds, or coping with stress. By naming the various reasons and motivations for sex, a healthcare provider can gain a psychological and social context for engaging in various sexual behaviors that would be very relevant for addressing risk and the prevention of disease or dysfunction, in addition to enhancing the overall health and well-being of the client or patient. This approach would also discuss practices by expanding the discussion beyond genitals, to include all body parts as part of sexuality.

Collaborating with Sexuality Specialists

An interdisciplinary approach to sexual concerns, including other professionals trained in various sexual medicine disciplines, including sex therapy, sex counseling, and sexual education, emphasizes the biopsycho-social systems approach that is inherent to a sex positive approach to healthcare. Interdisciplinary coordination offers greater opportunities for wrap-around care that is sex positive and inclusive.

There are a variety of sexuality specialists that can collaborate with primary healthcare providers. Sex therapists are mental health providers with advanced degrees who have clinical sexuality training in the cultural, behavioral, emotional, and/or psychological care of both simple and more complex sexual concerns, particularly concerns that may benefit from intensive therapy ("IT") described in the PLISSIT model. However, practicing as a licensed sex therapist is currently only regulated in one U.S. state, Florida. The American Association of Sex Educators, Counselors and Therapists (AASECT) certifies the largest number of sex therapists in the U.S. Whether in the U.S. or abroad, there are educational opportuni-ties for those with advanced degrees to become trained clinical sexologists and some may adopt the term sex therapist to describe themselves, even if not certified. Outside of Florida, there are no restrictions on the use of the term sex therapist by providers, reminding both patients and refer-ring healthcare providers to check on the training and experience of any sex therapist.

Sex counselors, particularly cross-trained professionals, provide client/patient-revolved interventions that are solution-focused and fall within the "PLISS" (permission, limited information and specific suggestions) portion of the PLISSIT Model. Pelvic floor physical therapists are licensed physical therapists (PT) who work to support pelvic floor health. Pelvic floor therapists specialize in the physical and functional integrity of the pelvic floor unit through the life stages of an individual, regardless of sex or gender, permitting an optimal quality of life through its multifunctional role (Pierce, 2015). Licensed Occupational Therapists (OT) work with a variety of patient habilitative and rehabilitative needs to address sexuality by utilizing core occupational therapy skills, such as communication, col-laborative problem solving, pacing, positioning, and adaptive equipment.

There are several other types of sexuality specialists that a healthcare provider might collaborate with, as the field of sexuality is a growing field with emerging professions that can provide expertise in a sex positive manner. Providing healthcare in a sex positive framework will continue to evolve as the field of sexuality expands and grows.

Conclusion

How can healthcare professionals enact a framework of sex positivity in their interactions with patients and clients, and in their collaborative work with other healthcare professionals? The long history of sex positivity in healthcare provides a framework and some guiding principles for interactions with clients and patients: open and clear communication that emphasizes a sense of empowerment, authenticity, and agency for clients and patients; an expansive view of human sexuality that focuses on the whole person and honors the wide range of sexual diversity that humans exhibit; and expanding beyond discussions of "the normal" and the focus on disease, dysfunction or disorder. New developments in the field of human sexuality would also expand opportunities for interdisciplinary collaboration to address the health and well-being of patients and clients. There are many resources and tools for healthcare professionals to incorporate and enact a positive sexuality framework, and the time to explore and develop this framework is now.

References

Altarum Institute. (2022). *Sexual health and your patients: A provider's guide.* Washington, DC: Author. Available at: https://nationalcoalitionforsexualhealth.org/tools/for-healthcare-providers/asset/Provider-Guide_May-2022.pdf

Annon, J. S. (1981). PLISSIT therapy. In R. J. Corsini (Ed.), *Handbook of innovative psychotherapies.* Wiley.

Berry, M. D., & Berry, P. D. (2013). Contemporary treatment of sexual dysfunction: Reexamining the biopsychosocial model. *The Journal of Sexual Medicine, 10*(11), 2627–2643.

Centers for Disease Control and Prevention (CDC) (2022). *A guide to taking a sexual history.* Atlanta GA. https://www.cdc.gov/std/treatment/SexualHistory.htm

Corrington, R. S. (2003). *Wilhelm Reich: Psychoanalyst and radical naturalist.* Farrar, Straus and Giroux.

Fikar, C. R., & Keith, L. (2004). Information needs of gay, lesbian, bisexual, and transgendered health care professionals: Results of an Internet survey. *Journal of the Medical Library Association*, 92(1), 56–65. http://www.ncbi.nlm.nih.gov/pmc/articles/pmc314103/

Gilbert, J. H., Yan, J., & Hoffman, S. J. (2010). A WHO report: Framework for action on interprofessional education and collaborative practice. *Journal of Allied Health*, 39 Suppl 1, 196–197.

Goldstein, I. (2012). Sexual medicine reflects the light of knowledge. *The Journal of Sexual Medicine*, 9(11), 2733–2735. https://doi.org/10.1111/j.1743-6109.2012.02991.x

Jannini, E. A., McCabe, M. P., Salonia, A., Montorsi, F., & Sachs, B. D. (2010). Controversies in sexual medicine: Organic vs. psychogenic? The Manichean diagnosis in sexual medicine. *The Journal of Sexual Medicine*, 7(5), 1726–1733. https://doi.org/10.1111/j.1743-6109.2010.01824.x

Kelder, I., Sneijder, P., Klarenbeek, A., & Laan, E. (2022). Communication practices in conversations about sexual health in medical healthcare settings: A systematic review. *Patient Education and Counseling*, 105(4), 858–868. https://doi.org/10.1016/j.pec.2021.07.049

Kinsey, A. C., Pomeroy, W. B., & Martin, C. E. (1948). *Sexual behavior in the human male*. Indiana University Press.

Kinsey, A. C., Pomeroy, W. B., Martin, C. E., & Gebhard, P. H. (1953). *Sexual behavior in the human female*. Indiana University Press.

Manthey, K., Novotny, M., & Cox, M. B. (2022). Queering the rhetoric of health and medicine: Bodies, embodiment, and the future. In K. Manthey, M Novotny, & M. Cox (Eds.) *The Routledge handbook of queer rhetoric* (pp. 438–444). Routledge.

Pierce, H., Perry, L., Gallagher, R., and Chiarelli, P. (2015). Pelvic floor health: A concept analysis. *Journal of Advanced Nursing*, 71(5), 991–1004. https://10.1111/jan.12628

Reich, W. (1973). *The function of the orgasm: Sex-economic problems of biological energy*. Farrar, Straus and Giroux.

Rose, I. D., & Friedman, D. P. (2013). We need health information too: A systematic review of studies examining the health information seeking and communication practices of sexual minority youth. *Health Education Journal*, 72(4), 417–430. https://doi.org/10.1177/0017896912446739

Roseman, M. J., & Reichenbach, L. (2010). International Conference on Population and Development at 15 years: Achieving sexual and reproductive health and rights for all? *American Journal of Public Health*, 100(3): 403–406. https://doi.org/10.2105/AJPH.2009.177873

Ross, L. (2020). Understanding reproductive justice. In C. McCann, S. Kim, & E. Ergun (Eds.) *Feminist theory reader: Local and global perspectives* (pp. 77–82). Routledge.

Sprott, R. A., Randall, A., Smith, K., & Woo, L. (2021). Rates of injury and healthcare utilization for kink-identified patients. *Journal of Sexual Medicine, 18*(10), 1721–1734. https://doi.org/10.1016/j.jsxm.2021.08.001

Taylor, B., & Davis, S. (2006). Using the extended PLISSIT model to address sexual healthcare needs. *Nursing Standard (Royal College of Nursing, Great Britain), 21*(11), 35–40. https://doi.org/10.7748/ns2006.11.21.11.35.c6382

Wakefield J. C. (2007). The concept of mental disorder: Diagnostic implications of the harmful dysfunction analysis. *World Psychiatry, 6*(3), 149–156.

Wakefield, J. C. (2016). Diagnostic issues and controversies in DSM-5: Return of the false positives problem. *Annual Review of Clinical Psychology, 12*, 105–132. https://psycnet.apa.org/doi/10.1146/annurev-clinpsy-032814-112800

4

INTUITIVE SEXUALITY

A Sex-Positive Model for Understanding and Treating Compulsive Sexual Behavior

Ari Lewis[1]

Introduction

Picture the following historical scene. You are at a professional conference. The focus of the conference is sexual health. Most attendees are either clinicians or researchers who work with individuals struggling with compulsive sexual behavior (CSB). You attend one workshop. The presenter refers to the members of his couples with the following two labels, "addict," and "victim." You attend another workshop. The presenter discusses the value of using a polygraph test on clients who cheated on their partners. At yet another workshop, one of the primary "symptoms" a presenting researcher has assessed for in her study includes, "number of sexual partners," unironically implying that a higher number of recent sexual partners must automatically indicate sexual pathology.[2] You check the date to learn how far back in time you must have traveled. The year is 2022.

DOI: 10.4324/9781032631820-5

This was my experience attending a sexual health conference. When I tell people that one of the focuses of my work centers around working with people with unhealthy relationships with their sexuality, people often want to know if I am talking about "sex addicts." I always assumed I would experience this among the general public, but I had hoped I could expect a higher level of respect among professionals. I was sorely let down. When my colleague and I began to present our own workshop at this conference on consensual non-monogamy (CNM) in therapy, a quarter of attendees stood up and left the room with distinctive frowns on their faces. Mingling with the crowd, other professionals who heard I worked with polyamorous clients, after needing me to explain the difference between polyamory and polygamy, wanted to know: "How do you teach these young people to protect themselves from STDs?" Before I could finish explaining that there does not seem to be a difference in the contraction rate of sexually transmitted infections between individuals practicing CNM and individuals practicing monogamy – and before I could even begin to explain that it is not so clear that older individuals engage in CNM that much less than younger individuals – I received another sex-negative question. I then realized that the person I was speaking to assumed that my goal must be to "cure" polyamory, as if polyamory was just another example of CSB. I always knew that clinicians working with CSB surely could benefit from the field of positive sexuality. However, on this particular day, I learned that many clinicians and researchers absolutely need it.

Defining CSB

Braun-Harvey and Vigorito (2015) define CSB as occurring when an individual repeatedly suffers from, or causes, harm due to that individual's failure to exert agency over "consensual" sexual activities, "thoughts," and "urges" (p. 48). There are numerous, somewhat conflicting definitions of CSB currently in use, but this chapter adopts the definition proposed above.

CSB is not the same as sex "addiction." CSB distinguishes the model proposed herein, the Intuitive Sexuality Model (ISM), from ideologies endorsed by proponents of the sex "addiction" model, which (incorrectly) assumes CSB to be an addiction (to be discussed shortly). Braun-Harvey and Vigorito (2015) technically refer to CSB as "out of control sexual behavior" (OCSB), thus they developed the OCSB Model. Indeed, ISM, proposed herein, derives much influence from the OCSB Model.

Serious Problems with the Sex "Addiction" 12- Step Model

Most of the attendees at the conference (described above) followed what is likely the best known and most applied model in current use among clinicians treating CSB: the sex "addiction"[3] model. The sex "addiction" model stems from Carnes' (2001) adaptation of the 12-step program developed via Alcoholics Anonymous. Studies validating the effectiveness of 12-step programs for CSB (e.g., Sex Addicts Anonymous, Sex and Love Addicts Anonymous, etc.) do exist (Efrati & Gola, 2018), but they typically suffer from significant methodological limitations. Furthermore, a prominent argument promoting them relies on these programs' cost-effectiveness rather than any demonstrated superiority over other therapeutic modalities, such as Cognitive Behavioral Therapy (CBT) or mindfulness-based approaches (Efrati & Gola, 2018). As of this writing, it appears systematic research is lacking regarding the potential harmful impacts 12-step and related programs may have on clients with CSB. Future scholarship should address this gap in the literature, given that several expert clinicians working with former 12-step participants for CSB have observed significant harmful impacts on clients from such interventions (e.g., M. M. Crocker, personal communication, July 2015; Neves, 2022).

Simply conceptualizing CSB as sex "addiction" may partly explain any assumed success reported from studies that examine particular outcomes of 12-step programs. Programs using the sex "addiction" model may inherently cause harm simply by their processes. This is because sex "addiction" programs include – under the purview of CSB – sexual behaviors that are not necessarily inherently problematic. By problematizing diverse sexual behaviors that may actually be normal and healthy, clinicians may succeed in reducing such behaviors, yet that would be an example of stigmatizing and grossly harming clients rather than helping them. For example, the sex "addiction" model includes language in its assessment tools that regard many kinks, visiting bathhouses, and particular sexual fantasies, as problematic behaviors.[4] Shaming these behaviors carries the potential to enact direct trauma on the client and severely diminish a client's well-being. Such practices, thankfully, are in direct contrast with values endorsed by such institutions as the World Health Organization (WHO, n.d.) and the American Association of Sexuality Educators, Counselors, and Therapists (AASECT; Kerner, 2016). It has been argued that 12-step programs – when used to treat CSB – are the new conversion therapy, but instead of attempting to change individuals' sexual orientations, this form of conversion therapy aims to change individuals' other sexual needs and desires (Kort, 2020; Neves, 2021, 2022). Future research should thus examine long-term effects, including likely harms, that such programs reportedly have on clients. Meanwhile, clinicians who wish to help their clients successfully address CSB are strongly advised to examine other available treatment models. The next section briefly reviews four, in particular.[5]

Positive Sexuality as an Answer to CSB (Mis)Treatment

Of the CSB models noted herein (see below), the OCSB Model (Braun-Harvey & Vigorito, 2015) has most strongly influenced the ISM. OCSB includes a sophisticated conceptualization of CSB that makes it advantageous over other models, but it limits CSB treatment to group therapy. Also, it addresses oppression and privilege as important to CSB and considers kink and sexual identity but at the expense of other important issues, such as race, gender, and ability status. Some of its other limitations will be highlighted shortly, including its lack of attention to both subjective life-meaning and interoception.

Although Coleman et al. (2018) use the term, "sex-positive," in the name of their CSB treatment model (Integrative Biopsychosocial and Sex-Positive Model of Impulsive/Compulsive Sexual Behavior, ICSB), this model reverts to a pathologizing stance in several ways. For example, the ICSB strongly emphasizes what it refers to as the biological factors of CSB, referencing research that the authors claim demonstrate neurological differences in the brains of individuals with CSB. The ICSB also staunchly advocates medication as one of the main avenues for CSB treatment. This focus on biological differences and pharmacological intervention presents CSB as pathological and medicalizes personal differences, which is not fully sex-positive.

Blycker and Potenza (2018) offer new and useful tools for treating CSB. Their Mindful Model of Sexual Health (MMSH), however, relies heavily on the use of mindfulness-based psychotherapy. Although mindfulness can be effective, limiting a treatment model to one particular modality makes it perhaps less useful for a wide variety of clients. MMSH also may be primarily useful to administer by therapists trained in that specific modality, or a closely related one, rendering the model less available for the majority of therapists, given most are typically trained from an eclectic approach (Bolton et al., 2022). An important aspect in common between the MMSH and the ISM concerns the importance of addressing interoception, which is one's sensory ability to detect and accurately interpret one's own body signals.

Finally, Neves (2021) offers a set of useful tools for sex positive clinicians working with clients with CSB, which he calls a pluralistic and sex positive treatment approach (PSTA). In particular, the PSTA emphasis on meaning in life for clients with CSB sets this model apart from other models. However, similar to deficits of the other models above, a more direct means of addressing power and privilege in therapy – as well as other underlying roots of clients' problems – could improve the comprehensiveness of PSTA.

A significant limitation shared by each of the above models concerns user-friendliness. A more coherent narrative tying the components of what leads to and sustains CSB is needed in order to help clients understand how CSB develops, and how this process subsequently shapes their personal struggles with sexual behaviors. Better client engagement and therapeutic communication is also needed, which is important to a robust, effective CSB model. Thus, ISM, proposed herein, draws from the strengths of other models, while also addressing current limitations.

ISM: Understanding Basic Processes of CSB

ISM conceptualizes CSB as resulting from a three-component cycle: toxic narratives, basic fears, and mechanics. Specifically, toxic narratives lead to and intensify an individual's basic fears – which produce emotional regulation issues, and, to quell those fears, an individual uses CSB. Increases in CSB, however, often further exacerbate an individual's toxic narratives, which thus produce a downward spiral. The underlying roots of the problems contributing to the client's CSB are the toxic narratives that others have held about the client (societally or on a personal level) and which the individual has usually internalized.[6] Toxic narratives often stem from interpersonal trauma (e.g., a man whose father routinely molested him growing up, thus teaching him such toxic narratives as, "you are meant to be exploited," and "you are worthless"), as well as from cultural power and privilege (e.g., a person may feel inferior due to their race or because of a physical disability). Importantly, both power and privilege can contribute to the toxic narratives that drive CSB. For example, men (who make up a majority of clients with CSB) often, in my experience, worry about being viewed as less masculine and, for them, part of the drive towards CSB stems from a desire to gain power through the masculinization they perceive they receive from sexual activity. These toxic narratives are what lead to the basic fears around CSB.

The basic fears of CSB are what drive the client's struggles with emotional regulation. The models discussed earlier herein all converge on this point: that emotional regulation can play a major role in causing and maintaining CSB; and research substantiates this (Lew-Starowicz et al., 2020). The models also frequently split emotional regulation issues into self-regulation and attachment regulation. Addressing CSB, accordingly, often involves either self-regulatory issues or relational issues. This conceptualization of self- and other-focused regulation strategies is popular in the current clinical milieu (e.g., Fern, 2020; Heller, 2019), but could benefit from an expanded perspective that incorporates subjective meaning in life and potentially other factors that drive emotional dysregulation (e.g., García-Alandete et al., 2019; Grech, 2021), especially when dealing with sexual issues (Kleinplatz, 2017).[7]

ISM thus conceptualizes emotional regulation as stemming largely from fear, and it draws from Existential Therapy (ET) to identify these fears. The first is a fear of living in isolation or of engulfment by one's partner (see Crocker, 2015). Such fear can lead to problems with self-regulation, as well as problems with attachment. The fundamental fear of isolation is thus addressed somewhat haphazardly by the models discussed earlier, since most of them target, in one way or another, self-regulation and attachment issues. However, when treating CSB-related emotional regulation issues, there are other important fears to address: meaninglessness, freedom, and death (Yalom, 2020). ISM posits that these fears are what produce emotional regulation issues. People may deal with these emotional regulation issues in a myriad of unhealthy ways, but, if the unhealthy coping mechanism a client develops is CSB, then CSB is perpetuated by its particular mechanics.

The mechanics of CSB involve the specific habits of using sexual activity to cope (problematically) with emotional problems. Fundamentally, ISM adopts the perspective of the Intuitive Eating (IE) Model, which posits that compulsive eating behaviors result from a lack of skill in determining when one truly feels hungry and when one feels satisfied. Similarly, ISM posits that CSB mechanics are perpetuated due to a lack of skill in determining when one truly feels lustful or erotically turned on and when one feels sexually satisfied. Overly restricting sexual activities can often exacerbate the problem, because it does not allow the individual with CSB to learn to recognize when they actually feel their feelings of lustfulness and sexual satiation. As CSB intensifies, this usually exacerbates particular toxic narratives, thus leading to continued problems.

Therapeutic Modalities and the ISM

A distinguishing factor of ISM concerns its employment of therapeutic modalities. Although it borrows from ET, IE, and Rational Emotive Behavior Therapy (REBT) in important parts of its conceptualization, implementation of ISM can and should involve deploying therapeutic modalities that the CSB therapist feels most comfortable using. This is an important feature of ISM, because studies that compare one established therapeutic modality to another generally determine little difference in treatment outcome (Cujpers et al., 2023). Other factors external to specific modality, such as competence and the therapeutic relationship, matter far more to outcome effectiveness (Friedlander et al., 2018; Norcross & Lambert, 2019). As of this writing, research validating specifically CBT interventions (i.e., REBT, Beckian CBT,[8] Positive Psychotherapy, etc.) and mindfulness-based therapies (i.e., Acceptance and Commitment Therapy, Mindfulness-Based Cognitive Therapy, Somatic Therapy, etc.) for the treatment of CSB (Efrati & Gola, 2018) might erroneously lead therapists with stronger backgrounds in other approaches to believe they are not well-suited to provide CSB treatment. However, the general evidence in the psychotherapy research literature strongly challenges such assumptions.

In reality, it can often be very difficult for clients to find therapists who fit their personalities and that they can relate to. Therefore, the flexibility in modality application is a central feature of the ISM.

ISM Treatment Principles

IE was created in the 1990s as a method of helping people heal their relationships with food and, since its inception, it has demonstrated impressive outcomes (Tribole & Resch, 2020). IE is based on ten principles that clinicians use in the treatment of compulsive eating issues, as well as other unhealthy attitudes about food. Because compulsive eating and CSB are both compulsions, ISM draws from IE principles and adapts them for application to CSB.

As mentioned above, the ISM is intended primarily for eclectic clinicians and, thus, does not marry itself to any one modality. However, two modalities warrant brief attention here. IE draws much of its rationale from REBT in its understanding of clients' unhealthy relationships with food. Because ISM borrows much of its organizing framework for addressing CSB from IE – and because I have trained in and use REBT a lot in my work with my own clients – many of the examples below include the use of REBT to help treat CSB. Similar to the IE approach, basic REBT theory is necessary for using ISM. However, examples using other modalities will also be included to illustrate the versatility of ISM.

Treatment Principle 1: Reject Toxic Narratives[9]

"Toxic narratives" are the underlying roots of CSB. When applying Principle 1, the clinician helps the client challenge both sociocultural narratives (e.g., shame due to internalized racism, internalized antisemitism, etc.) and personal narratives that may be psychologically harmful (e.g., subconsciously holding on to a message repeatedly conveyed by the client's father that the client is, as his father used to say over and over again, "useless"). Some clients may succeed in identifying their toxic narratives on day one of therapy whereas others may take years to uncover these. Clients may sometimes identify one or two toxic narratives early in therapy but take a much longer time to discover other toxic narratives. The ideal goal, here, is not to just reject the toxic narratives in principle, but to totally transform the client's internalized belief-system so as to eradicate the toxic belief and adopt or strengthen alternative, healthier beliefs. Eradicating toxic beliefs completely can sometimes be more aspirational than actually doable, since these beliefs can often be sourced to a young age, but aspiring to eradicate the belief can help the client feel motivated to more significantly diminish the toxic belief and strengthen alternative, healthier beliefs. And just recognizing that the belief is there can go a long way toward diminishing its power.[10]

Once a toxic narrative has been identified, I often employ a technique from REBT to address the toxic narrative head on. At the core of a toxic narrative, there often lies one of the fundamental irrational beliefs: "there is something wrong with me."[11] This irrational belief can come in the form of, "I am no good," "I am undesirable," "I am stupid," or any number of other unhealthy generalizations about oneself. I help the client learn to validate the underlying, healthy emotions that trigger these irrational beliefs. So, if the client says he feels stupid because he engaged in CSB again, I might teach the client to validate that he feels disappointed about acting out again, but then I may teach him to remind himself that that does not make him stupid, that he is not stupid, and that the only way he can be stupid is if he calls himself stupid again – I would only add this last part if I have a good enough rapport with the client to have confidence he will know this last part is a joke. REBT often works best when used with humor (Najafi & Lea-Baranovich, 2014).

I also typically encourage the client to find ways to do things that might trigger him to think the unhealthy thought, "I am stupid," so he can have more opportunities to challenge this belief with alternative healthier ones (this is called shame-attacking, Ellis & Dryden, 2007). He might accomplish this by, for example, intentionally getting an obvious fact wrong (like, whether Alaska is part of the U.S.) in front of a stranger. One might assume that it is good for clients to feel ashamed of their CSB, but it is not. Those feelings of shame only perpetuate the toxic narratives that drive CSB, as is demonstrated in countless studies of compulsive and addictive behavior (e.g., Bilevicius et al., 2018; Snoek et al., 2021).

To give a couple of examples of other modalities here, a Narrative Therapist might encourage the above client to uncover the narratives of his life and learn where "I am stupid" comes from, then the therapist might assist the client in replacing that narrative with alternative, healthier narratives through finding, for example, exceptions that disprove the unhealthy narrative (referred to by Narrative Therapists as unique outcomes). Similarly, a Beckian Cognitive Behavioral Therapist might help the client challenge the label of "stupid" (referred to in Beckian CBT as labeling).

In another example of a toxic narrative, a client I worked with, Sunil,[12,13] had been abstinent from porn, masturbation, and any dating for six months. He had become heavily involved in an online group known as NoFap, a harmful, toxically masculine forum where mostly heterosexual men often bully each other under the guise of supporting one another in healing from CSB by abstaining from masturbation (Prause & Binnie, 2023). In the NoFap community, these months-long abstentions from masturbation are referred to as "reboots." Sunil reported four reboots over the past five years, and each reboot would follow with an inevitable fall into intensified CSB episodes.

Over the course of therapy, our conversations uncovered an important toxic narrative. As a cisgender, South Asian man, Sunil felt emasculated by stereotypes his high school bullies imposed upon him as sexually inferior to other men. His compulsive use of porn helped Sunil imagine, for just a moment, that he was a "stud," but it would inevitably lead to intensified feelings of sexual inferiority, because his use of porn felt so out of control. Finding the NoFap community seemed like a way for Sunil to gain control over his CSB, but, as he learned through therapy, the racist and sexist beliefs held by many NoFap members only intensified Sunil's CSB in between reboots. Furthermore, Sunil's preoccupation with abstaining from masturbating only further isolated him. Helping Sunil reach these insights gradually helped Sunil untangle the toxic, masculine narratives he held so he could free himself from them, and it opened up our work to replace Sunil's reboots with a look at the basic fears of Sunil's CSB.

Treatment Principle 2: Cope with Your Emotions Without Using Sex[14]

Existential Therapy (ET), a modality that appears to work best when paired with other, structured approaches (Vos et al., 2015), operates on the principle that our clients' struggles stem from their fear of four fundamental things: freedom, isolation, meaninglessness, and death (Yalom, 2020).[15] In my work with CSB, I have observed that each of these fears also has a corollary, subverted manifestation, so: fear of freedom can often manifest as a fear of restriction; fear of isolation can appear as a fear of engulfment; fear of meaninglessness often shows up as a fear of selflessness; and fear of death (sadly, far too often in clients with CSB) can manifest as a fear of life (i.e., desire to end their lives). It is not at all necessary that the CSB therapist train in ET any more than that they train in REBT, so long as the CSB therapist can competently assess for and address these fears using whichever modalities the therapist knows best. The main goal when using the ISM is to move the client away from operating out of fear and, instead, to operate based on dreams, aspirations, and desires.

Jack,[16] a man in his 30s could not decide whether he wanted to stay with his partner, Amy, or not. Staying would mean too much restriction for him; Amy wanted monogamy and Jack did not. But leaving would mean facing his fear of freedom (fear of freedom and restriction). One day, Amy agreed to open up their marriage. Suddenly, Jack wished they would close it again, not because he felt jealous of Amy, but because the options now available to Jack tormented him. Jack ended up saying yes to too many of his dating prospects, and this would eat at his time for other important tasks, such as tending to his coursework and searching for internships.

Psychodynamic exploration helped Jack realize that his internal conflict kept him feeling a connection with both of his deceased parents. They had divorced when Jack was young. When Jack would stay with his mother, she would place draconian restrictions on him, which he realized he associated with monogamy. Jack's father, on the other hand, exercised a lot of toxic masculinity in his parenting style. He would not just encourage Jack to go out to unsupervised parties. He would pressure Jack to "score" kisses, dates, and phone numbers at those parties and shame Jack if Jack "underperformed." Recognizing these connections with his parents helped Jack realize he wanted to better process his complicated grief over his parents' early deaths. He also began to realize that he was using life (engaging sexually with as many people as wanted to with him) to skirt his fear of death. These realizations helped Jack understand that he did want CNM, but he did not want to use CNM to date as recklessly as he had when he had been single either. Insights like these gradually led to a more intentional and balanced lifestyle. In this manner, Jack gradually replaced his fears with movement towards his desires. This helped facilitate a greater focus on the mechanics of CSB, addressed in Principles 3 through 7.

Treatment Principle 3: Honor Your Sexual Desire[17]

The ISM borrows from IE its emphasis on supporting clients in building their interoceptive awareness. In CSB treatment, building interoceptive skills means teaching clients to more accurately identify their body's signals. For example, this means noticing when one's body sensations may indicate that the client needs to use the restroom, feels hungry or full, or feels sleepy. Often, individuals with CSB lack interoceptive awareness (as indicated by multiple studies linking sexual issues with interoception, e.g., Poovey et al., 2023, as well as with other compulsive issues, e.g., Herman, 2023). The MMSH shares this focus on building interoceptive awareness to treat CSB, but the MMSH's approach to building interoception relies heavily on mindfulness, despite mixed evidence for using this method (Khalsa et al., 2020), especially on its own. Given the important role interoception likely plays in the demonstrated success of IE (DeVille et al., 2021), the ISM adopts IE's emphasis on building interoceptive awareness. Principles 3 through 6 outline exactly how.

It may seem counterintuitive to encourage clients with CSB to honor their sexual desire. Indeed, IE can seem similarly counterintuitive by encouraging clients, for example, who binge food frequently, to honor their hunger cues. But asking clients to honor their hunger cues can prove immensely helpful in treating binge eating (Cella et al., 2019), and I have found that the same is true for CSB. The clinician (and the client) must distinguish, however, between true sexual desire and a sexual craving. A craving might be to relieve boredom, numb emotional pain, or procrastinate, for example, or it could just be habitual (e.g., always masturbating to porn to mark transitions), whereas true sexual desire derives from feelings of lust.[18] Similar to individuals who struggle to differentiate between true hunger for food and stress-related food cravings, clients with CSB may often have much trouble differentiating lustful feelings from sexual cravings. This is where discussing what those feelings feel like to the client may prove helpful and encouraging the client to journal about these sensations as they arise is another method I often employ (as findings support, Sohal et al., 2022). When the client decides to engage in a sexual activity, the client is encouraged to pay extra attention to how it feels before, during, and afterwards, to help the client observe (without judgment) what the sensations feel like when they truly enjoyed the experience and when they engaged in sexual activity for non-sexual reasons.

This approach works without need for modification as long as there are no major consequences to a single act of CSB. For example, a client who regularly pays people for sex (and can afford it) or spends many hours watching pornography may suffer consequences as a result of the amount of their sexual activity, but there is less urgency with each, specific act of sexuality.[19] For clients cheating in monogamous relationships or paying for sex they cannot afford, modifications can be employed. For example, having the client imagine going through with the act in session and encouraging the client to really feel how it feels all the way through, including afterwards at the point when the client may feel regretful or disappointed. I then instruct the client to go through this visualization exercise – to really go through with the activity in the client's imagination – all the way through, when the client experiences a craving to do something they could later regret.

In many cases, however, the client may continue engaging in CSB that has harmful consequences regardless of therapist recommendations. If they do, the clinician is strongly advised not to judge the client as this will only exacerbate the client's shame and thus the problem (Knox, 2019). Instead, the clinician can engage with curiosity and use the episode as an opportunity for honoring the client's desire. Importantly, by doing this, the therapist is not endorsing cheating behavior or irresponsible spending. The therapist is helping the client truly explore their feelings about their sexual activities. With CSB, if the client engages in truly honoring their sexual desire (and noticing when their desire is not truly desire), the CSB becomes less tempting over time.

Sometimes, through this process, the client may identify that they truly desire the CSB and that the desire cannot be described as a craving. In many of these cases, I have found that the client will still concede that it often is a craving, but I have still found it important to validate that not all CSB can be chalked up only to cravings. The analogy here might be true hunger in the middle of a funeral. It is not a craving, but it also is not an appropriate place to eat food. The method of visualization can still help here. At the end of the day, true lust and a craving may not be that different if the activity is something the client will regret after engaging in it.

Treatment Principle 4: Make Peace with Sex[20]

Whereas Principle 3 is about learning to detect sexual desire, Principle 4 is about acting on sexual desire. This is how the client learns to differentiate between truly lustful sensations and cravings. As the client chooses to engage in sexual activity, they are encouraged to pay attention to how it feels, both during the activity and afterwards. Oftentimes, when clients act on cravings, they will report feeling nothing at all, bored, or even impatient to finish the activity or to engage in the next sexual activity they have planned. This is one clue the client may not truly have felt lustful. As mentioned in Principle 3, clients who may face more consequences for acting on their cravings may have to use other methods such as imaginative techniques with the therapist or journaling out an entire imagined experience when they feel tempted to do something they may later regret.

Treatment Principle 5: Challenge the Sex Police[21]

In cases where no one is harmed by the CSB (other than the client, due to losing time, money, etc.), applying the IE version of this principle is straightforward. Strongly dissuade clients from using "good" or "bad" or implying either of these judgments to their sexual behaviors. If the client spent an entire night engaging in cam sex instead of looking for a job, this might be regrettable, but the key here is that – assuming the client is single or CNM – this is not really a moral issue. They wasted time and it makes sense that they wish they could have that time back, but the key is to teach the client not to persecute themself for engaging in CSB.

REBT can be one handy tool when challenging the sex police. Either this will be how I learn what bad things the client calls themselves (revealing, perhaps, more toxic narratives), or I might learn that the client uses what REBT therapists call demands. Demands are beliefs that things must be a specific way (e.g., "I cannot engage in cam sex.", "I have to apply for a job every day or else I'm a loser.", etc.). When I learn about the latter type of irrational belief, I would validate the client's disappointment and teach the client to remind themself that things do not have to/need to.etc. anything.

This principle still applies in cases where a client's CSB does, in fact, violate the client's moral code. This can happen in cases where the client's CSB harmed someone else (e.g., if the client is cheating or excessively spending shared funds). It can also happen if the client is religious. Many Jews, Muslims, and Christians, for example, believe it is sinful to masturbate. In either event where, according to the client's belief system, they are, in fact, doing something morally wrong, the clinician is still advised to encourage the client to think and speak in specific terms instead of using condemnatory language. For example, "I feel guilty for breaking my relationship agreement and going behind my girlfriend's back," would be a healthy reaction. On the other hand, a toxic narrative emerges in the statement, "I am such a terrible person for cheating. What's wrong with me?" Clients in this case can often have a hard time with the idea that they are not bad people for doing bad things (or that nothing should/has to be, etc.). Here, I often employ another technique from REBT called the functional argument (R. A. DiGiuseppe, personal communication, September 2023). This is where I remind the client that condemning themself or demanding things in life actually increases the likelihood that they will keep engaging in the CSB they want to eliminate. This often motivates clients to more actively challenge their toxic beliefs.

Of course, REBT is one of many methods a therapist can use to successfully implement Principle 5. For example, a relational method that I sometimes use is to share with the client how I feel when I hear the client condemn his own behavior so harshly. A social justice lens that I often apply involves helping the client trace where his ideas of "good" and "bad" come from (societally) and, similarly, a psychodynamic approach that I often employ also involve helping the client to trace where his ideas of "good" and "bad" come from (looking to the client's history); I often use the second and third methods synchronously. For example, one client with CSB traced her ideas of "good" and "bad" to what her religious community growing up and her parents deemed to be "not-gay" and "too gay."

Treatment Principle 6: Discover Sexual Satisfaction[22]

As the client learns to remove judgment from their beliefs about sexual activity and, instead, strengthens their awareness of what genuinely feels good – not just in the moment, but after engaging in sexual activity as well – the client begins to recognize when they feel sexually satiated. This is a central awareness for the client to build, because feeling sexually satisfied plays a major role in whether one's sexual sensations signal lustfulness or a craving. For some individuals with CSB, feelings of satisfaction may be especially important to investigate after engaging in sexual activity. For others, it could also be important to investigate this during sexual activity as some with CSB may struggle to know when they want to stop sexually engaging. For this part of treatment, I often employ a positive psychotherapeutic technique known as savoring (also used in many mindfulness-based approaches). This is where the client really notices and enjoys the pleasant feelings they experience both during and after engaging in sexual activity (and I might encourage clients to practice this with other activities, such as when eating one of their favorite foods). The corollary feeling to sexual satisfaction in IE is fullness. Just as one knows they are not hungry if their stomachs feel full or satisfied, one knows they are not lustful if they feel sexually satisfied.

An important difference between savoring food and savoring sex concerns physical versus emotional enjoyment. Although there certainly are plenty of emotional aspects to enjoying food, such as eating with good company or taking in the ambiance of the room, the physical pleasure of food likely plays a more important role. When Kleinplatz et al. (2009) asked participants what they appreciated most about their favorite sexual experiences, they tended to focus much more on the emotional aspects (e.g., feeling close with their partner, laughing together, or learning something new) and they typically hardly at all mentioned the physical aspects (e.g., physical pleasure, attraction to their partner). For this reason, when I ask about clients' sexual experiences, I make sure to not only ask about pleasure. If a client only mentioned pleasure or the attractiveness of their partner, I gently push the client to think what else they enjoyed or did not enjoy about a given sexual encounter.

Treatment Principle 7: A Gentle Approach to Sexual Health[23]

Similar to IE, the ISM strongly emphasizes the previous principles over the final principle; this is because an over-emphasis on sexual health can lead to more judgement and shame. The ISM includes the final principle, however, because clients with CSB are, after all, replacing unhealthy behaviors with healthier one. Many of those healthier behaviors may not involve sexuality, but many of them might. Clients (and their therapists) thus naturally want to know what distinguishes healthy sexual activity from CSB. Current sexual health models tend to focus more on what healthy sexuality is not rather than what it is, so I do not use them, but instead, I focus on how my clients' sexual activities contribute to or detract from their overall well-being. To guide this exploration, I often use the PERMA Model (Seligman, 2018), which defines well-being as consisting of five components: pleasant emotions, engagement, healthy relationships, meaning in life, and accomplishment. As I go through Principles 3 through 6 in my treatment approach, I encourage clients to consider their desires not just in the immediate sense, but also in the grander sense. Maybe they may feel pleasant emotions with a particular activity, for example, but then feel regret the next day, due to an impact on something else that is important to their sense of purpose in life.

Conclusion

Sometimes, one cannot have too much of a good thing. Such may be the case when applying positive sexuality to CSB treatment. Although the various sex positive treatment models discussed earlier in this chapter do employ positive sexuality to one degree or another, ISM does so more fully, which is an important strength. Like PSTA, the ISM does not only focus on the problems of CSB, but it also explores the meaningful aspects of sexuality, especially through exploring clients' basic fears (Principle 2). However, it also draws from IE to address pleasurable and enjoyable aspects of sexuality, and it utilizes the good and enjoyable parts of clients' sexualities to address problematic aspects of their sex lives (through Principles, 3, 4, 5, 6, and 7). Furthermore, (through Principle 1) the ISM takes a more explicitly comprehensive social justice angle to targeting the roots of clients' CSB by not just looking at sexual identity and kink (as is done in the OCSB model), but, instead, exploring the many power and privilege related problems that fuel so much CSB. In addition to each of these sex positive elements, the ISM is further bolstered (through Principle 1) by its embrace of the link between interpersonal trauma and CSB (Crocker, 2015; Efrati & Gola, 2019).[24] Finally, through its adaptation of IE principles, the ISM provides an organizing framework that makes it relatively easy to learn, implement, and teach to clients, thus empowering them with information. Indeed, while ISM is rooted in contemporary research and theory, its application is user-friendly for both clinicians and clients.

Notes

1 I would like to dedicate this chapter to Dr. Michael M. Crocker, who has taught me so many of those things one could never learn from books, but who has also helped me immensely with finding the right books. Michael has trained me in CSB treatment (as well as in providing treatment in general) for nearly three years. Without his immense wisdom, care, and modeling, I would not be able to write this chapter.

2 Another "symptom" included extra-relational sex without any attempts to differentiate between cheating monogamous partners and partners in consensually non-monogamous relationships.

3 Throughout this chapter, "addiction" is placed between quotation marks to denote the physiological inaccuracy of characterizing CSB as an addiction (e.g., as discussed by Kerner, 2016, and Neves, 2021).

4 As discussed by Kort (2020), who, as a result of the prevalence of harm incurred by 12-step programs, has developed a treatment approach that helps former 12-step members recover from their often-traumatic experiences.

5 It is important to note, here, that many excellent clinicians do use the 12-step/sex addiction model. Kort (2020), for example, was once one of them. This section's critique is aimed squarely at the sex addiction model, itself, and not at all clinicians who use it. This is particularly important for clients who may not have other options.

6 Although specific research investigating the links between power, privilege, and stigma to CSB is sorely needed, the broader meaning of toxic narratives as stemming from internalized messaging is based on the well-documented link between CSB and interpersonal trauma (e.g., Crocker, 2015; Efrati & Gola, 2019; Neves, 2021).

7 As an aside, I think it is worth considering that it is Western culture's overemphasis on individualism that makes it possible for attachment theory to be as popular as it is today. A less individualistic perspective would consider relationality as too obvious to have its own component and would, instead, weave relationality into all aspects of treatment, much like some have begun to do recently with social justice.

8 Frequently referred to, simply, as "CBT," as if no other CBT exists.

9 In Tribole and Resch's (2020, p. 21) IE model, "Reject the diet mentality."

10 This is an organizing principle behind most insight-oriented therapies.

11 The official term for this irrational belief is "global evaluation." Irrational beliefs are beliefs clients often have that exacerbate their distress to unhealthy levels. Addressing irrational beliefs successfully does not eliminate all distress, but when clients successfully challenge them over time, this does reduce distress adequately enough to eliminate unhealthy degrees of distress as well as unhealthy behaviors, such as CSB (Ellis & Dryden, 2007). In addition to the belief that there is something wrong with oneself, global evaluations can also involve beliefs that other people, like a client's partner, are flawed, which tends to result in unhealthy anger.

12 All client vignettes are fictitious composites of my clinical experiences so as to protect my real clients' identities. No single narrative described in this chapter is real, but the details have been left just close enough to reality to retain a realistic depiction of CSB.

13 The reader may notice I use cisgender men in examples much more than women or non-binary individuals. This is intended to reflect the reality that men appear to represent a large majority of clients with CSB.

14 In Tribole and Resch's (2020, p. 27) IE model, "Cope with Your Emotions Without Using Food."

15 Yalom (2020) refers to these fears as the inevitabilities of life.

16 The following narratives are fictitious composites of sessions, and they are primarily intended to illustrate the ISM and its applications of its

treatment principles. Since they are intended for illustrative purposes, the treatment aspects of the narratives are highly simplified.

17 In Tribole and Resch's (2020, p. 22) model, "Honor your hunger."

18 Tribole and Resch (2020) do not use the term, "craving," in the same manner, but the concept of true desire versus desire that is based on alternative, unmet needs is borrowed from them.

19 It is important to note, here, that engaging with sex workers does not at all equate to CSB. See CSB definition included in "A Note on Terminology."

20 In Tribole and Resch's (2020, p. 23) IE model, "Make Peace with Food."

21 In Tribole and Resch's (2020, p. 24) IE model, "Challenge the Food Police."

22 This draws from two principles in Tribole and Resch's (2020) IE model: "Discover the Satisfaction Factor" (p. 26), and, "Feel your fullness" (p. 25).

23 In Tribole and Resch's (2020, p. 30) IE model, "Honor Your Health – Gentle Nutrition."

24 This element is not specific to positive sexuality, but it is a strength of the ISM all the same.

References

Bilevicius, E., Single, A., Bristow, L. A., Foot, M., Ellery, M., Keough, M. T., & Johnson, E. A. (2018). Shame mediates the relationship between depression and addictive behaviours. *Addictive Behaviors, 82,* 94–100. https://doi.org/10.1016/j.addbeh.2018.02.023

Blycker, G. R., & Potenza, M. N. (2018). A mindful model of sexual health: A review and implications of the model for the treatment of individuals with compulsive sexual behavior disorder. *Journal of Behavioral Addictions, 7*(4), 917–929. https://doi.org/10.1556/2006.7.2018.127

Bolton, K. W., Hall, J. C., & Lehman, P. (2022). Introduction. In K. W. Bolton, J. C. Hall, & P. Lehman (Eds.), *Theoretical perspectives for direct social work practice: A generalist-eclectic approach* (4th ed.). Springer Publishing.

Braun-Harvey, D., & Vigorito, M. A. (2015). *Treating out of control sexual behavior: Rethinking sex addiction.* Springer Publishing Company.

Carnes, P. J. (2001). *Out of the shadows: Understanding sexual addiction.* Hazelden Publishing.

Cella, S., Cipriano, A., Giardiello, C., & Cotrufo, P. (2019). Relationship between self-esteem, interoceptive awareness, impulse regulation, and binge eating: Path analysis in bariatric surgery candidates. *Clinical Neuropsychiatry*, *16*(5–6), 213–220. http://doi.org/10.36131/clinicalnpsych2019050604

Coleman, E., Dickenson, J. A., Girard, A., Rider, G. N., Candelario-Pérez, L. E., Becker-Warner, R., Kovic, A. G., & Munns, R. (2018). An integrative bio-psychosocial and sex positive model of understanding and treatment of impulsive/compulsive sexual behavior. *Sexual Addiction & Compulsivity*, *25*(2–3), 125–152. https://doi.org/10.1080/10720162.2018.1515050

Crocker, M. M. (2015). Out-of-control sexual behavior as a symptom of insecure attachment in men. *Journal of Social Work Practice in Addictions*, *14*(4), 373–393. https://doi.org/10.1080/1533256X.2015.1091000

Cujpers, P., Miguel, C., Harrer, M., Plessen, C. Y., Ciharova, M., Ebert, D., & Karyotaki, E. (2023). Cognitive behavior therapy vs. control conditions, other psychotherapies and combined treatment for depression: A comprehensive meta-analysis including 409 trials with 52,702 patients. *World Psychiatry*, *22*(1), 105–115. http://doi.org/10.1002/wps.21069

DeVille, D. C., Erchull, M. J., & Mailoux, J. R. (2021). Intuitive eating mediates the relationship between interoceptive accuracy and eating disorder risk. *Eating Behaviors*, *41*, 101495. https://doi.org/10.1016/j.eatbeh.2021.101495

Efrati, Y., & Gola, M. (2018). Compulsive sexual behavior: A twelve-step therapeutic approach. *Journal of Behavioral Addictions*, *7*(2), 445–453. https://doi.org/10.1556/2006.7.2018.26

Efrati, Y., & Gola, M. (2019). The effect of early life trauma on compulsive sexual behavior among members of a 12-step group. *The Journal of Sexual Medicine*, *16*(6), 803–811. http://doi.org/10.1016/j.jsxm.2019.03.272

Ellis, A., & Dryden, W. (2007). *The practice of rational emotive behavior therapy*. Springer Publishing Company.

Fern, J. (2020). *Polysecure: Attachment, trauma and consensual nonmonogamy*. Thornapple Press.

Friedlander, M. L., Escudero, V., de Poll, Welmers-van de Poll, M. J., & Heatherington, L. (2018). Meta-analysis of the alliance-outcome relation in couple and family therapy. *Psychotherapy*, *55*(4), 356–371. http://doi.org/10.1037/pst0000161

García-Alandete, J., de Tajada, B. G. H., Rodríguez, S. P., & Marco-Salvador, J. H. (2019). Meaning in life among adolescents: Factorial invariance of the purpose in life test and buffering effect on the relationship between emotional dysregulation and hopelessness. *Clinical Psychology & Psychotherapy, 26*(1), 24–34. https://doi.org/10.1002/cpp.2327

Grech, G. (2021). An existential model of addiction. *European Psychiatry, 64*(S1), S495–S495. http://doi.org/10.1192/j.eurpsy.2021.1323

Heller, D. P. (2019). *The power of attachment: How to create deep and lasting intimate relationships.* Sounds True.

Herman, A. M. (2023). Interoception within the context of impulsivity and addiction. *Current Addiction Reports, 10,* 97–106. https://doi.org/10.1007/s40429-023-00482-7

Kerner, I. (December 2016). From a scientific perspective, sex addiction is not real. Statement, *AASECT.* www.aasect.org/sites/default/files/AASECT_Press_Release_on_Sex_Addiction.pdf

Khalsa, S., S., Rudrauf, D., Hassanpour, M. S., Davidson, R. J., & Tranel, D. (2020). The practice of meditation is not associated with improved interoceptive awareness of the heartbeat. *Psychophysiology, 57*(2), e13479. https://doi.org/10.1111/psyp.13479

Kleinplatz, P. J. (2017). An existential-experiential approach to sex therapy. In Z. D. Peterson (Ed.), *The Wiley handbook of sex therapy.* John Wiley & Sons.

Kleinplatz, P. J., Menard, A. D., Fontaine-Paquet, M.-P., & Paradis, N. (2009). The components of optimal sexuality: A portrait of "great sex." *The Canadian Journal of Human Sexuality, 18*(1), 1–13.

Knox, J. (2019). The harmful effects of psychotherapy: When the therapeutic alliance fails. *British Journal of Psychotherapy, 35*(2), 242–262. https://doi.org/10.1111/bjp.12445

Kort, J. (January 2020). Recovering from sex addiction treatment: Sometimes the cure is worse than the diagnosis. *Psychology Today.* www.psychologytoday.com/gb/blog/understanding-the-erotic-code/202001/recovering-sex-addiction-treatment

Lew-Starowicz, M., Lewczuk, K., Nowakowska, I., Kraus, S., & Gola, M. (2020). Compulsive sexual behavior and dysregulation of emotion. *Sexual Medicine Reviews, 8*(2), 191–205. https://doi.org/10.1016/j.sxmr.2019.10.003

Najafi, T., & Lea-Baranovich, D. (2014). Theoretical background, therapeutic process, therapeutic relationship, and therapeutic techniques of REBT and CT; and some parallels and dissimilarities between the two approaches. *International Journal of Education and Research, 2*(2), 1–12. www.ijern.com/journal/February-2014/13.pdf

National Institutes of Health (January 2012). Breaking bad habits: Why it's so hard. *NIH News in Health.* https://newsinhealth.nih.gov/2012/01/breaking-bad-habits

Neves, S. (2021). *Compulsive sexual behaviors: A psycho-sexual treatment guide for clinicians.* Routledge.

Neves, S. (2022). The religious disguise in "sex addiction" therapy. *Sexual and Relationship Therapy, 37*(3), 299–313. https://doi.org/10.1080/14681994.2021.2008344

Norcross, J. C., & Lambert, M. J. (2019). Evidence-based psychotherapy relationship: The third task force. In J. C. Norcross & M. J. Lambert (Eds.), *Psychotherapy relationships that work* (3rd ed.). Oxford University Press.

Poovey, K., de Jong, D., & Rancourt, D. (2023). Women's disordered eating and sexual function: The role of interoception. *The Journal of Sexual Medicine, 20*(6), 859–870. https://doi.org/10.1093/jsxmed/qdad038

Prause, N., & Binnie, J. (2023). Iatrogenic effects of Reboot/NoFap on public health: A preregistered survey study. *Sexualities.* https://doi.org/10.1177/13634607231157070

Seligman, M. E. P. (2018). PERMA and the building blocks of well-being. *The Journal of Positive Psychology, 13*(4), 333–335. https://doi.org/10.1080/17439760.2018.1437466

Snoek, A., McGeer, V., Brandenburg, D., & Kennett, J. (2021). Managing shame and guilt in addiction: A pathway to recovery. *Addictive Behaviors, 120*, 106954. https://doi.org/10.1016/j.addbeh.2021.106954

Sohal, M., Singh, P., Dhillon, B. S., & Gill, H. S. (2022). Efficacy of journaling in the management of mental illness: A systematic review and meta-analysis. *Family Medicine and Community Health, 10*(1), e001154. http://doi.org/10.1136/fmch-2021–001154

Tribole, E., & Resch, E. (2020). *Intuitive eating: A revolutionary anti-diet approach* (4th ed.). St. Martin's Essentials.

Vos, J., Craig, M., & Cooper, M. (2015). Existential therapies: A meta-analysis of their effects on psychological outcomes. *Journal of Consulting and Clinical Psychologies, 83*(1), 115–128. https://doi.org/10.1037/a0037167

World Health Organization (n.d.). Sexual and reproductive health and research. *World Health Organization.* http://www.who.int

Yalom, I. D. (2020). *Existential psychotherapy* (ebook ed.). Basic Books.

5

"THE TERM 'LIFE' SHOULD BE RETURNED TO US"[1]

Achieving a More Just Society through Sex-Positive Criminology

Aimee Wodda and Vanessa R. Panfil

Introduction

Sex-positive criminology employs an interdisciplinary approach to theorizing about sexuality within the *crimino-legal complex* – a term that points to the relationship between criminal law, the criminal punishment system, and criminology (Young, 1996). At the core of sex-positive criminology is a focus on identifying and *calling out* sex-negativity within the crimino-legal complex and in Western society while *calling in* sex-positive approaches that reduce harm, increase agency, and support access. We *call on*[2] scholars and practitioners interested in our approach to adapt it to serve their own needs and the needs of their communities.

Sex-positivity supports agency and bodily autonomy, consent, education, and medical and other forms of access (Wodda & Panfil, 2021a). Sex-positive criminology relies on core organizing frameworks which include positive sexuality (Williams et al., 2015), thick desire (Fine & McClelland, 2006), and it incorporates anti-racist, critical,

DOI: 10.4324/9781032631820-6

disability-inclusive, feminist, harm reductionist, intersectional, and queer/ed and feminist criminological orientations. Accordingly, respect for sexual difference and a commitment to inclusivity are cornerstones of sex-positive criminological theory and praxis (Wodda & Panfil, 2021a). The positive sexuality framework supports our humanizing ethic, awakens our sensitivity to strengths and well-being, and inspires us to include multiple ways of knowing in our research and writing (Williams et al., 2015). Likewise, the "thick desire" organizing framework asserts that people have the right to "unhindered access to structural and institutional supports, such as education, health care, and protection from coercion" (Fine & McClelland, 2006, p. 325). These frameworks align with our focus on agency, bodily autonomy, and access and our reinforce our desire to contribute to the "everyone for everyone" ethic embodied in the INCITE!-Critical Resistance statement which links struggles for personal transformation and healing with social justice, as the creators write,

> We seek to build movements that not only end violence, but that create a society based on radical freedom, mutual accountability, and passionate reciprocity. In this society, safety and security will not be premised on violence or the threat of violence; it will be based on a collective commitment to guaranteeing the survival and care of all peoples.
>
> (2001, italics in original)

In contrast, the crimino-legal complex has not been interested in guaranteeing survival or care – much less thriving, well-being, or desire. Sex-negativity – an attitude that regards expressions of sexuality outside of prescribed cisheteronormative ideals as morally wrong and/or deviant – aligns with carceral attitudes that may animate direct harms including barriers to necessary medical care, criminalization of marginalized populations, state violence, and morality-based enforcement of laws prompted by moral panics – specifically, sex panics (Wodda & Panfil, 2021a; Wodda, 2018).

Despite the long history of law, punishment, and institutions of social control used to stifle sexual diversity and expression (i.e., sex-negativity), a better way is possible. Sex-positive criminology taps into critical criminological perspectives that look into how the state perpetuates harm and constructs deviance (DeKeseredy & Dragiewicz, 2018). It connects with queer criminology's desire to reduce inequality and related criminalization, victimization, and marginalization of lesbian, gay, bisexual, trans, and queer (LGBTQ+) populations (Buist & Lenning, 2022; Peterson & Panfil, 2014). It builds upon feminist criminology's understandings of the criminalization and regulation of girls' and women's sexuality (Pasko, 2010) and engages with the many possibilities offered by scholars working on reproductive justice (Flavin, 2009; Ross & Solinger, 2017) and intersectionality within criminology (Potter, 2015). Sex-positive criminology is consistent with abolitionist approaches that center goals such as decriminalization, destigmatization, and Liberatory Harm Reduction (Hassan, 2022; Schenwar & Law, 2020). To be clear, sex-positive criminology is founded upon a bedrock of scholarly and activist knowledge – without the work of previous scholars and activists in these areas, sex-positive criminology would not be possible.

In this chapter, after we describe the sex-positive criminology framework in greater detail, we discuss sex-positive social and legal change in Latin America prompted by Marea Verde/The Green Wave, a bold social/political movement from which we can learn much. We provide recommendations for policy, especially those that relate to restorative and transformative justice, decriminalization, widening access to education, protecting bodily autonomy, and expansion of general safety nets. Finally, we conclude with practical suggestions for allies and accomplices who wish to align themselves with our sex-positive criminological approach and vision for the future.

Major Tenets/Goals of Sex-Positive Criminology

Agency, Bodily Autonomy, and Consent

Issues related to agency (choice/power), bodily autonomy, and consent are major concerns for sex-positive criminologists. Consent relates to the idea that people should be in control of their own bodies (i.e., they should have agency and bodily autonomy). In order to make agentic decisions about whether to give, refuse, or negotiate permission about what happens to us – whether the "ask" involves sexual activity, nonsexual touching, medical procedures, and so on – a few conditions must be present: our decisions must be free from coercion, they must be informed (i.e., we must be able to access appropriate and accurate information), and clear communication and a clear understanding about what one is being asked to consent to must be present. It follows, then, that in cases where bodily autonomy and personal agency are not allowed or respected, consent may be difficult or impossible. Agentic consent practices that respect bodily autonomy are not limited to negotiations between individuals – for sex-positive criminologists, agency, bodily autonomy, and consent matter – not just among private citizens, but also when people find themselves entangled with state and other institutions of control. Instances where agency, bodily autonomy, and consent are troubled by the state and other systems include (but are not limited to) carceral settings such as jails, prisons, juvenile detention, group homes, probation and parole, and immigration detention centers (Wodda & Panfil, 2021a).

Education

Sexual education is a right. We can best exercise agency, assert bodily autonomy, and make informed decisions about our bodies and lives when we receive factual and inclusive information related to our sexuality, health, relationships, and well-being (Fine & McClelland, 2006). Medically accurate sexual education is crucial; however, in the U.S., at present, only 18 states require sexual education to be medically accurate (Guttmacher Institute, 2023). Sex-positive criminology advocates for comprehensive sexual education (CSE) as part of a framework of harm reduction where thick desire, wanting, and pleasure are regarded as essential (Fine & McClelland, 2006). Unlike abstinence-only mis-education, which is currently the most prevalent form in the U.S. and has been linked with higher rates of school drop-outs, youth pregnancy, and victimization – especially for lower-income youth – CSE tends to provide age-appropriate, culturally sensitive, and medically accurate sexual education (Denford et al., 2017; Wodda & Panfil, 2021a). Additionally, CSE largely supports intersectional sex-positive goals, providing information that reduces stigma, is inclusive, and is more likely to normalize different ways of being in relationship – not merely those that align with the cisheteronormative paradigm. Truly, CSE has the power to change culture. As we argued in an earlier piece,

> . . . a deep and precise understanding of human sexuality is crucial for human liberation. True gender equality, racial justice, and queer liberation can only be achieved within the context of inclusive,

comprehensive/holistic forms of sex education. Sex-positive sex education supports lasting social change by promoting discussions that acknowledge and affirm the spectrum of sexual orientations and gender identities. It also allows for deep and nuanced reflection about agency, boundaries, consent, gendered expectations, relationships, respect for cultural differences, and self-esteem.

(Wodda & Panfil, 2021b, p. 5)

Sex education is an understudied phenomenon in criminology, yet sexuality educator, researcher, and activist Jennifer Pollitt and educator and criminal defense attorney Richard Shore put forth a compelling argument about why CSE may serve as "one of the most important tools in revolutionizing our criminal-legal system in the fight towards sexual freedom, equality and transformational justice" (2019). They write,

When done well, sex ed deconstructs privilege and power, engenders sexual and erotic agency, reduces shame and creates space for accountability, empathy and compassion. These are the things we need most in our criminal-legal system. Comprehensive sexuality education is anti-violence education – violence done to ourselves and others, state-sanctioned violence and violence committed by upholding patriarchy and white supremacy.

(Pollitt & Shore, 2019)

Indeed, research suggests that CSE guided by the National Sexuality Education Standards (NSES) may prevent violence, especially when age-appropriate curricula spans grades K-12 (Schneider & Hirsch, 2020). In fact, because "unequal gendered access to power is an underlying cause of sexual violence" (Schneider & Hirsch, 2020, p. 446), CSE that is "gender-transformative" may decrease the likelihood of both victimization and perpetration; it does this by "[reconfiguring] gender roles in the direction of more gender equitable relationships" (Dworkin et al., 2013, p. 2486, cited in Schneider & Hirsch, 2020, p. 446). By addressing power imbalances, teaching critical thinking around gender, gender roles, and gender inequality, and learning about healthy relationships, communication skills, power dynamics, gender identity, gender expression, and sexual orientation, respect for and valuing difference, expressing and managing feelings and preferences, and understanding consent, young people are given tools that could help them identify boundary breaches and abuse, avoid perpetrating harm, as they build strong connections and share empathy with others (Schneider & Hirsch, 2020).

Resources that Foster Well-being, such as Medical Access

Sex-positive criminology highlights the importance of resources that foster well-being. As the "thick desire" principle argues for a politic of wanting (Fine & McClelland, 2006), we contend that access to resources (including medical care) is crucial to ensure the well-being and survival of all. For example, while arguments in support of reproductive rights often rely on the language of choice, it's important to note that "choices" may be constrained by ableist, cisheterosexist, classist, racist, and misogynist social structures and institutions – these factors produce disparities in health and wellness (Price, 2010). BIPOC women have long contended that framing reproductive rights in terms of "choice" ignores institutionalized disparities facing marginalized populations and fails to account for the fact that those who lack access to reproductive services and supports tend to be people of color, LGBTQ+ populations, and people with less access to economic resources (Price, 2010). Rather than focus on supporting "a right to choose" that may be inaccessible for marginalized populations, foundational reproductive justice scholars and activists (and scholar/activists) like Byllye Avery, Loretta J. Ross, Luz Martinez, Luz Rodriguez, Marlene Fried, Katsi Cook, Nkenge Toure, and Carmen Vazquez (Price, 2010, p. 51) recommend a focus on access and reproductive justice instead of relying on choice narratives to sway voters. Access to medical care that improves well-being – including reproductive healthcare – is a human right. Access to what we need supports bodily autonomy and facilitates health and wellness. Both sex-positive criminology and reproductive justice are interested in agency, bodily autonomy, education, consent – including informed consent and accurate information regarding medical procedures – and in examining how inequality, poverty, and lack of access directly relate to social stratification and prevent people from getting what they need to survive and thrive.

Harm Reduction

Harm reduction is a core value of sex-positivity and a focus on institutional harm underscores the framework (Wodda & Panfil, 2021a). Because it typically focuses on "crime" and not "harm," mainstream criminological scholarship often focuses on reducing offending, recidivism, and crime prevention rather than on harm reduction. Scholars and activists working in the area of gender, sexuality, and the law who are critical of criminalization tend to offer recommendations that include decriminalization and/or legalization as a first step in order to reduce harm (Wodda & Panfil, 2021a).

For scholars interested in sex-positive criminology and harm reduction, we recommend exploring the Liberatory Harm Reduction framework – a radical approach that emerged from peer support, community-based support, and mutual aid networks (Hassan, 2022). As Shira Hassan, former director of the Young Women's Empowerment Project (YWEP) and co-founder of Just Practice Collaborative, puts it,

> Liberatory Harm Reduction believes that we should have all the information and education we want and need to make the choices that work best for us . . . for many of us, our tools and strategies are criminalized. Let me say it again: our survival is criminalized.
>
> (Hassan, 2022, p. 124).

Liberatory Harm Reduction regards "harm reduction" as co-opted by public health and the nonprofit-industrial complex, which have sanitized and stripped harm reductionist approaches of their liberatory potential and ignored its BIPOC roots (Tourmaline, 2022). Unlike institutionalized forms of harm reduction that "cannibalize the people's practices" (Hassan, 2022, p. 117), Liberatory Harm Reduction incorporates Transformative Justice, Disability Justice, and Healing Justice and acknowledges its roots as coming from the people – specifically, queer and trans BIPOC folks (brown, 2022, p. xv). As Hassan writes,

> In many ways, the everyday practice of harm reduction is how we make a world without violence because it gives us steps, tools, and rituals to strengthen our community interdependence, build our collective power, and reduce our need for state systems and social services.
>
> (Hassan, 2022, pp. 261–262)

This philosophy is often in direct contrast to public health harm reduction models that rely on a "'law-and-order politic' that disregards the safety and security of the most vulnerable and instead protects itself" (Hassan, 2022, p. 263). For Hassan, liberatory forms of harm reduction are worlds apart from a professionalized harm reduction model, which

> views us as an assemblage of risks to be managed and is primarily concerned with its own liability at the expense of self-determination, bodily autonomy, and liberation of BIPOC who are sex workers, queer, transgender, using drugs, people with disabilities and chronic illness, street-based, and sometimes houseless.
>
> (Hassan, 2022, p. 122)

Institutionalized harm reduction approaches often contribute to criminalization, pathologization, and may place vulnerable and marginalized populations at risk of exploitation by law enforcement or may result in unwanted sterilization, medication, and institutionalization – those who turn to a site for help may find themselves experiencing harm and control (Hassan, 2022, p. 123). In contrast, Liberatory Harm Reduction approaches tend to be abolitionist and decriminalizing, accepting risk as part of life and working to meet people where they are.

Integration of the Positive Sexuality Framework

We created a sex-positive criminological framework because we wanted to push back against the crimino-legal complex's historical and continuing treatment of sexuality as destructive, problematic, and in need of constant regulation. We wanted to trouble the regulation of sexuality that emerges from a sex-negative, narrow, and repressive religious ethic that not all of us share. We wanted to call out laws, institutions, and social structures that are invested in punishing and criminalizing and are at odds with harm reduction.

Sex-positive criminology joyfully embraces the eight key dimensions of the positive sexuality framework (Williams et al., 2015) summarized in the introduction of this book. In fact, this framework was foundational for us. We have taken deep inspiration from its overall ethos of focusing on strengths, well-being, happiness, humanization, open and honest communication (i.e., education), peacemaking, and inclusion, and integrate these into all of our recommendations for policy and attitudinal changes. We created a framework that allows us to practice our ethics as queer and feminist scholars, communicate our aims honestly and openly, and which continually reminds us that we are human.

We also prioritize reducing harm while acknowledging possible risks. In this way, our approach echoes and highlights the work of those engaging in Liberatory Harm Reduction, a practice that has difficulty existing within systems as they are currently structured (Hassan, 2022). We believe, moving forward, that much of the work of caring for ourselves and each other, holding each other accountable, supporting each other, reducing harm and stigma, increasing agency, and creating social change will come through transformative and liberatory approaches that necessarily work outside existing institutions. Indeed, our current crimino-legal system is currently not set up to support sex-positive, liberatory harm reductionist practices (Hassan, 2022; Kaba, 2021).

Criminologists typically analyze social harm in relation to populations, whether we are looking at lawbreaking/offending, criminalization, or victimization – however, our integration of the positive sexuality framework has prompted us to highlight individual strengths in our work whenever possible. For example, in alignment with Audre Lorde, we recognize that the erotic has power (1978/2007). Lorde teaches us that the erotic is related to a lust for life, passion for work, hobbies, friendship, self-care and more. When we expand our notion of the erotic and its potential for our lives, we become powerful. Part of that power lies in the connections we forge with others; with the joyful collaborations we engage in – both in intimate spaces and in our daily lives. Lorde observes that capitalism, patriarchy, and white supremacy are the polar opposite of the erotic. These frameworks often work through denial – denial of authentic pleasure and denial of power. Lorde's vision of the erotic represents satisfaction in shared experiences, connection with ourselves, with others, with our work, our passions. The erotic emanates from within and represents "power with" instead of "power over." Capitalism prefers us to be alienated from our work. Patriarchy wants us to be bound up in tight nuclear family units with little access to community support. White supremacy would like us to believe we got where we are all on our own. The power of the erotic pushes back and says – *Collaborate! Connect! Change things! Savor! Be passionate! Desire the world!* Lorde's urgency is reflected in anti-racist, critical, disability-inclusive, feminist, intersectional, and queer/ed and feminist criminological orientations that shape the web of understandings embedded within sex-positive criminology.

"Strong, Brave, and Valuable": What We Learn from Marea Verde/The Green Wave and Solidarity Models

Like critical criminologist Jeff Ferrell, we recognize that any time is a good time to fight the power. He writes, "Now. Now is the time to resist" (Ferrell, 2019, p. 603). In an article published online first in 2019 – three years before the right to access abortion in the U.S. was imperiled with the overturning of *Roe v. Wade* – Ferrell urged his readers to action,

> . . . even if you're reading this 2 years or 20 years after its writing, now's still the time to resist. In part, this is because no amount of progressive social change can cleanse completely the present social order of its institutionalized ills. It's partly because any radically alternative social order, no matter how just and inclusive, will remain susceptible to the next generation of bullies and brutalizers – and so will remain in need of those ready to resist their rise.
>
> (Ferrell, 2019, p. 603)

We heed Ferrell's call for readiness – especially since the U.S. is backsliding when it comes to rights related to gender, sexuality, and reproductive justice. Conversely, other countries have been experiencing major victories in access, rights, and recognition – mostly due to the efforts of activists who have worked collectively for decades (Lopreite, 2023). Now is the time to learn from the exciting Latin American socio-legal phenomenon called Marea Verde/The Green Wave and solidarity models in places like Greece. This section discusses how collective action movements like these align with the positive sexuality ethic embedded within sex-positive criminology, especially the inclusive, collaborative, creative, feminist aspects of this form of making change.

In 2007, Mexico City decriminalized abortion; 12 years passed before another state, Oaxaca, did the same. By August 2023, however, 10 more Mexican states had decriminalized abortion (Espadas Barros Leal, 2023). By September 2023, the Supreme Court in Mexico ruled that abortion should be removed from the federal penal code (Center for Reproductive Rights, 2023, Kitroeff, 2022, Sánchez & Janetsky, 2023). Mexico's 2023 ruling is part of a wave, as journalists Fabiola Sánchez and Megan Janetsky observe, "After decades of work by activists across the region, the trend picked up speed in Argentina, which in 2020 legalized the procedure. In 2022, Colombia, a highly conservative country, did the same" (Sánchez & Janetsky, 2023).

Marea Verde borrowed strategies from the Mothers of Plaza de Mayo in Buenos Aires who began to demonstrate in 1977 with regular presence up until 2006 (Schmidt, 2022). Those vigils inspired Argentinian abortion activists who decided that collective action was the way forward. In 2003, lawyer and activist Susana Chiarotti suggested that green should be the color of abortion rights – as Samantha Schmidt reports, "The color represented nature, growth, life. Facing off against a movement described as 'pro-life,' Chiarotti thought, 'The term "life" should be returned to us'" (2022). Mexican Chief Justice Zaldívar would later tell the court, "We are all in favor of life . . . The only thing is, some of us are in favor of the life of women being one in which their dignity is respected, in which they can fully exercise their rights" (Kitroeff, 2022). Deeply entrenched social structures persist despite decriminalization, which is why many legal scholars argue that decriminalization alone is not enough. As Venezuelan attorney Fanny Cata Gómez-Lugo, Director of Research and Advocacy programs at the Women's Equality Center in Washington D.C., observes,

> One thing is a legal decriminalization, and the other is actually a social decriminalization . . . Abortion continues to be highly stigmatized in countries even that have decriminalized it. And that really is part of embedded patriarchy and just a system that views women and people who can get pregnant as vessels for another purpose, as opposed to human beings themselves.
>
> (Espadas Barros Leal, 2023)

As mentioned earlier, CSE provides young people with a "gender-transformative" education that teaches about gender equity, power imbalance, and bodily autonomy – destigmatizing as well as decriminalizing.

Journalist Isabela Espadas Barros Leal describes a humanizing and destigmatizing medical situation as she writes,

Every recovery room at Fundación ILE, an abortion clinic in Mexico City's Roma Sur neighborhood, is equipped with a small bed, blankets, sanitary pads and a turquoise journal. The journals are filled with letters written by women minutes after having had abortions. . . [one letter said] 'Eres fuerte . . . Eres valiente . . . eres valiosa,' which means 'You are strong . . . you are brave . . . you are valuable'.

(Espadas Barros Leal, 2023)

An asynchronous community of care forms when people who access abortion at the clinic write in the shared journal. Unlike the sterile, un-agentic, and often humiliating treatment many patients experience in medical facilities, Daniel Lopez, an administrator at the clinic, told the reporter,

[The journals are] part of the medical support we give them . . . We try to make it more of an accompaniment than just a medical treatment by making sure they don't feel alone – we want our clients to understand that abortion can be experienced without pain . . . We want women to know that they have resources.

(Espadas Barros Leal, 2023)

Lopez's statement demonstrates that at Fundación ILE care is conceptualized differently – not just typical "medical" assessments and treatments, but normalizing the process and looking after well-being while intentionally creating a community feeling similar to that of Greek solidarity clinics that emerged in response to the 2008 economic crisis. Likewise, Colombian feminist and the Regional Director for Latin America and the Caribbean at the Center for Reproductive Rights, Catalina Martínez Coral describes how the Causa Justa Movement employed various strategies in order to achieve their legislative win. These included "advocacy, communications, and mobilization strategies," to ensure that everyday people were having conversations about abortion access and rights ("Let's Talk Repro," 2023). In Argentina, it seemed everyone was talking about abortion "in the home, in the neighborhoods, in the bakery"; advocacy became so popular, the country began to run out of green fabric (Schmidt, 2022). If could happen in Argentina, Colombia, and Mexico, it could happen elsewhere, as Martínez Coral points out,

I think the win in Argentina inspired the win in Mexico, and the win in Mexico inspired the win in Colombia, and we hope that all of these will be also an example for other countries worldwide. In the Global South we are learning valuable lessons on strategy and making real change that we hope can inspire other countries, including in the Global North. Comparative law, policies, and mobilizations can inspire others to act.

("Let's Talk Repro," 2023)

Mobilization and action often means taking matters into one's own hands. As another example, in response to around three million people in Greece having limited access to health care following the economic crisis, activists, ordinary people, and unemployed medical staff formed "solidarity clinics" to provide necessary medical care (Evlampidou & Kogevinas, 2019; Hasa, 2021). Architect, educator, and co-founder of Fatura Collaborative Elisavet Hasa describes a document collectively authored in 2013:

Acting as a strategy document, the Charter of Constitution outlined the codes and ethics of a 'network of social protection built to counteract any form of state violence that was reproduced and exacerbated through austerity.' The ultimate aim, as described in the charter's introduction, was to build 'an archive of resistance.' Intent on registering the social movements around health care in Greece, the archive would record and collect testimonials from activists engaged in the struggle against mass deprivation – a struggle that continues to transform and retransform the city.

(Hasa, 2021)

What could it look like for sex-positive criminologists to contribute to our own archive of resistance? What might it look like to apply principles of solidarity in models such as Marea Verde and Greek solidarity clinics to the current socio-legal crises in the U.S.?

What Sex-Positive Criminology Suggests for Policy + Praxis

Sex-positive criminology suggests decriminalizing or overturning criminalizing law and policy wherever possible – especially when no harm has been caused. When harm *has* been caused, we recommend restorative and/or transformative justice approaches – accountability in the form of mediation, meaningful restitution, and education can have positive outcomes for victims/survivors, even when dealing with sexual victimization. We applaud activist groups and nonprofit organizations who are working to decriminalize commercial sex among consenting adults and to ensure the removal of criminal penalties that apply to HIV nondisclosure/exposure – especially where HIV was not transmitted (Wodda & Panfil, 2021a).

We recommend widening access to education, not narrowing it. For example, many organizations are pushing back against "Don't Say Gay" laws (e.g., Arkansas, Florida, Indiana, Iowa, and North Carolina), regressive sexual education policies, and book banning in the U.S., which tends to target books with minoritized main characters, such as BIPOC and LGBTQ+ people. Groups in the U.S. are also working to push back against state obscenity and misnamed "harmful to minors" laws that allow for the prosecution of educators, college and university faculty, educators, librarians, and museum professionals simply for speaking factually about the range of human sexuality (Everylibrary, 2024).

Additionally, we recommend removing the possibility of criminal punishment for young people where punishment only compounds harm. For example, when minors sell or trade sex to adults, their survival tactic is often treated as a crime – even in U.S. states with Safe Harbor laws where young people may be arrested "for their own good" (Wodda & Panfil, 2021a). Relatedly, in the U.S., young people below the age of consent where they live who are caught exchanging sexts (or even those who have nude images of themselves on their own phones) may be subject to abusive searches, detainment, and sex offender registration (Wodda & Panfil, 2021a; Wodda & Panfil, 2018). Like many other scholars, we assert that minors should not be charged with producing and distributing child pornography, for taking and potentially sharing digital images of themselves; currently in some jurisdictions, young people are illogically considered both the legal perpetrator and victim of the same crime (Wodda & Panfil, 2018). Applying harm reduction principles to consensual teen sexting would involve teaching young people about safer sexting, consent when sexting, healthy boundaries, communication, and the importance of privacy. There would be a clear difference in social response between consensual sexting and abusive sexting. Following from that frame, sexts that are not consensually shared, are not deleted when requested – say, after a break-up – and sexts that are shared with a third party (or parties) without explicit permission would be violating a young person's right to privacy, would be considered abusive sexting, and would be addressed with restorative justice approaches. For these reasons, we support the decriminalization of consensual youth sexting and also of young people who participate in the sex trade. Instead of criminalization, we favor efforts to prevent possible harms to young people, such as providing resources and support for youth in precarious economic positions and education about the harm that abusive sexting entails.

Finally, we strongly advocate for the protection of bodily autonomy. We recommend the institution of policies and programs that protect and expand reproductive justice rather than narrow it – as the fallout from *Dobbs v. Jackson Women's Health Organization* (2022) has done. We urge policymakers to reject attempts to restrict medical access for LGBTQ+ people, and reject framing trans-affirming care for young people as "child abuse." Consistent with the "thick desire" principle, we recommend the expansion of social safety nets including: universal healthcare (e.g., at a minimum, expansions in Medicare or Medicaid), universal basic income, broader efforts at accessibility and support for people with disabilities, and resources for youth in crisis.

Conclusion

Our approach is inspired by queer, feminist, anti-racist, and disability-inclusive frameworks from across the globe – it was designed to integrate with the positive sexuality framework (Williams et al., 2015) and employs the "thick desire" perspective, which encourages wanting (Fine & McClelland, 2006, p. 325). This chapter illustrated how personal agency, bodily autonomy, education, access to resources such as medical care, and harm reduction are supported by sex-positive criminology and its conceptual building blocks.

Because we are scholars from the U.S., we come to sex-positive criminology with an admittedly narrow focus and we look forward to embracing sex-positive criminological scholarship created by our colleagues across the globe. The legal and social landscape in the U.S. at the moment we are writing this can seem bleak. As of March 2024, anti-trans legislation trackers have flagged 523 bills; 10 have passed, 426 are active and 87 have failed; this legislation aims to regulate or oppress trans people and suppress their rights (Trans Legislation Tracker, 2024). Additionally, according to the Guttmacher Institute's legislation tracker, around 332 laws have been introduced as of March 2024 that ban, criminalize, and/or limit or deny access to abortion or criminalize abortion providers in the U.S. (2024). Globally, many factors present considerable reproductive health challenges, including violent unrest, oppression, and occupation (Elnakib et al., 2024), environmental pollution (Liddell & Kington, 2021), and climate change (Haley & Arrigo, 2022).

And yet, if we shift our focus away from the lawmakers for a moment, away from the people who wear suits and ties (or red hats), and look towards our global community – particularly those in the Global South wearing green – we are inspired by collective liberation and mutual aid efforts. While the U.S. population has legislatively regressed into what often seems like a dark age of oppression and injustice as a result of conservative religious values that do not reflect the majority, Latin American countries with largely religious (Christian) populations are moving in the direction of supporting bodily autonomy and agency, and are affirming the right to access education, medical care, and other resources that support well-being and reduce harm. As Catalina Martínez Coral, Regional Director of the Center for Reproductive Rights in Colombia puts it, "The United States has rarely looked south and asked what they can learn from us . . . We're part of the same movement" (Schmidt, 2022). We are eager to learn and to continue working towards change. We invite allies to join us as we work to affirm our desire for bodily autonomy – for control of our own lives. We can remind each other along the way how strong, brave, and valuable we are.

Notes

1 This 2003 quote comes from Argentinian lawyer and activist Susana Chiarotti as she reflected on the generative ways grassroots movements for reproductive justice operated, as compared to the "pro-life" anti-abortion movement (Schmidt, 2022).

2 Here, we draw from Sonya Renee Taylor's calling out/calling in/calling on framework (2021).

References

brown, a. m. (2022). [Foreword]. In S. Hassan, *Saving our own lives: A liberatory practice of harm reduction* (p. xv). Haymarket Books.

Buist, C. L., & Lenning, E. (2022). *Queer criminology* (2nd ed.). Routledge.

Center for Reproductive Rights (2023, September 7). Historic Decision: Mexico's Supreme Court Decriminalizes Abortion. https://reproductiverights. org/mexico-supreme-court-decriminalizes-abortion-federal

DeKeseredy, W. S., & Dragiewicz, M. (Eds.). (2018). *Routledge handbook of critical criminology* (2nd ed.). Routledge.

Denford, S., Abraham, C., Campbell, R., & Busse, H. (2017). A comprehensive review of reviews of school-based interventions to improve sexual-health. *Health Psychology Review, 11*(1), 33–52. https://doi.org/10.1080 /17437199.2016.1240625

Dworkin, S. L., Treves-Kagan, S., & Lippman, S. A. (2013). Gender-transformative interventions to reduce HIV risks and violence with heterosexually-active men: A review of the global evidence. *AIDS and Behavior, 17*(9), 2845–2863.

Elnakib, S., Fair, M., Mayrhofer, E., Afifi, M., & Jamaluddine, Z. (2024). Pregnant women in Gaza require urgent protection. *The Lancet, 403*(10423), 244.

Espadas Barros Leal, I. (2023, November 2). Abortion is decriminalized in Mexico, but the social and cultural stigma remains. *NBC News.* https://www. nbcnews.com/news/latino/mexico-abortion-legal-social-cultural-stigma-remains-rcna123029

Everylibrary (2024, 22 April). Legislation of concern in 2024 [Webpage]. https://www.everylibrary.org/billtracking

Evlampidou, I., & Kogevinas, M. (2019). Solidarity outpatient clinics in Greece: a survey of a massive social movement. *Gaceta Sanitaria, 33*(3), 263–267.

Ferrell, J. (2019). In defense of resistance. *Critical Criminology, 30,* 603–619. https://doi.org/10.1007/s10612-019-09456-6

Fine, M., & McClelland, S. (2006). Sexuality, education, and desire: Still missing after all these years. *Harvard Educational Review, 76*(3), 297–338.

Flavin, J. (2009). *Our bodies, our crimes: The policing of women's reproduction in America.* NYU Press.

Guttmacher Institute. (2023, September 1). HIV and sex education [State Laws and Policies]. https://www.guttmacher.org/state-policy/explore/sex-and-hiv-education

Haley, S., & Arrigo, B. (2022). Ethical considerations at the intersection of climate change and reproductive justice: Directions from green criminology. *Critical Criminology*, 30(4), 1001–1018.

Hasa, E. (2021). In the absence of care: Building solidarity in Athens. *The Avery Review*, 54, 1–11. https://averyreview.com/issues/54/in-the-absence-of-care

Hassan, S. (2022). *Saving our own lives: A liberatory practice of harm reduction*. Haymarket Books.

INCITE!-Critical Resistance (2001). Statement on gender violence and the prison industrial complex. https://incite-national.org/incite-critical-resistance-statement/

Kaba, M. (2021). *We do this 'til we free us: Abolitionist organizing and transforming justice*. Haymarket Books.

Kitroeff, N. (2022, July 9). How Mexico's top justice, raised Catholic, became an abortion rights champion. *New York Times*. https://www.nytimes.com/2022/07/09/world/americas/mexico-abortion-chief-justice.html

"Let's talk repro" series: Making waves in Colombia with Catalina Martínez Coral (2023, February 27). Center for Reproductive Rights. https://reproductiverights.org/lets-talk-repro-catalina-martinez-coral/

Liddell, J. L., & Kington, S. G. (2021). "Something was attacking them and their reproductive organs": Environmental reproductive justice in an Indigenous tribe in the United States Gulf Coast. *International Journal of Environmental Research and Public Health*, 18(2), 666.

Lopreite, D. (2023). The long road to abortion rights in Argentina (1983–2020). *Bulletin of Latin American Research*, 42(3), 357–371.

Lorde, A. (1978/2007). Uses of the erotic: The erotic as power (pp. 53–59) In *Sister outsider: Essays and speeches*. Crossing Press.

Pasko, L. (2010). Damaged daughters: The history of girls' sexuality and the juvenile justice system. *Journal of Criminal Law and Criminology*, 100(2), 1099–1130.

Peterson, D., & Panfil, V. R. (2014). Introduction: Reducing the invisibility of sexual and gender identities in criminology and criminal justice. In D. Peterson, & V. R. Panfil (Eds.), *Handbook of LGBT communities, crime, and justice* (pp. 3–13). Springer.

Pollitt, J., & Shore, R. (2019, August 17). Sex education as a radical tool for criminal justice reform [Workshop]. Woodhull Foundation.

Potter, H. (2015). *Intersectionality and criminology: Disrupting and revolutionizing studies of crime.* Routledge.

Price, K. (2010). What is reproductive justice? How women of color activists are redefining the pro-choice paradigm. *Meridians, 10*(2), 42–65.

Ross, L. J., & Solinger, R. (2017). *Reproductive justice: An introduction.* University of California Press.

Sánchez, F. & Janetsky, M. (2023, September 6). Mexico decriminalizes abortion, extending Latin American trend of widening access to procedure. *Associated Press News.* https://apnews.com/article/mexico-abortion-decriminalize-d87f6edbdf68c2e6c8f5700b3afd15de

Schenwar, M., & Law, V. (2020). *Prison by any other name: The harmful consequences of popular reforms.* The New Press.

Schmidt, S. (2022, July 3). How green became the color of abortion rights. *The Washington Post.* https://www.washingtonpost.com/world/interactive/2022/abortion-green-roe-wade-argentina/

Schneider, M., & Hirsch, J. S. (2020). Comprehensive sexuality education as a primary prevention strategy for sexual violence perpetration. *Trauma, Violence, & Abuse, 21*(3), 439–455.

Taylor, S. R. (2021). Let's replace cancel culture with accountability. TedX Auckland. https://www.youtube.com/watch?v=3vCKwoee27c

Tourmaline. (2022). [Introduction]. In Hassan, S., *Saving our own lives: A liberatory practice of harm reduction.* Haymarket Books.

Trans Legislation Tracker (2024). https://translegislation.com/

Williams, D., Thomas, J. N., Prior, E. E., & Walters, W. (2015). Introducing a multidisciplinary framework of positive sexuality. *Journal of Positive Sexuality, 1,* 6–11.

Wodda, A. (2018). Stranger danger! *Journal of Family Strengths, 18*(1), 1–33.

Wodda, A., & Panfil, V. R. (2021a). *Sex-positive criminology.* Routledge.

Wodda, A., & Panfil, V. R. (2021b). Sex-positive criminology: Possibilities for legal and social change. *Sociology Compass, 15*(11), e12929.

Wodda, A., & Panfil, V. R. (2018). Insert sexy title here: Moving toward a sex-positive criminology. *Feminist Criminology, 13*(5), 583–608.

Young, A. (1996). *Imagining crime.* Sage.

6

POLYAMOROUS ELDERS

The "Original Gangsters" of Sex-Positivity

Elisabeth Sheff and Kathy Labriola

Introduction

Because of their advanced age and pioneering actions, we describe poly-amorous elders as the "Original Gangsters," or "OGs,"[1] of sex-positivity. Polyamory is a form of consensual non-monogamy (CNM) in which practitioners openly conduct emotionally and/or sexually intimate relationships with multiple partners (Labriola, 2022; Sheff, 2014). In their youth from the 1950s through 1970s, these OG sex-positivists rejected centuries of a cultural imperative of sexual repression that restricted sex to marriage and compulsory monogamy. They created groups and organizations, and cultivated attitudes promoting sex-positivity. Polyamorous activist Dr. Ken Haslam named an online community "Polygeezers" in 2005, and many poly elders adopted this term as a positive expression of age and relationship diversity. They form the core of the OG sex-positive consensual nonmonogamists.

DOI: 10.4324/9781032631820-7

Regarding our particular professional backgrounds and expertise necessary for writing this chapter, we have decades of research and clinical practice experience on CNM (Labriola, 1999, 2011, 2013, 2022; Sheff, 2005,
2006, 2007, 2010, 2011, 2014, 2015, 2016a, 2016b; 2020, Sheff &
Smith, 2022; Sheff & Tesene, 2015; Sheff & Wolf, 2015; Sheff et al.,
2021).We prioritize data from the *Longitudinal Polyamorous Family Study* or
LPFS (Sheff, 2014) and decades of specialized clinical practice (Labriola,
2022). This chapter, then, summarizes the impact of sex-negativity on
CNM pioneers/founders of the second wave of CNM in the U.S., along
with the ways they deployed sex-positivity as a coping mechanism and
shield against stigma. We define elders as 55 years or older, both because
that is how the law and government agencies define "senior citizens," and
because around that age, many people experience the effects of aging and
begin making changes in their lifestyles.

Throughout their entire adult lives, polygeezers have faced stigma,
discrimination, and hostility for rejecting culturally sanctioned monogamy and for embracing a sex-positive lifestyle (Labriola, 2022). Many
polyamorous elders have noted the irony of being shamed, demonized,
and rejected by their parents and family members from their adolescence
all the way through their 60s, and then facing renewed polyphobia later
in life from their adult children! (Labriola, 2022). This lifelong struggle against sex-negativity sustained persistent sex-positivity in numerous
polyamorous elders.

We begin by introducing polyamorous elders, reviewing literature on
aging and CNM, describing some of the characteristics of polyamorous
elders, and summarizing their issues within a broader social and gen-
erational context. We then identify some of the common personal and
social issues polygeezers face and the sex-positive strategies they evolve to
manage those challenges. We also share some of the surprising findings
from our respective data, and we conclude with a few recommendations
for future research.

Research on Aging in Polyamorous Relationships

Research demonstrates that one in five adults (21.9%) in North America
have tried a CNM relationship and that approximately 5% of all North

Americans are currently practicing some form of CNM (Conley et al., 2011; Haupert et al., 2017; Levine et al., 2018). There is scant literature on aging in polyamorous relationships, partly because younger people are more likely to attempt CNM relationships than their elders (Balzarini et al., 2019; Moors et al., 2021). These findings indicate that OG polyamorists are especially distinct, both as pioneers and early adopters of the second wave of CNM in the U.S., but also among anyone who is willing to engage in CNM. The few studies that exist point to the positive implications of the larger social network associated with polyamorous relationships.

Three primary studies provide information about polyamorous elders. Fleckenstein and Cox (2015) surveyed 4,000 Americans over 55 who were currently engaged in some form of CNM, and then focused on over 500 of them, comparing them to 700 people from the 2012 U.S. General Social Survey. Spears and Lowen (2010) studied 86 long-term, gay male couples currently engaged in some form of CNM relationship. Almost half (44%) of their respondents were at least 55, and their average age was 52.7 (Spears & Lowen, personal communication, 2010). These couples had been in a committed relationship for an average of 16 years, with many being coupled for over 30 years and a few couples cohabiting more than 40 years.

Both Fleckenstein and Cox (2015) and Spears and Lowen (2010) found that sex was important to their respondents, and that both high frequency of sex and high-quality sex were crucial to their happiness and their relationship satisfaction. Fleckenstein and Cox's (2015) findings indicate that, "Polys reported more frequent sex, more sex partners, and greater happiness, and better health" (p. 94) than the controls from the General Social Survey. All genders reported wanting sex at least once a week, but not everyone achieved that goal (Fleckenstein & Cox, 2015). Poly elders appear to have significantly more sex than respondents to the National Social Life, Health, and Aging Project, and that the average CNM man 57 and older reported sexual frequencies of 3.1 times monthly and women reported 1.74 times monthly (Fleckenstein & Cox, 2015).

Labriola's (2022) book, *Polyamorous Elders: Aging in Open Relationships*, is the most in-depth work on aging and CNM. The book draws from interviews and case studies from decades of counseling to provide the first exploration of older polyamorous people's lives, sexuality, families, relationships, health, politics, and changes due to aging. From retirement to grandchildren, sex and celibacy, *Polyamorous Elders* demonstrates that polygeezers face some of the same challenges in aging as their monogamous peers, while using their unique relational orientations, skill sets, and resources for resilient aging.

Characteristics of Polygeezers

The Greatest Generation and the Baby Boomers

Polyamorous elders span two somewhat overlapping age groups – the "Greatest Generation" (1925–1945) and the "Baby Boom" (1946–1964) – that share some strong similarities and some vastly different experiences. Polygeezers encompass polyamorous people from ages 55 to 100. The Greatest Generation or "older elders" grew up during the Great Depression and World War II during a socially and politically conservative era. They have had a very different life experience than the Baby Boomer "younger elders" born during the post-war era of the late 1940s to 1960s. While both groups are "polygeezers," they are distinguished by different life stages and different outlooks on life due to the respective eras in which they were born.

A large percentage of the "younger elders" from 55 to 75 are still working, and many have caregiving responsibilities for their elderly parents. Most are able-bodied and lead active lives. Many are involved with their adult children and grandchildren, and some still have teenagers or young adult children at home. A few have primary custody of grandchildren because the children's parents have lost custody. Many are in the process of transitioning towards retirement after long careers, and others have recently retired and are adjusting to a new post-career life.

The older elders over 75 were born from the 1920s to the early 1940s, and most have already lost their parents. Almost all older elders have adult children, with whom they are unlikely to cohabit unless the child has suffered a catastrophic life event or returned to provide care for a disabled parent. Most have retired and established a post-work life, and nearly all are grappling with increasing health problems and disabilities. Many are caregivers for partners or siblings who are ill or disabled, and some have moved from their homes into senior living. These eldest also encountered the most virulent sex negativity and began paving the way for later relationship nonconformists.

The older elders are living longer than any generation before them. The Baby Boomers born 1946–1964 are more numerous than any generation before them and likely to live even longer than the older elders, due to advances in medical care and healthier lifestyles. All the Boomers have now become senior citizens, with the youngest turning 60 this year and the oldest will turn 78. While a significant portion of Boomer polygeezers are lifelong radicals who came of age in alternative subcultures of the 1960s, others spent decades in traditional monogamous marriages before becoming polyamorous.

Complex Lives

The lives of older people are quite complicated, and polygeezers' lives are even more so. In addition to the usual issues of aging, polygeezers combine the complexities of juggling multiple relationships. These can include managing medical conditions and disabilities (their own and/or their partners'); caregiving responsibilities for loved ones; grieving the deaths of parents, siblings, and partners; retiring; helping raise grandchildren; and/or moving from a long-time home into some form of assisted living arrangement.

The vast majority of the Greatest Generation poly older elders have adult children, grandchildren, and often step-children and step-grandchildren. The majority of the younger elders, the Baby Boomers, also have adult children and some have grandchildren. Many of those younger elders who do have children postponed childbearing until their late 30s and early 40s, so many do not yet have grandchildren.

A statistically small, but historically significant, percentage of Boomers do not have children, and they are much more likely to describe themselves as childless or childfree than the older poly elders. As the first generation of women in history to have access to safe and effective birth control, polygeezer women often chose paid employment and more limited childbearing than their foremothers, who did not have this option. Choosing not to have children significantly changed the life trajectories of Boomers of all genders, allowing them the time, energy, and financial resources to focus on work, travel, multiple relationships, political activism, and other passions.

Polygeezers from both generations face the challenges of repeatedly deciding whether to disclose their polyamorous relationships to their families, professional associates, healthcare providers, and other caregivers. Their well-founded fears of discrimination mean that many are cautious about coming out, and most disclose this only selectively.

Personal Issues: Aging and Sexual Health

Our collective research identified similar challenges facing polygeezers, and this section focuses on the personal issues that poly elders reported. Personal issues related mostly to relationships and sexuality, body image, medical problems of aging, and specific changes in sexual functioning and experience.

Changing Bodies (Generally)

Like most elders in a youth-obsessed culture, polygeezers struggled to accept weight gain, hair loss, and wrinkles. Many opined that feeling sexually desirable is a prerequisite to being able to feel sexual desire or to make or respond to sexual overtures, so their changing bodies impaired their feelings of sexiness and desire for sex.

Maintaining healthy self-esteem about sexual desirability was particularly difficult for elders who had a surgery or a medical condition that caused them to feel disfigured. Mastectomies, prostate surgeries, erectile dysfunction, and menopausal symptoms can all contribute to an elder feeling less desirable. These personal issues can be especially acute for those who never had to cope with illness or disability before. Polygeezers expressed feeling vulnerable to outdated, prejudiced attitudes about sex and disability, finding it difficult to see themselves as viable sexual beings. This insecurity about sexual attractiveness can be amplified if a partner has other partners who are younger or more physically fit. Some reported feeling threatened by the other partner who they may see as sexier or having more sexual prowess due to their youth or more robust health. Furthermore, menopause introduced a host of sexual issues for most women. Older poly women described needing more stimulation to get sexually aroused after menopause, as well as increased difficulty reaching orgasm.

Lower Libido

While some people experience a sexual revival in their older years, many elders' sex drives decline as they age. Low libido often results from medical problems that cause pain and other symptoms that interfere with mobility or pleasure. Indeed, chronic pain, fatigue, acid reflux, and respiratory problems certainly are not conducive to jumping into bed for wild sex!

Older people with histories of heart attacks or other cardiovascular issues often experience severe fatigue, and they worry that having sex could worsen their cardiac symptoms. The stress and exhaustion of caregiving responsibilities for an elderly parent or a disabled partner also undermines sexual desire, as does mourning the death of loved ones (Price, 2010).

Impact of Medications on Sexual Functioning

Many older people found it challenging to adapt to the changes in their sexual functioning. Erections became more difficult to attain and sustain, and many men[2] found that they required more stimulation to reach orgasm. Drugs like Viagra have changed the sexual landscape considerably, enabling people of all ages with penises to have more reliable erections. However, many men found that these drugs lost efficacy with prolonged use, and it became more difficult to obtain and maintain an erection and to reach orgasm.

Adding to these challenges, doctors routinely prescribed medications to elders that caused sexual side effects without even informing older patients about these side effects (Nimbi et al., 2021). Many medications for cardiac issues, ulcers, cholesterol, and even antihistamines can inhibit erections and orgasm (Kaplan-Marans, 2022). Some antidepressants, such as SSRIs, also lower libido for people of all genders, reduce sexual arousal response, and make it difficult to reach orgasm (Rothmore, 2020).

Social Issues: Oppression, Family Stigma, and Inadequate Healthcare

Social issues commonly experienced among polygeezers result from inequality and sex- negativity. Primary social issues include discrimination resulting from intersectional identities, challenges with families of origin, and difficulty finding culturally competent healthcare.

Intersectional Identities and Oppression

We noted earlier herein that polygeezers' lives are inherently complex. Our research found that their stories demonstrated the crushing effects of racism, poverty, homophobia, sexism, ableism, and ageism. Even those who remained closeted regarding their relationships and orientations frequently experienced multiple forms of oppression. Coping with financial insecurities, discrimination, and sometimes even violence resulting from belonging in an oppressed group burdens polygeezers and their relationships. Polygeezers struggling with multiple forms of marginalization and oppression are much more vulnerable to the risks of coming out and often have fewer overall resources than others with greater race, class, gender, and heterosexual privileges (Sheff & Hammers, 2011). As a result, they are more likely to be closeted about their poly lives than heteronormative or White polygeezers from more affluent social and economic classes. Furthermore, all poly elders face both ageism and polyphobia, regardless of other forms of oppression they may experience.

Stigma from Adult Children

Polyamorous people in all age groups experienced stigma and societal ostracism. However, many poly elders no longer worried about being fired, because they were retired, or losing custody of their children, because their children were grown (Sheff, 2014). Instead, polygeezers' adult children were often scandalized when, for example, Mom told them that "her friend and tennis partner" was actually a long-time lover or, similarly, that a "close friend that used to go on our family camping trips" had been Dad's sweetie for decades.

We both found from our research studies that sometimes this stigma from adult children translated to controlling access to the grandchildren. For some adult children with especially negative reactions to polyamory, this meant restricting their parents from seeing the grandchildren completely. In other instances, it meant that the grandparent could see the grandchildren under limited circumstances, often with parental supervision and only in the absence of any polyamorous partners. This, not surprisingly, created unique strain for polygeezers, who subsequently felt targeted, shamed, and belittled when their adult children insisted on supervised visitation of grandchildren and excluded polygeezers' CNM partners from family gatherings.

Obstacles to Sex-Positive Healthcare

In addition to sex-negativity from adult children, poly elders reported difficulty accessing culturally competent healthcare. Labriola's research and interviews revealed significant gaps in health care for poly elders, due to several factors. First, many doctors and medical providers, unfortunately, share the common belief that older people do not, or perhaps should not, have sex. Most medical practitioners receive little training about the most common sexual problems affecting elders, and thus fail to diagnose and treat these medical conditions (Ezhova et al., 2020). Furthermore, many clinicians lack appropriate training in sexuality and demonstrate bias against sex and gender minorities (McDowell et al., 2020). Many physicians fail to screen their older patients for sexual concerns or even discuss sexual health, perhaps simply assuming that elders have magically become celibate (Van Epps et al., 2023).

Elders in Labriola's studies often reported that their doctors dismissed requests for STI testing, saying it was unnecessary and that protocols did not include STI testing for patients over 55. This sex-negative attitude within healthcare leaves sexually active elders, their partners, and metamours vulnerable to the repercussions of untreated STIs. Polygeezers repeatedly described doctors becoming embarrassed and shaming them for having sex at all, and even more so for having sex with multiple partners. While all elders face potential conflict with their adult children and may experience ageist medical care, polygeezers' experiences show that there is an added layer of social injustice due to widespread sex-negativity.

Resilient Responses

Lasting Relationships

Labriola's research indicates that an overwhelming majority of poly elders live in couple relationships, either married or cohabiting, while simultaneously maintaining additional significant romantic relationships outside their domestic partnership. A small number of participants were divorced or widowed after decades-long marriages or cohabiting relationships. The majority of polygeezers practiced some form of hierarchical polyamory, living with a primary partner and sustaining casual and/or committed relationships with other non-cohabiting partners. A considerably smaller group resided in triads or quads consisting of three or four domestic partners.

Most polygeezers reported having some short-term and casual sexual relationships when they were younger, then transitioning to multiple serious relationships that have lasted for decades. Explaining that they no longer had room in their lives for new relationships due to health problems, limited energy, or caregiving responsibilities for disabled spouses or family members, the vast majority of participants from our collective research frequently indicated that they were not seeking new partners. Of those who continued to enjoy new sexual relationships, most described themselves as kinksters. These polygeezer kinksters reported that they attended play parties and sometimes used dating apps, and/or other online means of finding sexual and/or BDSM opportunities outside of their current domestic partnerships.

Reframing Sexuality

We both found that the many changes that elders experienced around sexuality meant that their conceptualization of sex had shifted over time, even while remaining firmly rooted in a general attitude of sex-positivity. This could involve moving from a primary focus on intense orgasmic sex to a more affectionate or comforting version of sexuality. Sheff's body of research found that most poly elders continued having sex in some form, but that sex itself was not as central as it once was to their relationships. Some long-term couples transitioned to platonic companionable marriages while continuing to have sexual relationships with outside partners.

While many older monogamous couples break up due to lack of sex, poly couples can stay together and outsource the sex.

Labriola concurs, finding that some polygeezers report having better sex because they no longer needed to use birth control or worry about pregnancy. Furthermore, many had greater privacy and more time for sex now that they were retired, and their children had left home. Several older poly women in Labriola's (2022) interviews stressed that these factors helped them feel much freer, less inhibited, more open to sexual exploration.

Timing

Nearly all people with penises experience a significant increase as they age in the *refractory period* needed between the time they have one erection and orgasm and when they can get a reliable erection again (Zhang et al., 2023). For older polyamorous men, this can mean that if they had sex today with one partner, they couldn't reliably get an erection tomorrow or the next day with another partner. Labriola's clients learned to adapt by timing their dates appropriately if they intend to have intercourse with various partners. These polyamorous men recommended being transparent with each partner so they would not take it personally if an erection was not forthcoming. Some reported scheduling dates further apart, so they would be able to enjoy sex with each partner without worrying about erection problems.

Expanding Sexual Ideas and Practices

Aided by their lifelong sex positive attitudes, many poly folks of all genders reported enjoying a wide range of sexual activities that do not require an erect penis. Polygeezers developed a range of sexual skills over their lives of interacting with diverse lovers, which proved especially useful as the reliability of erections declined. Some emphasized other ways to stimulate each other manually, orally, using toys, and other strategies to pleasure their partners. Others used uniquely multiplistic techniques, including one of Labriola's respondents who enjoyed having orgasms during intercourse and would sometimes arrange dates with both male partners at the same time so that neither partner felt pressured to get or keep an erection.

The presence of additional partners helped some polygeezers navigate the changes in their own sexual relationships. One of Labriola's clients explained the comfort her husband felt when he found out from her boyfriend that they used copious amounts of bottled sexual lubricant, because he was able to reframe his wife's decreased lubrication from a problem about him to a natural outcome of aging, since this was an issue with other partners as well. The same comparison held true for others who experienced declining libido with multiple partners, and creative strategies were discussed to satisfy everyone's sexual needs. Polygeezers' willingness to reframe sexuality opened their minds to new experiences, allowing them to continue enjoying sex, even with significant changes in their bodies and relationships. Expanding what they thought of as sex, being aware of timing, and communicating clearly about their sexual desires and needs became effective strategies these elders used for resilient and sex-positive aging.

Valuable Insights from our Collective Research

Shifting to Monogamy

In addition to expanding sexual possibilities and attending to timing, many polyamorous elders also expanded their relationship options as they aged. Ironically, for some this meant a shift to monogamy. Some of Labriola's respondents described this transition to monogamy as accidental or situational, but for others it is a conscious decision.

Sheff found a similar trend among a small percentage of what she terms "the persistent polyamorists" – long-term poly couples, triads, and other poly configurations that have been together for over 25 years – and some as long as 60 years. Some have now chosen what one termed "conscious monogamy," either because they have less energy for relationships or because one or more partners have left the relationship or a partner has died. LPFS findings demonstrate that some poly relationships shift naturally to non-sexual friendships, but those relationships remain central in their lives. Polygeezers can transition from sexual to platonic relationships and still love each other, live together, and grow old together. Some relationships may become monogamous because other relationships may no longer be sexual, yet these non-sexual polyaffective relationships often remain a key part of chosen family.

Some older couples break up after many years in a poly relationship because one person wants monogamy. Often this is because they have never really wanted polyamory but complied with it in order to make their spouse happy, or they felt coerced if their spouse insisted on it. They may have had conflicts for many years due to one person wanting monogamy, eventually causing the relationship to end. Other former polygeezers may become monogamous because they both lose interest in having other partners, or their priorities may change as they age.

Becoming Celibate

In further irony, some polyamorous elders' expansion of sexuality means they include celibacy or asexuality into their sexual repertoire and/or identity. Both of us found a small number of poly elders who are no longer having sex with *any* partner. Some elders who stop having sex questioned whether they could still call themselves polyamorous. Polygeezers who had been very sexually active all their adult lives sometimes no longer desired sex or became physically unable to engage in sexual activity. The majority of older celibate polys were actively engaged in one, two, or three relationships with long-time lovers or spouses, and those relationships continued apace, albeit without sex. Most poly elders who stopped having sex altogether identified medical problems, impaired mobility and dexterity, fatigue, and/or chronic pain as the cause. Others reported that an inability to get an erection or increasing difficulties reaching orgasm had "taken a lot of the fun out of sex." Most described this development as part of the organic evolution of their relationships. Anecdotal evidence suggests that the majority of poly elders continue to engage in some kind of sexual activity with one or more partners. However, being celibate is a legitimate choice, and most geezers who stop having sex remain involved in committed, long-term poly relationships.

Older Poly-Mono Couples

Older heterosexual women, both monogamous and poly, lament the difficulty of finding older men for sex and relationships (Watson & Stelle, 2021). Men are usually at least three years older than their wives, and women generally outlive their husbands by 10 years. After their partners have passed away, women far outnumber men. Most of the surviving older men are married or partnered, or prefer to date younger women (Carr & Utz, 2020).

While both monogamous and polyamorous women have expressed this frustration, poly women have an advantage. Because they can date men who are partnered, they have a much larger dating pool than monogamous women who are seeking a single man for an exclusive relationship. Some older women in Labriola's research had previously viewed themselves as very monogamous, but eventually entered polyamorous relationships because available older men were already in CNM primary relationships. Many of these women embarked upon a polyamorous relationship because of the shortage of available men, but were then surprised by how well polyamory worked for them. Labriola noticed significantly more successful "mono/poly" relationships in older, heterosexual couples than younger people who were under age 55. Among aging heterosexuals, it was usually the woman who had a monogamous orientation, and she then adapted to a male partner who already was in a primary relationship. Sometimes the woman subsequently became polyamorous herself, but more often she simply became comfortable with her partner's other relationship(s) yet did not want other partners herself.

It appears that some issues directly related to aging make it easier for monogamous women to enjoy poly relationships. Older women's children are grown and gone, so they don't see themselves as competing with another woman for a man's involvement in the labor and financial responsibilities of child-rearing. Many older women spend a lot of their time with their adult children and grandchildren. Furthermore, aging women report that their needs for affection, closeness, and companionship are met through their relationships with family members, so they have a lot less need for a man's time and attention. Importantly, some women have postponed pursuing important life goals such as art or pursuing a college degree (Carr & Utz, 2020). A poly relationship, where they are not as restricted as being with a full-time spouse, has made it easier for many women to pursue personal dreams that they deferred, rather than raising children and making a living.

Additionally, Sheff's research indicates that some older monogamous women may opt for a relationship with a married or partnered man to avoid the caretaking responsibilities of a monogamous, heterosexual relationship. Most who made such decisions have been married and raised children, but do not want to cook and keep house for a man, nor be a primary caregiver if he becomes ill or disabled. Older women may seek love, companionship, sex, and emotional connection, but might not want a full range of spousal responsibilities. Some of these unique advantages related to aging seem to change the cost-benefit ratio for older women who have always been monogamous. Such advantages can make a polyamorous married or partnered man much more attractive.

Of course, not every monogamous older woman becomes a convert to polyamory. Many have experimented with open relationships and have eventually decided that the benefits of having a loving relationship are not worth the jealousy and distress provoked by sharing their partner with other women. Collectively, these findings indicate that polyamory can be a successful strategy for some older women who want some of the benefits of a partnership without the traditional expectations of marriage. Independent women with a strong support system are usually happiest with this, while those who crave exclusive partnership and more time together usually find polyamory unsatisfying.

Suggestions for Further Research

While our collective findings indicate that polygeezers often employ sex-positive strategies that might be useful for a wide range of elders, additional research is required for a more comprehensive understanding of polygeezers' lifestyles. It remains unclear why such a large gap exists between the comparatively[3] high number of younger people who engage in some form of CNM, and the much smaller number of those who sustain ongoing CNM relationships, thus there is a need for more research in this area. Like many other studies on CNM, the few extant samples of polygeezers have been mostly White in Sheff's studies, yet somewhat more diverse in Labriola's research. Further studies should utilize a more demographically diverse sample of elders.

Similarly, it is not clear whether or not poly elders' sexual orientations mirror those of all elders. Our professional experience suggests that a higher percentage of poly elders identify as queer than elders in the monogamous world. It is possible that polygeezers are simply more open than others about both their sexual orientations and their polyamorous lifestyles. More research would be needed to confirm this anecdotal evidence.

Families' responses to their elders who disclose unconventional sex or gender lives deserve significantly more study than has been received. This need is partly because elders are only now becoming far more diverse in their sexual relationships and gender presentations. Polyamorous and other relational nonconformists today owe these elders a debt for braving sex-negativity, with its stigma and discrimination, to make a social presence for CNM, which has increased substantially in recent decades. Insights gained from research with diverse elders can be a valuable window into the future as subsequent generations more fully embrace sex and gender diversity.

Finally, it is important to consider the protective features of sex-positivity for elders of all sorts, and especially for demographically diverse elders. Lifelong sex-positivity helped these OG polygeezers to withstand the stigma, discrimination, and hardship associated with being pioneers in relationship nonconformity. For these elders, the flexibility and willingness to try new things, while respecting the wide range of diversity that is endemic in sex-positivity functioned as a strong buffer against the effects of marginalization and oppression associated with sex-negativity. In our professional opinion, positive sexuality can provide the same protections for other elders, too!

Notes

1 While originally coined by urban gang members on the West coast of the U.S. to pertain to their own founding or elder members, the term OG has filtered into mainstream language to mean anything that is "old school" or anyone who is a long-time expert at something (Westhoff, 2016).

2 While we are aware that not all people with penises identify as men, the tendency for these respondents and indeed most members of the Baby Boom and Greatest generations is to associate man with penis so we use that here for shorthand to indicate that these respondents are largely cisgender.

3 Using comparison here we mean that people who have attempted a CNM relationship represent a comparatively high percentage of the

general population (21%) in relationship to other sex and gender minorities, such as people who identify as LGBTQ+ and whose combined numbers comprise only around 5% of the population (Haupert et al., 2017)

References

Balzarini, R. N., Dharma, C., Kohut, T., Holmes, B. M., Campbell, L., Lehmillier, J. J., & Harman, J. J. (2019). Demographic comparison of American individuals in polyamorous and monogamous relationships. *The Journal of Sex Research, 56*(6), 681–694. https://doi.org/10.1080/0022 4499.2018.1474333

Carr, D., & Utz, R. L. (2020). Families in later life: A decade in review. *Journal of Marriage and Family, 82*(1), 346–363. https://doi.org/10.1111/jomf.12609

Ezhova, I., Savidge, L., Bonnett, C., Cassidy, J., Okwuokei, A., & Dickinson, T. (2020). Barriers to older adults seeking sexual health advice and treatment: a scoping review. *International Journal of Nursing Studies, 107,* 103566. https://doi.org/10.1016/j.ijnurstu.2020.103566

Fleckenstein, J. R., & Cox II, D. W. (2015). The association of an open relationship orientation with health and happiness in a sample of older US adults. *Sexual and Relationship Therapy, 30*(1), 94–116. https://doi.org/10.1 080/14681994.2014.976997

Haupert, M. L., Moors, A. C., Gesselman, A. N., & Garcia, J. R. (2017). Estimates and correlates of engagement in consensually non-monogamous relationships. Curr. Sex Health Rep. 9, 155–165. https://doi.org/10.1007/ s11930-017-0121-6

Kaplan-Marans, E., Sandozi, A., Martinez, M., Lee, J., Schulman, A., & Khurgin, J. (2022). Medications most commonly associated with erectile dysfunction: evaluation of the Food and Drug Administration national pharmacovigilance database. *Sexual Medicine, 10*(5), 100543–100543. https://doi.org/10.1016/j.esxm.2022.100543.

Labriola, K. (1999). Models of open relationships. *Journal of Lesbian Studies, 3*(1–2), 217–225. https://doi.org/10.1300/J155v03n01_25

Labriola, K. (2011). *Love in abundance: A counselor's advice on open relationships.* Greenery Press.

Labriola, K. (2013). *The jealousy workbook: Exercises and insights for managing open relationships.* Greenery Press.

Labriola, K. (2022). *Polyamorous elders: Aging in open relationships*. Rowman & Littlefield.

Levine, E. C., Herbenick, D., Martinez, O., Fu, T. C., & Dodge, B. (2018). Open relationships, nonconsensual nonmonogamy, and monogamy among U.S. adults: Findings from the 2012 national survey of sexual health and behavior. *Archives of Sexual Behavior, 47*, 1439–1450. https://doi.org/10.1007/s10508-018-1178-7

McDowell, M. J., Goldhammer, H., Potter, J. E., & Keuroghlian, A. S. (2020). Strategies to mitigate clinician implicit bias against sexual and gender minority patients. *Psychosomatics, 61*(6), 655–661. https://doi.org/10.1016/j.psym.2020.04.021

Moors, A. C., Gesselman, A. N., & Garcia, J. R. (2021). Desire, familiarity, and engagement in polyamory: Results from a national sample of single adults in the United States. *Frontiers in Psychology, 12*. https://doi.org/10.3389/fpsyg.2021.619640

Nimbi, F. M., Galizia, R., Rossi, R., Limoncin, E., Ciocca, G., Fontanesi, L., Jannini, A. A., Simonelli, C., & Tambelli, R. (2021). The biopsychosocial model and the sex-positive approach: An integrative perspective for sexology and general health care. *Sexuality Research and Social Policy*, 1–15. https://doi.org/10.1007/s13178-021-00647-x

Price, J. (2010). *Naked at our age: Talking out loud about senior sex*. Seal Press.

Rhoten, K., Sheff, E., & D. Lane, J. (2021). U.S. family law along the slippery slope: The limits of a sexual rights strategy for polyamorous parents. *Sexualities, 27*(4), https://doi.org/10.1177/13634607211061485

Rothmore, J. (2020). Antidepressant-induced sexual dysfunction. *Medical Journal of Australia, 212*(7), 329–334.

Sheff, E. (2005). Polyamorous women, sexual subjectivity and power. *Journal of Contemporary Ethnography, 34*(3), 251–283. https://doi.org/10.1177/0891241604274263

Sheff, E. (2006). Poly-hegemonic masculinities. *Sexualities, 9*(5), 621–642. https://doi.org/10.1177/1363460706070004

Sheff, E. (2007). The reluctant polyamorist: Auto-ethnographic research in a sexualized setting. In M. Stombler et al., (Eds.), *Sex matters: The sexuality and society reader* (pp. 111–118). Springer.

Sheff, E. (2010). Strategies in polyamorous parenting. In *Understanding non-monogamies* (pp. 181–193). Routledge.

Sheff, E. (2011). Polyamorous families, same-sex marriage, and the slippery slope. *Journal of Contemporary Ethnography*, 40(5), 487–520. https://doi.org/10.1177/0891241611413578

Sheff, E. (2014). *The polyamorists next door: Inside multiple-partner relationships and families*. Rowman & Littlefield.

Sheff, E. (2015). Not necessarily broken: Redefining success when polyamorous relationships end. In T. S. Weinberg & S. Newmahr (Eds.), *Selves, symbols, and sexualities: An interactionist anthology* (pp. 201–214). Sage.

Sheff, E. (2016a). *When someone you love is polyamorous: Understanding poly people and relationships*. Thorntree Press LLC.

Sheff, E. (2016b). Resilience in polyamorous families. In R Karian (Ed.), *Critical & experiential: Dimensions in gender and sexual diversity* (pp. 257–280). Resonance Publications.

Sheff, E. (2020). Polyamory is deviant—but not for the reasons you may think. *Deviant Behavior*, 41(7), 882–892. https://doi.org/10.1080/01639625.2020.1737353

Sheff, E., & Hammers, C. (2011). The privilege of perversities: Race, class and education among polyamorists and kinksters. *Psychology & Sexuality*, 2(3), 198–223. https://doi.org/10.1080/19419899.2010.537674

Sheff, E., Rhoten, K., & Lane, J. (2021). A whole village: Polyamorous families and the best interests of the child standard. *Cornell Journal of Law & Public Policy*, 31, 287–330.

Sheff, E., & Smith, H. A. (2022). Social class and polyamory. In M. D. Vaughan & T. R. Burnes (Eds.), *The handbook of consensual non-monogamy: Affirming mental health practice* (pp. 315–331). Rowman & Littlefield.

Sheff, E., & Tesene, M. M. (2015). Consensual non-monogamies in industrialized nations. In J. DeLamater & R. F. Plante (Eds.), *Handbook of the sociology of sexualities* (pp. 223–242). Springer.

Sheff, E., & Wolf, T. (2015). *Stories from the polycule: Real life in polyamorous families*. Thorntree Press LLC.

Spears, B., & Lowen, L. (2010). The couples study: Beyond monogamy: Lessons from long-term male couples in non-monogamous relationships (unpublished).

Van Epps, P., Musoke, L., & McNeil, C. J. (2023). Sexually transmitted infections in older adults: Increasing tide and how to stem it. *Infectious Disease Clinics*, 37(1), 47–63. https://doi.org/10.1016/j.idc.2022.11.003

Watson, W. K., & Stelle, C. (2021). Love in cyberspace: Self presentation and partner seeking in online dating advertisements of older adults. *Journal of Family Issues, 42,* 2438–2463. https://doi.org/10.1177/0192513X20982024

Westhoff, B. (2016). *Original gangstas: The untold story of Dr. Dre, Eazy-E, Ice Cube, Tupac Shakur, and the birth of West Coast rap.* Hachette UK.

Zhang, F., Yang, Z., Li, X., & Wang, A. (2023). Factors influencing the quality of sexual life in the older adults: A scoping review. *International Journal of Nursing Sciences, 10*(2), 167–173. 10.1016/j.ijnss.2023.03.006

7

SEX WORK AS A FORM OF ART

Using Arts-Based Research to Understand
the Profession

*Moshoula Capous-Desyllas, Victoria Loy,
Arutyun Ambartsumyan, and
Marcos Chavez*

Introduction and Purpose

The purpose of this chapter is to uplift the voices of people working in the sex industry while showcasing the transformative power of arts-based research. We embody sex-positive and artistic approaches when presenting the personal narratives of sex workers to share their stories through their own art and from their own perspectives. This chapter aims to challenge stereotypes, stigmas, and negative discourse surrounding sex work to provide safe spaces for sex workers to be respected and admired for their labor. We emphasize the power of photovoice as a radical and revolutionary arts-based method with the capacity to liberate sexuality and reveal the positive aspects of sex work. We highlight the ways in which photovoice methodology can serve as a beneficial tool to build allyship and a sex-positive culture for people working in the sex industry. In doing so, we hope to shift the discourse on sex work and move society toward a brighter future where sex work is admired as an art form worthy of admiration, compassion, and respect.

DOI: 10.4324/9781032631820-8

Our Positionality and Social Locations

As cisgender queer people of color from working-class backgrounds, varying sexual orientations, and spanning roles of academics, artists, activists, social workers, legal scholars, and intersectional feminists, we bring diverse engagement levels and layered experiences with trading sex for material gain at various times in our lives. We recognize that the experiences of individuals who work in the sex trades deeply vary and exist on a broad spectrum from feelings of empowerment to experiences of oppression, informed by the positionality and social location of individuals. Understanding sex work through a positive sexuality lens embraces diversity, empowerment, and choice. While acknowledging its risks, we maintain the importance of sexual pleasure, freedom, and diversity (Williams et al., 2015). Drawing from personal experiences and years of formal and informal discussions with individuals in the sex industry, this chapter highlights sex work as a form of artistic self-expression.

Theoretical and Methodological Framework

Sex Work from a Sex-Positive Lens

Sex work has long been stigmatized and criticized as immoral, degrading, and oppressive to individuals, communities, and societies. This type of sex-negative perspective tends to frame sexuality and sexual practices primarily as risky, dangerous, difficult to manage, and harmful (Williams et al., 2015). A sex-positive, or positive sexuality, perspective acknowledges these concerns while also emphasizing the importance of sexual pleasure, freedom, and diversity in experiences (Williams et al., 2015). Our personal and political perspective aligns with this perspective, recognizing sex work as a legitimate form of labor. We also acknowledge the intersections of race, class, gender, ethnicity, sexuality, citizenship status, ability status, and the imbalance of power on an institutional, communal level. There is a wide range of individuals involved in the sex industry, a myriad of ways in which sexual services and sexual fantasies are bought and sold, and much variety in the relationships that are developed in the workplace (Benoit & Shaver, 2006, p. 249). Embodying a positive sexuality framework is critical for highlighting sex workers as active agents with self-determination. We believe that the complexity of sex workers' sexual agency can best be illustrated by sex workers themselves, especially through art.

Art as a Way of Knowing

Art is a unique medium for understanding ourselves and the world around us. Art promotes a form of understanding that is derived or evoked through empathic experience; thus, the artist provides a means through which feelings can come to be known (Eisner, 2008, p. 7). Susanne Langer explains this by writing:

> What does art seek to express? . . . I think every work of art expresses, more or less purely, more or less subtly, not feelings and emotions the artist has, but feelings which the artist knows; their insight into the nature of sentience, their picture of vital experience, physical, emotive and fantastic.
>
> (Langer, 1957, p. 91)

From this perspective, art represents an artist's ability to create something to mirror human experiences and feelings. Eisner (2008) discusses four contributions of the arts to knowledge. First, the arts address the qualitative subtle differences in situations. For example, art has the potential to address what is subtle but significant about the world that someone might not notice if they didn't know how to look. A second contribution relates to emphatic feeling. Images created in artistically expressive form generate a type of empathy that makes action possible. A third contribution the arts make to knowledge has to do with the fresh perspective they offer so that our old habits of mind don't dominate our reactions with typical, collected responses. The arts offer new ways in which to perceive and interpret the world that would otherwise go unknown. Finally, the arts tell us something about the capabilities of individuals to experience the affective responses to life that the arts evoke:

> If the arts are about anything, they are about emotion, and emotion has to do with the ways in which we feel. Becoming aware of our

> capacity to feel is a way of discovering our humanity. Art helps us connect with personal, subjective emotions, and through such a process, it enables us to discover our own interior landscape.
>
> (Eisner, 2008, p. 11)

Art enables our understanding of what we actually believe, feel, and experience while also providing a process and a form of inquiry within research.

A Positive Sexuality Framework and the Intersection of Arts-Based Research

The key dimensions of the positive sexuality framework, created by Williams et al. (2015), intersect with arts-based research approaches to illuminate how sex work can be seen as a form of art and self-expression. The first dimension *acknowledges that the "positive" in positive sexuality refers to strengths, well-being, and happiness.* This recognizes that people have an assortment of personal strengths and unique sexualities, and they are capable of drawing from their existing strengths to resolve problems, be happier, and feel more fulfilled. By developing their sexual identities and expressing their sexuality, sex workers can enhance their overall well-being and quality of life. Engaging in the arts provides sex workers with the opportunity to explore their strengths and assert their agency through their artistic visions, voices, and the opportunity for creative self-presentation (Capous-Desyllas, 2013). Representing oneself through artmaking can also offer ways for representing and envisioning well-being and what that looks like individually and collectively.

The second dimension of the framework emphasizes that *individual sexuality is unique and multifaceted.* Williams et al. (2015) draw from the World Health Organization to recognize that sexuality involves a "diverse array of aspects including roles and identities, preferences and orientations, relationships and activities, pleasures and desired, scripts and fantasies, as well as values and beliefs" (2006, p. 8). The process of artmaking and engaging in arts-based research with sex workers has the potential to illustrate the multi-layered experiences and unique sexual histories of sex workers and how the arts can contribute to illustrating unique sexual narratives that challenge stereotypes and stigmas about sex workers (Capous-Desyllas, 2013).

The arts-based, creative inquiry process is defined by openness to the extensive possibilities of the human imagination. Butler-Kisber (2008) states that there is growing interest in using arts-based inquiry to "counteract the hegemony and linearity in written texts, to increase voice and reflexivity in the research process, and to expand the possibilities of multiple, diverse realities and understandings" (p. 268). It has the potential to offer ways of re-visioning issues that are unique and multifaceted and are simply not possible through descriptive linear language. This also aligns with the third dimension of the framework that maintains positive sexuality embraces multiple ways of knowing.

Arts-based research is grounded in a multi-sensory perspective that acknowledges diverse ways of knowing and expressing knowledge and experience through the arts. The concept of creative, artistic, and alternative forms of data representation acknowledges the variety of ways through which our experience is coded (Eisner, 1997). Engaging in arts-based research allows meanings to take shape in different ways and invites us to engage with experiences in new ways. It provides opportunities to go beyond the limitations of our usual frame of reference and beliefs so that new associations are created. Creative and artistic forms invite us to see differently and develop insights that would otherwise be inaccessible. Some human experiences are so complex and intensely emotional, that creative forms of representation can reflect their texture more powerfully and make a greater impact.

The fourth dimension of the framework connects positive sexuality to professional ethics. This approach reflects the importance of professional ethical principles that promote diversity, and honor the voices, needs, choices, experiences, and lives of every individual. While many do not recognize sex work as a profession, we view sex work as a legitimate form of labor that adheres to codes of conduct from a sex-positive lens. Similarly, arts-based research maintains methodological integrity by intersecting with anti-oppressive and indigenous/decolonizing approaches to research to harmonize the heart, mind, body, and spirit. Key to this intersection is the focus on interconnectedness, our relationship to ourselves, to one another, to our environment, and to our earth while using the arts as a form of social justice.

The fifth dimension illuminates how positive sexuality promotes open and honest communication. This moves beyond discussions of sexual preferences, attitudes, and behaviors, to also allow and account for freedom of language, concepts and ideas that may differ from personal perspectives or social norms. This openness helps to establish trust and safety that are critical for personal and collective growth and well-being. Arts-based research facilitates open and honest communication, as the interpretive license lies within individuals to create meaning from experience through art. Each creator, viewer and consumer of art is granted the freedom to interpret the art from their own lens and positionality, creating space for multiple interpretations and meanings to co-exist.

The sixth dimension asserts that *positive sexuality is humanizing*. This approach recognizes the diversity of challenges associated with sexuality and helps to address them while also maintaining the importance of attending to language that devalues people and perpetuates stigma. Regardless of the problematic behavior that people may engage in, acknowledging the humanness of others through the use of positive language reflects social justice and inclusiveness. This is critical when engaging in research with sex workers who are inherently "othered," dehumanized and stigmatized. A central purpose of arts-informed research is to enhance the understanding of the human condition through alternative processes and representational forms of inquiry (Cole & Knowles, 2008).

The seventh dimension of the framework maintains that *positive sexuality encourages peacemaking*, which entails attending to language and approaching issues from a humanistic and inclusive stance from a place of honesty and openness. Peacemaking is rooted in love and compassion (Pepinski, 2013) and facilitated by self-control, communication, deep listening, empathizing, learning, and creativity (Hahn, 2014). The eighth dimension reflects *positive sexuality as being applicable across all levels of social structure*, from the individual to the collective to the societal, with the potential to help address issues of power and inequality that exist. These last two dimensions intersect with arts-based research's goal to challenge hierarchies and inequalities by reaching multiple audiences through art by making scholarship more accessible. Arts-based inquiry is committed to connecting the work of academia with the lives of people in the community through research that is accessible, evocative, empathetic, and stimulating (Cole & Knowles, 2008). It aims to democratize research and place control in the hands of the people. The arts-based researcher aims to provide tools and opportunities for participants to perform inquiry through creative

mediums. Arts-based processes invite participants to reflect on their performances, and to preserve, create, and rewrite their experiences and culture in dynamic, local spaces (Finley, 2008). Artful representations by
participants can provoke honest and reflective dialogue and meaningful
participatory action to change society at all levels.

Photovoice and the Use of Visual Images in Research

The process of photovoice entails giving cameras to individuals who
use photography to identify, represent, and enhance their communities
(Wang & Burris, 1997). Participant-generated images provide an opportunity for traditionally silenced populations to document their lives and
environments (Hubbard, 1994). As a form of self-expression, visual techniques provide a window into the participants' (sex workers') immediate
environment, significant relationships, feelings, and perceptions of self
(Hubbard, 1994). Through photovoice, the power of the visual image is
used to communicate life experiences and perceptions, which then has
the power to influence social policy. An arts-informed paradigm states
that by handing over creativity (the contents of research) and its interpretation (the explanation of its contents) to the research participants, they
are empowered, and the content is more culturally exact and explicit, utilizing emotional and cognitive ways of knowing (Sclater, 2003). Photovoice has the potential to challenge negative perceptions, stereotypes, and
stigma of sex workers, as well as empower participants and educate the
community through art. Through our research, the photovoice method
allowed sex workers to represent themselves, their lives, and their needs
through photography.

Images are invaluable to research because they can convey multiple messages, pose questions, and point to both abstract and concrete thoughts
(Weber, 2008). Visual images are constantly subject to reconstruction
and reinterpretation, holding multiple meanings. Barthes (1981) takes
the photographic image and explains that images have two main levels
of meaning: denotative and connotative. The denotative meaning of an
image refers to its literal, descriptive meaning; the visible truth, evidence,
or objective reality that the image documents. The connotative meaning of
that same image refers to the cultural and historical context of a specific
image, in addition to the social conventions, codes, and meanings that

have been attached to or associated with that image in a particular context (Weber, 2008). Images can act as useful metaphors, providing themes and patterns to form ideas and explanations (Simons & McCormack, 2007). In addition, metaphors provide an opportunity to connect images and ideas in different ways. This can reshape the text from being one-dimensional to having multiple layers and meanings. The ability of images to express multiple messages contributes to the potential for obtaining rich data about human experiences and perspectives. Arts-based research approaches that incorporate visual images operate at a symbolic, meta-phoric level, which invites multiple ways of understanding (Franz, 2005).

Weber (2008) advocates the use of visual images in research to help capture the indescribable, hard-to-put-into-words of knowledge often overlooked. Images hold the power to engage us into viewing humanity from varying perspectives. Images can elicit emotional and intellectual responses (Weber, 2008). These various responses make images more memorable, easier to disseminate, and accessible to a wider audience. Visual images can help us adopt someone else's point of view, enhancing empathic understanding (Eisner, 1997; Weber, 2008). They encourage embodied knowledge; "people are not ideas, but flesh and blood beings learning through senses and responding to images through their embod-ied experiences" (Weber, 2008, p. 46). There is also the power of images to provoke action for social justice (Wang, 1999; Weber, 2008), sparking critical dialogue and encourage individual and collective action.

Participants

A total of 32 individuals participated in qualitative and photovoice research studies, with this chapter focusing on testimonies and photo-graphs from 17 sex workers living and working in Southern California and the Pacific Northwest. Participants, aged 21–37, included 12 cis women, three trans women, one cis man, and one trans man. Six were white, four Black, five Latinx, and one South Asian. Sexual orientations with the participants varied, with seven identifying as heterosexual, two as queer, two as pansexual, three as sexually fluid, two as gay, and two as bisexual. The participants worked in diverse sectors of the sex indus-try, including BDSM work/pro dominatrix work, exotic dancing, erotic modeling, pornography, webcam work, phone sex, sexual massage, stripping, sugar baby, and street work, with experience ranging from 6 months to 18 years.

Findings

The lived experiences of sex workers are unique, diverse, and encompass varying degrees of complexities, intimacies, and pleasures. In this section, we explore the brilliant mindsets and artistic perspectives of sex workers through their own creative photographs and testimonies of the meaning behind their work. The themes that emerged from our research illuminated sex work as: (1) a form of art, freedom of expression and empowerment; (2) as facilitating fantasy, play and desire; (3) as an opportunity for integration, growth, and self-knowledge; and (4) as a form of reciprocity, care, and connection. These themes are not mutually exclusive, but rather interconnected and overlapping, and we only present a snapshot of the various visual voices shared with us.

Sex Work as a Form of Art, Freedom of Expression and Empowerment

Examining sex work from a sex-positive lens allows us to view sex work as a form of art and self-love that evokes a deeper sense of self. Some individuals start sex work with previous artistic experience with dancing, writing, poetry, and modeling. This is the reality for Lady Purfection, an entertainer in the sex industry who engages in the profession not just for money but also to amplify her art. As a spoken-word poet and sex work artist, she has been featured in magazines and admired for her talents as an entertainer and dancer. When asked about her experiences in the sex trade, she expressed the urgent need for society to grant sex workers respect, admiration, and compassion for the work they participate in. The judgments projected by society, and especially from state officials, creates a sex-negative culture which harms sex workers, damages the credibility of their careers, and removes their agency to do what they want with their bodies. For Lady Purfection, sex work is empowering and fulfilling, a career choice that grants her agency and artistic freedom. Lady Purfection captured these sentiments in the photograph of herself dancing at the club (Figure 7.1).

Figure 7.1

When asked about her engagement in the sex industry, Lady Purfection expressed:

> I'm in the sex industry because it's fun. It's an experience you won't ever get anywhere else unless you partake in it. I love what I do, I love art and [entertaining] is a form of art to me. One day I hope to be famous. For my art, not just for my sex work.

Lady Purfection represents this notion through her self-portrait, depicting her resilience, confidence, and her desires to be treated with humanity and respect. Her sexual labor is a form of artistic activism because it challenges a sexually repressed society and politically asserts her right to bodily autonomy. Similarly, Megan, who works as a stripper and sugar baby, shared, "I'm an Aries, so I like freedom of expression. I love to dance, so I passionately like to strip. I like to be on the pole. Not so much strip, but dance on the pole." Mouse, who works as a stripper, erotic model and escort posed for a photograph (Figure 7.2) that she titled "Beautiful Landscape" and shared:

No matter what kind of sex work you do, it is a kind of art. And I mean when I think of stripping, I really do try to treat it like an art. I mean everything, from the movements that you do while you are dancing, to the image that you project when you are interacting with other people because a big part of the job is the way you talk to people and the way that you flirt with the customers at the restaurant.

Sex work offers more than just creative expression but also a sense of power and empowerment. Tiff, who works as a stripper and sugar baby, shared, "When I go to work, I feel like I have powers, because, you know, how I talk to them [clients] and to get them to give me stuff, you know, that makes me feel like I have powers." Through her work as an escort, stripper and sugar baby, Kimberly echoed these sentiments detailing how power and money from sex work brought about liberation and independence. She expressed:

I am a boss, I'm in charge of my life, I make my own hours. The money was empowering because there was a lot of it. It was the most money I ever made in my life. You know, of course when you have more money, you feel like you have more power. I felt in complete control.

Figure 7.2

When discussing empowerment, Lily, who works as a high-end escort and dominatrix, shared, "I took a great deal of selfies . . . I was transfixed by the idea that women could reclaim their power taken from them via the patriarchy by owning their sexual power." Feelings of empowerment were also connected to sex work as a space to feel desired and validated, particularly for those who were trans-identified. When discussing the benefits of escorting and the love she has for her work, Moon, who works as an escort, stated:

> Schedule, autonomy, power, control, and then, just feeling desired too. Yeah, yeah, I felt very desired. I mean, I've always felt desired. I don't think – I think even before the sex work, I think I always felt desired just because . . . I felt very confident the entire time, and sexy and I liked that. I've always been a sexual person. It seemed to make sense. I was like, 'Well, I'm having sex anyway. Why not get paid for it.'

Domino, a pro dom involved in BDSM work shared:

> I came out five years ago as trans, and when I came out, it never, in a million years, would have crossed my mind that I would be able to even blend in society, or a term that many refer to as passing, I don't care for that term. It definitely never crossed my mind that anyone would find me attractive. To be in this field where, whether it'd be professional domination, or whether it'd be direct sex work, or any other field, being able to be affirmed in my identity.

The theme of feeling affirmed and desired was a driving force in the participants' views of sex work as a form of empowerment and creative self-expression.

Sex work as Facilitating Creativity, Fantasy, Play and Desire

Many participants shared how their work provided them with the opportunity to be creative, as they sought out more opportunities for play, engaging in fantasy and fostering desire with their clients. Nikkita-Jones, a trans woman who worked as an escort, sugar baby and street worker shared her experience.

We are providing this fantasy for people when a lot of situations, it's a lot of women living their truth. Trans women. We are lending our bodies and time the glamour, the pop, you know, that's just who we are . . . we are sought out because we provide this fantasy situation.

For some, the power of self-representation was a form of artistic self-expression. Having the opportunity to dress up and be adored was an important and enjoyable aspect of their work. Krystal, who worked as an escort, street worker and dominatrix, expressed, "I loved being able to put on an outfit and feel sexy and walk the street and get people's heads to turn. I had like an addiction to that, the entertainment." For many participants, feeling affirmed and desired created the space to be imaginative and engage in fantasy, performance, and play. Skyler, a gay escort who identified as an artist, shared:

I studied fashion design . . . this is going to sound really strange, but when it comes down to it, I am a very visual person and I'm very obsessed with the way that I look and the way that I project myself, physically. For me, this job, it's almost like a validation of that. Because people are willing to come here to pay to be with me, because of my physical appearance. I'm very happy with who I have become as a person. I've realized that it's because I get so much validation from the people, these clients and whatever. Because, then, two or three years ago, I was dating this guy and he really wanted me to stop. I was going to stop but then I was like, 'If I stop, who's going to tell me that I'm beautiful every day? Where am I going to get these people that are coming over here to pay me, to be with me?' It's not even just the money that I was worried about, it was that validation that every human being needs.

Feeling empowered, connected, desired, and admired, while fulfilling other people's fantasies, opens up space for meeting basic human needs and moving towards self-actualization. Mouse took a photograph (Figure 7.3) and discussed her aspirations for privacy and playfulness in her life as a sex worker. She captured a picture of a seesaw with her lingerie hanging around the ledges.

When asked about the meaning of the photo, Mouse stated:

Figure 7.3

> How public my private life feels when I am dancing because I mean, just literally being physically naked or scantily clad in front of other people. There is really no privacy, and I would like to retain a little more privacy, I think in my life. But on the other I was also thinking about the idea of play, again, which I was thinking about with dogs and how I wanted to have more playful approach to my life.

The playfulness of the seesaw signified desire to revert to an innocent understanding of life that incorporates play. The symbolism of her photograph shows the intense physical and social labor of sex work and her goals of finding more of a balance between the joys and pleasures of the lightness of being while navigating the weight of existing. An interesting perspective was shared by Domino, who expressed:

> For me, professional domination . . . I'm a lifestyle kinkster, first and foremost. I love to play; no, I don't pay, I get paid . . . what I get paid for the time investment and the flexibility of that time investment allows me to engage in so many other things that really fuel me and fulfill me. Not to say that sex work itself doesn't fuel me and fulfill me, it does, in so many ways.

Having the ability to be creative through fantasy and play allows one to thrive and grow sexually, emotionally, professionally, and artistically.

Sex work as an Opportunity for Integration, Growth, and Self-Knowledge

Many participants discussed their work in the sex industry as an opportunity for cultivating their inner self. Strawberry, who was an escort, also did webcam work, nude modeling, porn performance, stripping and phone sex, and described how sex work enhanced her sense of self and the opportunity to develop other parts of herself. She shared,

> [sex work] totally opened up my mind. It made me more comfortable in my own skin. It made it easier for me to be – in my own personal relationships, to talk about sex. I learned a lot how to make someone else feel comfortable, and also what I enjoy, or what I like.

Similarly, Scar, who engages in stripping and twerking videos, shared the following thoughts on learning about herself because of her work in the industry,

> I used to be energetic and really sweet and nice, but now I'm energetic and aggressive too. That's how I manage dancing with these guys. I observe first where everybody is seating [or] if they are standing. I look at their body language. I ask like, does it look like he'll give in. I have to be aggressive, or sweet, or show some boobies. I gotta twerk some!

Multiple sex workers shared how sex work provided them with the opportunity to learn more about themselves, their sexuality, and their bodies.

For example, Grahm, a stripper and dominatrix, photographed her friend reading a book on a bed (Figure 7.4) to represent empowerment through knowledge of herself and her body.

Grahm accompanied her photograph with the following explanation:

> These are a couple of photos of my friend sitting on a bed and reading *The Ultimate Guide to Anal Sex for Women*. I took this photo because I wanted to have an opportunity to mention a lot of sex workers' literature. Tristan Taormino wrote that book and she's an

interesting pornographer, like, a sort of 'empowering, learn about sex, take your health into your own hands' sort of culture that I think is, in a lot of ways, related to sex work, even if you go way back to Nina Hartley's instructional videos. They are instructional porn and the beginnings of feminist porn that are related to teaching people about their bodies.

For Grahm, knowing about her own body was a source of empowerment and books represented a way to share skills and knowledge to improve her life and the lives of her clients. She went on to share her belief in the power of information sharing. Grahm expressed:

Talking about sex is skill-sharing in this context – it's not that talking about sex is inherently liberating or whatever, but I do believe that openness is valuable as a way of learning how to communicate about things that are difficult. In talking about things explicitly, we begin to get comfortable articulating our own boundaries, protecting ourselves and learning to have the type of sex – with clients or lovers or whoever or with ourselves – that we want to have.

Figure 7.4

For Moon, who was also in medical school at a prestigious university, sex work provided the chance to integrate parts of herself and challenge stereotypes. She shared:

> I have friends in school who, if I told them, they'd probably flip out because there is negative connotations against being a whore or a slut or just dirty and those stereotype of just maybe not being smart. Like, 'Oh, you have to use your body for money? Why can't you use your brain?' That bothers me a lot. Because a lot of people, I think they assume, well, if you can't use your brain to make money, maybe you're going to use your body, you know? I think I could do both, easily. And I think that's what makes me unique. I'm trying to disprove that stereotype, you know? When I meet people at bars and stuff they assume, 'Oh my gosh, she's this dumb blonde.' Or, whatever. They don't realize I'm in a graduate program and progressing in my career, you know? I think that's something – I like that aspect of me a little bit, too, is that I can be sexy and also smart at the same time.

Skyler expressed the importance of feeling whole and integrated through sex work, and not just "being some worker in an office job that is valued for their mind."

The intimacy of sex work labor encompasses intense emotional, physical, and spiritual aspects for people working in the industry. The photograph below is captured by Mouse (Figure 7.5), who views her work in the sex industry as a way to explore her sexuality and express her identity as a gutter-punk.

When asked about her needs and aspirations, Mouse expressed how romanticism, sexuality, and love are interwoven in both her private and work life. She encapsulates these feelings by taking a photo of a heart-print, black and white thong entangled in and draped over a thorny rose bush. Mouse shared:

> The thong is obviously kind of symbolic of sexuality and then the rose is commonly thought as a symbol of love. And I want to be more assured of the fact that these things are still so intimately connected because that was something that I worried about a lot when I started this work . . .

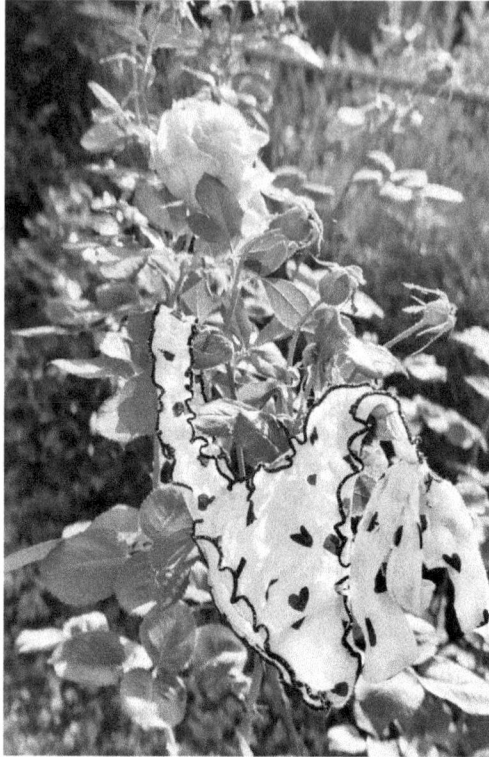

Figure 7.5

Mouse recounted the times when she worried about whether getting naked in front of people would impact her private sexual intimacies with those she was romantically involved with. She expressed her internal fears of love rendering itself meaningless if the sexuality and physical labor of her sex work life could not be untangled from her romantic private life. Figure 7.5 provided an intense realization to Mouse that the two could not be separated. She went on to state, "It kind of does detract from some of the specialness I think. But I don't think that's something that I can't get past, so I want to kind of meld those things back together again- romanticism and my sexuality."

Sex work labor has a profound impact on the personal and private lives of sex workers and their integration of self; sometimes feelings are integrated, other times they are compartmentalized. The photograph allowed Mouse to make sense of this challenge and reflect on the ways she has closed off romanticism from her life to perform sexually for money. Her photo illustrates her need to merge love and sex back together for herself to create more balance and personal growth in her life so that she can continue opening herself up to the idea of love, even if it hurts, and even if it is difficult to do while engaged in sex work labor. She expanded on the imagery of the roses and shared, "I always thought [roses are] a funny and kind of appropriate analogy for love. Because it is beautiful and it smells wonderful, and you know, but it hurts. It hurts a lot." The rose serves as an analogy for love to express the beauty, pain, and wonder that comes with life experiences, especially for individuals who exist in the sex work realm. Similarly, Sexy Red, who gave sexual massages, shared,

> Well it's like being somebody that you're not on a daily basis. You gotta live another life. You gotta act like another person. Your other double person. Have a more adventurous sexy side of you. It's acting, it's role-playing pretty much. That's how I see this type of work.

For many participants, their work in the sex industry provided them with the opportunity to reflect upon and integrate various aspects of themselves.

Sex work as a Form of Reciprocity, Care, and Connection

There is love in sex work practice, existing in micro-forms of caring, self-expression, therapizing, and nurturing clients' needs. Many of the sex workers discussed the significance of caring for others and being cared for as part of their work. They discussed the art of caring and building meaningful connections through their diverse interactions with clients. Lily shared:

> I love very easily. I can see the best parts of people without trying too hard, the things that make them delightful, their talents, their vulnerabilities. I love making people feel cared for. Perhaps that is a large part of why I started doing sex work in the first place.

She continues to discuss the art of connection through giving pleasure. Lily expressed,

That's my favorite part of my work – my clients feeling pleasure. Feeling their tension, their desire, playing with it, directing it, touching them, and stroking them to keep them on the edge of climax . . . giving pleasure is my fantasy as well.

When discussing her role as a sex worker, Roxanne, who worked as a stripper and escort, commented, "We are just there to have people feel better about themselves, you know, guys that are lonely or whatever, that they can't just go up to girls and talk to them."

Quite a few sex workers discussed their work as a form of therapy. Ambrosia, who worked in porn, exotic dancing, web cam work, and phone sex shared, "there are a lot of people that do come in that have mental issues that you can – like you can see that. Sometimes you're a therapist to these people." In the context of her work, Scar shared,

I'm a real comforter. Like, I comfort people in any which way that I can. So, like all the time I would just tell him [client] the things I knew he wanted to hear, and a lot of times I guess I would do for people as I wish I was done as a little kid, so that comforter thing in me is like super, super big.

Similarly, Domino, who was enrolled in a Master of Social Work program, expressed:

Even though I'm two months away from getting my degree, I think I have enough experience both academically, professionally, to know what a therapist is. If what I do as a professional dominatrix, or what I do as a direct provider is not a form of therapy, then I don't know what is. I've had clients come to me, many clients over the years able to share intimate details of their lives that they haven't been able to share with anyone. Not their wives, not their parents, not their therapists, no one, and it is healing to them. It is more than just about whipping someone, or beating someone, or sleeping with someone, that it is about human connection.

Skyler echoed these sentiments when he said:

I think that's one of the things that I get from this job that another job probably would not offer me. Is validation in who I am, both physically and emotionally, as a person, you know what I mean? Because my clients don't just come here and just have sex with me and leave. We sit and talk and bond.

Having the art of connection with their clients was also a way to incorporate healing into their sex work. Lily went on to express, "I'm the type of sex worker, and there are many of us, who delight in strange requests from clients, who read about psychology and sexuality and apply it all in our bookings, approaching work as a type of therapy." Sex work as a form of art through therapy evoked a deeper sense of oneself and of others.

Integrating Ideas and Concluding Thoughts

This chapter shared the personal narratives of diverse sex workers using photovoice to illustrate how arts-based methodologies provide cathartic, therapeutic, and healing elements for sex workers to creatively reflect and artistically connect with the world and their inner selves By centering their diverse stories through photography and testimonies, we provide a deeper understanding of sex work and how it can be represented as a form of art, embodying intimate feelings, deep connections, and intense introspections.

Ambiguity, complexity, polyphony, and polysemy – embracing multiple voices, meanings, and perspectives – lie at the heart of arts-based research methods. Arts-based research encourages the expression of multiple truths, the interactions of these truths to create new individual and collective meanings, and raise further questions. Moreover, arts-based research methods problematize the relationship between knowledge and power in our society, exposing knowledge as socially constructed, creating diverse modes and mediums that strive to amplify the voices of marginalized populations, our understanding of cultural issues, and our efforts toward social justice.

Using photography as a methodological tool in sex work scholarship profoundly influences our perception of the profession and serves as a methodological tool for artistic and social exploration. By looking through the lens of sex work as a form of art, we enable sex workers to externalize and express sentiments that are oftentimes internalized and misunderstood, enhancing our understanding of their influence and power.

The visual voices of the sex workers presented here illustrate their multi-faceted roles as artists, entertainers, social workers, and spiritual workers who understand their sex work as embodying the potential for emotional, physical, social, and spiritual growth of self and others. Sex work as a form of artistic expression can facilitate the exchange of connection through discussion, play, fantasy, and pleasure, offering opportunities for growth and empowerment. The diverse voices featured in this chapter highlight the art of connection, healing, communication, performance, and sexual pleasure. Fantasy, play, and desire cultivate a space of reciprocity and exchange, carving a path toward self-love and exploration within the context of sex work. Using the eight dimensions of positive sexuality as a framework for informing creative research methodologies allows us to reimagine sex work as an art form for advancing social, emotional, physical, and spiritual connection.

References

Barthes, R. (1981). *Camera lucida: Reflections on photography.* Noonday.

Benoit, C. & Shaver, F. (2006). Critical issues and new directions in sex work research. *The Canadian Review of Sociology and Anthropology, Special Issue, 43*(3), 243–252.

Butler-Kisber, L. (2008). Collage as inquiry. In G. Knowles & A. Cole (Eds.) *Handbook of the arts in qualitative research: Perspectives, methodologies, examples & issues* (pp. 265–276). Sage Publications.

Capous-Desyllas, M. (2013). Using photovoice with sex workers: The power of art, agency and resistance. *Qualitative Social Work, 13*(4), 469–492.

Cole, A. & Knowles, G. (2008). Arts-informed research. In G. Knowles & A. Cole (Eds.) *Handbook of the arts in qualitative research: Perspectives, methodologies, examples & issues* (pp. 55–70). Sage Publications.

Eisner, E. (1997). The promise and perils of alternative forms of data representation. *Educational Reader, 26*(6), 4–10.

Eisner, E. (2008). Art and knowledge. In G. Knowles & A. Cole (Eds.) *Handbook of the arts in qualitative research: Perspectives, methodologies, examples & issues* (pp. 3–12). Sage Publications.

Finley, S. (2008). Arts-based research. In G. Knowles & A. Cole (Eds.) *Handbook of the arts in qualitative research: Perspectives, methodologies, examples & issues* (pp. 71–82). Sage Publications.

Franz, J. M. (2005). *Arts-based research in design education.* In Proceedings AQR Conference, Melbourne. https://eprints.qut.edu.au/9106/1/9106.pdf

Hahn, T. N. (2014). *The art of communicating.* HarperOne.

Hubbard, J. (1994). *Shooting back: A photographic view of life by Native Americans.* The New York Press.

Langer, S. (1957). *Problems of art: Ten philosophical lectures.* Scribner.

Pepinski, H. (2013). Peacemaking criminology. *Critical Criminology, 21,* 319–339.

Sclater, D. (2003). The arts and narrative research. *Qualitative Inquiry, 9*(4), 621–625.

Simons, H. & McCormack, B. (2007). Integrating arts-based inquiry in evaluation methodology: Opportunities and challenges. *Qualitative Inquiry, 13*(2), 292–311.

Wang, C. & Burris, M. A. (1997). Photovoice: Concept, methodology, and use for participatory needs assessment. *Health Education & Behavior, 24*(3), 369–387.

Wang, C. (1999). Photovoice: A participatory action research strategy applied to women's health. *Journal of Women's Health, 8*(2), 185–192.

Weber, S. (2008). Visual images in research. In G. Knowles & A. Cole (Eds.) *Handbook of the arts in qualitative research: Perspectives, methodologies, examples & issues* (pp. 41–54). Sage Publications.

World Health Organization (2006). *Defining sexual health: Report of a technical consultation on sexual health.* World Health Organization.

Williams, D.J., Thomas, J., Prior, E., & Walters, W. (2015). Introducing a multidisciplinary framework of positive sexuality. *Journal of Positive Sexuality, 1,* 6–12.

8

POSITIVITY SEXUALITY AS PRAXIS

A Collaborative and Intergenerational Discussion on the Training and Mentoring Experiences of Sexuality Educators

Bianca I. Laureano, carrie "cherry" kaufman, Em Thev, Laura Ramos Tomás, and Scotney Young

Introduction

When done well and in a culturally relevant way, divesting from all forms of oppressive supremacy, sexuality education has the potential to save lives! (Dixon et al., 2021). In the U.S. if an educator is seeking to become a certified sexuality educator (CSE) they must complete a series of requirements in education, professional development, and mentorship/ supervision. This chapter focuses on if/when/and how sex positivity is present in the training of CSEs. Our approach herein is from a subjective, intersectional lens that embraces a relational approach implemented in teaching and learning as well as anti-oppressive strategies utilized in training sexuality educators.

This chapter is a collaborative, intergenerational, roundtable conversation between Bianca I. Laureano, and four of her former supervisees who

DOI: 10.4324/9781032631820-9

completed their requirements to become CSEs. Together they explore how and if sex positivity was a part of their training and professional development. Each of us works with, supports, and advocates for work with demographically diverse communities, schools, and individuals in the U.S. and globally that offer an abundance of opportunities to consider how sex positivity may shift, change, or be present beyond a Western, U.S.-dominant, colonial lens.

Author Introductions and Social Positioning

Bianca I. Laureano is a queer, fat, LatiNegra, disabled, gender expansive femme sexuality educator, curriculum writer, sexologist, and AASECT CSE and CSES (certified sexuality educator supervisor). She is the foundress of the virtual freedom school ANTE UP!

carrie "cherry" kaufman is a queer, multiply disabled, white, Jewish artist, organizer, and kitchen witch. She is in love with supporting other disabled survivors and sought AASECT and ANTE UP! certification to continue offering sexuality education grounded in the principles of Disability Justice. Cooking, ritual, and poetry are her current tools for connection and healing. She is also a certified Death Doula. Her work explores disabled embodiment, erotics, survivorship, care, and intimacy as well as Jewish magic and spirituality. She is the creator of DisabledParts.com, a website featuring stories about disabled sexuality. She is full of fire, water, and honey.

Em Thev; Prior to her recent passing, Em Thev was an AASECT CSE Relationship and Mindfulness Educator. She lived with invisible disabilities and was a purity culture survivor. Through her organization, Honey Rose Haven, she helped thousands of people worldwide overcome sexual shame and cultivate healthy, passionate relationships through one-to-one educational sessions and workshops.

Laura Ramos Tomás is an AASECT CSE of European origin, working in non-formal education spaces in Latin America through her organization TabuTabu. She co-creates programs on sexual wellbeing and justice with communities of the global majority who usually haven't had access to affirming and pleasure-based sexuality education.

Scotney Young is a Black American and Chicana AASECT CSE committed to offering practical tools and information to help people better understand

and enjoy their bodies and relationships. As an ANTE UP! certified sexuality professional, her work is rooted in community collaboration and justice with a special focus on elevating youth voices and experiences. She has worked in five countries across three continents implementing culturally relevant sexual and reproductive health and justice initiatives.

Discussion Narratives: Becoming Sex Educators, Conceptualizations, and Training

Our discussion herein is comprised of brief personal narratives how and why we became sexuality educators, our personal definitions of sex positivity, tensions and challenges to incorporating sex positivity in our communities and globally, then we discuss our training as sexuality educators, the impact of erasure, projects we have been a part of that utilize the sex positivity we envision in the world, lessons learned in doing our work, and joys of offering sexuality education across the globe!

Bianca: I learned about certification in 2008. I thought I'd become a CSE and decided to attend a conference in Arizona in 2009 and was one of 19 people of the global majority at the conference of over 400 people in a state that is indigenous land with a thriving Mexican community! The other 18 women of color present, mostly Black women, we chose to support one another. We created the Women of Color Sexual Health Network (WOCSHN). I left that conference knowing I did not fit in, was not welcome, and my Black, Caribbean, and immigrant communities were not valued. Five years later I reconsidered certification where I could bypass supervision. I did not want to spend money on supervision with a white person who was non-disabled, did not understand or work with my communities, and I worried I would be teaching my supervisor rather than learning from them. This was the same reason many WOCSHN members delayed completing their certification. For this reason I chose to become a supervisor with the goal to offer support to those choosing certification.

Scotney: I pursued certification because you, Bianca, let me know it was safe to do so. "Safe" in that I would not have to navigate challenges, discrimination, or obstacles from white-led organizations alone and unprotected. I had gone through a marginalizing experience at a Sexual Health Certificate Program (SHCP) in the Midwest. I felt emotionally and financially burned. I wasn't eager to engage with another organization where I would have to hide my authentic self, prove my experience, and pay for professional development that would not be applicable to the populations I work with. I knew certification would give me the validity and legitimacy to access certain work opportunities. I looked for more inclusive and relevant training and found you and began taking some courses through ANTE UP! Sharing your experiences let me know you could help me through the process and navigate the obstacles. It is not an exaggeration to say I would not have pursued certification without you. I do not say this to flatter you, Bianca, but to highlight the importance of mentorship, allyship, solidarity, representation, and support that is essential to making the professional sexuality world inclusive and expansive.

Em: I grew up neurodivergent in a conservative, religious environment where I had to navigate purity culture. Two decades ago I received a diagnosis of a rare disease which gives me the same quality of life as someone on kidney dialysis. Recognizing the need for inclusive sex education within these intersecting spheres of my life, I embarked on a journey to provide comprehensive sex ed to my community in a culturally relevant manner. My work was received so well, I started my own organization where I teach workshops and provide personalized educational interventions. Several years ago, a colleague shared with me the profound impact certification had on her professional life. I was interested in being part of an organization upholding high standards of practice.

Due to my chronic illness, travel is a significant challenge for me, so I had to wait many years to pursue certification until the COVID-19 pandemic (2020) prompted more online training, making the process accessible to me. I was also thrilled to find the safe space Bianca creates, so I could pursue certification authentically and not feel isolated. Becoming credentialed with such a prestigious organization is a wonderful achievement, and within Bianca's inclusive supervision I felt valued and my support needs were always met.

cherry: I'm pursuing certification because I want to learn as much as I can about reproductive justice and sexuality education. My goal is to provide community space and support for disabled people, especially disabled survivors, to explore, heal, and connect to their sexuality, bodies, and partners. The more I can learn about sex, sexuality, kink, pleasure, and reproductive justice, the more competent I will be at holding space for people with many different disabilities, identities, and experiences. I'm already doing the work I seek to do in terms of writing and education; Bianca advised me to consider certification because the credentials provide me with credibility as well as protection from people who might seek to discredit or refute the work I put out into the world.

Laura: Working in Brazil and Honduras, comprehensive sexuality education is not a part of curricula and often faces opposition. I knew training with well-established institutions would offer credibility and ground my work. I had been unsuccessful in finding more regionally relevant accrediting bodies training sexuality *educators*. My first formal experience in the field was at a (SHCP) in the Midwest U.S., which covers a large part of the certification requirements. After completing this program, I reached out to Bianca, who had been recommended as the only supervisor who would be able to authentically support my work in Latin America with cultural sensitivity and awareness. Supervision guided my work, specifically as a white European educator working with Latin American communities of color. I later pursued certification for the original purpose of added credibility and formalizing the work I was already doing.

Sex-Positivity Conceptualizations and Important General Issues

Bianca: When I was first introduced to sex positivity as a concept, framework, and movement, it was very much from a U.S., non-disabled white feminist lens. I had to seek out Black feminists who introduced me to Indigenous, Latina, and Caribbean experiences and those definitions did not neatly fit or align with what white US feminists were stating. My definition of and framing for sex positivity today is constantly shifting shape.

Scotney: Sex educator Goody Howard says sex positivity is about creating space for people to explore and express their sexuality without shame and judgment. I like this and what stands out to me is the word "space" because it is never one thing, place, or time. As someone who works in multicultural and international settings, sex positivity must be flexible, adaptable, and unique to the individuals or communities. The way sex positivity is restricted by different systems of oppression impacts my approach. Sex positivity is connected to liberation which is inherent to our being; I cannot give or create it, we must define it for ourselves. I integrate sex positivity into my work by creating spaces to enhance critical understanding of the systems and power dynamics that are responsible for imposing shame and judgment on our ability to explore and express our sexuality and gender freely. Deconstructing the impact of those imposing forces allows sex positivity to fit our lives and realities.

Em: I advocate that sex positivity isn't the "anything goes" approach – which, in my mind, suggests a less thoughtful approach to sex, and it's not the repressed notion of sex many of us were raised with. The sex positive education I provide is a connected, informed, and accepting approach that empowers individuals to make wise choices regarding their sexual lives. It embraces inclusivity and celebrates the rich tapestry of human sexuality, addressing topics like consent, pleasure, diversity, effective communication, attachment, sexual health, and supporting informed decision-making.

cherry: I think sex positivity is a response to sex historically being taboo, stigmatized, oversimplified, weaponized, and steeped in heteronormativity. It asserts sex is something to be enjoyed by everyone, and something we should all be free to talk about and express. It is a framework seeking to remove shame from the conversations around sex, and give people room to exist in the fullness of their humanity. It requires a culture of consent and self-awareness. From this place it can allow for conversations about sex to be free of shame, fear, and hierarchy.

I think sex positivity has often been a buzzword giving blanket permission for people to speak openly about sex whenever it pleases them, or even for people to address and touch others in unwelcomed ways, because the assumptions are: everyone loves sex, talks about it all the time, and wants to be sexy and sexualized uncritically.

Laura: I agree, sex-positivity is an ever-evolving concept that changes – and rightly so, as people learn about sexuality and connection in the spaces they move in. To me, sex-positivity seeks to tackle very common, oppressive, and limiting "death and disease" narratives, especially found in the so-called "Global North". Sex-positivity is inherently linked to a pleasure-based approach, which advocates for people being able to choose if and how to feel pleasure in a way that acknowledges their individuality, desires, and rights.

Em: Sex positivity is meant to be inclusive, yet I often find myself and my clients excluded from the movement. For example, the movement lacks representation and resources for my clients recovering from purity culture, navigating neurodiversity, and living with in/visible disabilities. It also presents a steep learning curve for many in my community who had no prior exposure to its concepts and terminology. Sadly, there is a notable absence of bridge-building and offering resources for purity culture survivors or people experiencing sexual shame. The movement's neglect to address the deep-seated shame experienced by so many survivors of purity culture speaks to the significance of the work I do with that community.

Scotney: I struggle with the way sex positivity as a concept is sometimes presented within the sexuality field in two different ways. The first is there can be an emphasis on destigmatizing sex and sexuality through exposing individuals to all things sexual without being intentional about relationship building and understanding participants personally, culturally, or socio-economically. Second is the white-washing, oversimplification, and monetization of cultural- and ethnic-based sexual practices.

Some colleagues believe exclusively multi-gender conversations with youth to be sex positive. However, working with newly arrived immigrants to the U.S. made conversations about sexuality extremely challenging. The "new" experiences were so compounded for them as they tried to heal from significant trauma during their journey to the U.S. Understandably, they did not want to engage with the material. We may have retraumatized some participants. I learned a lot about considerations to have when trying to create sex positive spaces.

There can be a tendency for western sexuality professionals to pick things from different cultures, strip them of their deeper cultural meanings, repackage them without any cultural context or credit given, and sell them under their own brand of sex positivity. Highlighting a diverse array of sex positive practices from around the world must be done in a culturally humble and ethical way to avoid further perpetuation of oppressive systems. Providing broader cultural context, giving credit/attribution, as well as compensating and uplifting the voices of people from the respective cultures are some places to begin. These are the things I am intentional about incorporating into my work and why having a diverse professional network is helpful because I have people who can check me when I make a mistake.

cherry: I struggle with the concept because sex is not something that always feels inherently positive to me. Sometimes the framework asks us to celebrate sex in a way that might not leave room for a complicated or nuanced experience of sex and sexuality. Sexuality has often felt complex and burdensome due to my visible disability, I feel I've often been in the position of proving or asserting to others – especially healthcare providers and peers in the queer community – my sexuality exists. It has felt exhausting at best and dehumanizing at worst.

I'm a survivor of sexual abuse, and due to this trauma, sex is often not something I desire. It can be hard for those of us who don't want to celebrate or have sex to feel comfortable. Sex positivity conjures a very body-centered focus, on physical attractiveness and sexiness, and on what we are doing/able to do with our bodies. For those of us with complicated relationships to our bodies, sex positivity can be a very alienating culture. Sex positive conversations have focused on the mechanics of sex and of undoing stigma and shame. I lament this focus takes away from many other aspects of pleasure and sexuality, including kink, erotics, and communication/connection.

Laura: Sex-positivity isn't quite as universal as it must be. It is usually reserved for certain people, whether it be white, cisgender, non-disabled, more wealthy, and more educated people. Working with groups I often don't belong to, I find it crucial to take a human rights- and pleasure-based approach. It resonates organically with participants because sexuality and the choice to experience pleasure are integral aspects of being human! When I talk about my work in spaces with people who, like me, haven't faced as much erasure and exclusion, my work gets elevated for the mere fact of prioritizing these approaches. The correlation between sex-positivity and privilege persists. Agency over one's sexuality is a universal human right, and historically the mainstream sex-positivity movement hasn't elevated all voices. This won't change until we all acknowledge our biases and the importance of comprehensive sexuality education as a tool for social justice.

Sexuality Education Training Programs

Bianca: My sexuality education journey began through peer education in 1996 when I went to the University of Maryland. Through the University Health Center I was trained as a peer educator to offer substance and sexuality education to campus communities. I changed my major three times until my junior year when I created my own: a mashup of public health, gender, and Latin American studies. Putting my unique major together taught me how to fill in gaps, this helped for my graduate work in the sexuality program at NYU where *every single professor* I had was a white person over 50 years old. I was one of two people of the global majority in my cohort of about 20 students. I didn't claim disability as an identity then and there was one disabled student in my cohort. This student was the only person who brought in a disability perspective in classes and readings and it was specific to their disability.

Scotney: My sexuality training is always on-going and I am intentional about seeking opportunities that fill gaps in my knowledge. My formal learning era at a SHCP was in 2017. I expected information and training on strategies for working with people from different backgrounds. However, much of the content and materials were about and taught by upper class white non-disabled individuals. It was frustrating and invalidating because it did not represent the communities I work with and was not reflective of my own identities and experiences. When I and the other four Black students in a cohort of over 100, highlighted these gaps we were repeatedly shut down and ostracized by faculty and students. I learned academic and medical concepts and vocabulary which are passwords to get past gatekeepers who attempt to restrict access to sexual health information. When I searched for opportunities to fill the gaps that remained from the first training program, I found you, Bianca, and your ANTE UP! certificate program and began my "formal unlearning era." The courses gave me concrete tools to remove the lens of white supremacy, colonization, ableism, and oppression and consider ways to work with and for the diverse communities I serve. These courses gave me strategies, critical frameworks, and the historical context I needed to think intentionally about who is in my class and who is not, what cultural and historical experiences are brought to the space, and how to create inclusive and relevant sex education. I continue to seek training that expands the critical and anti-oppression frameworks I use.

Laura: My sexuality education training has evolved in three streams – the formal, non-formal, and informal training. I sought formal training offering various perspectives and the staff and peers had different lenses from my own. I completed courses at a university in Colombia before completing my SHCP in 2021, and have most recently enrolled in a

Master's in Public Health in London. Non-formal learning opportunities included supervision with you, Bianca, and my Fellowship and collaboration with The Pleasure Project, which offered training in pleasure-based sexual health. Most importantly is the knowledge, perspective, and skills I have gained from collaborating with communities in Latin America. Through working with – rather than in or for – these communities, perspectives shift in ways only possible outside of academic, theoretical frameworks, and models. Through collaboration, I continue to learn to listen deeply and confront my own biases with more clarity.

Scotney: The most important part of sex positivity, especially in training, is allowing individuals to find or create a space to explore all the aspects of sexuality without shame and judgment, while remembering the process may be different for others. At times, there's a compulsory sexuality approach, and as cherry shared, a lack of acceptance or acknowledgement some people might not want to engage in sex. Some may identify with the spectrum of asexuality or aromanticism, some live where it is difficult or illegal to find space without shame and judgment, and others may need more time and healing.

The traditional sexual attitude reassessment (SAR) tries to promote a sex positive perspective, yet does not consider the context participants may be coming from or working within. My SAR experience was several hours of watching pornography to "desensitize" and "familiarize" us to different sexual practices, expressions, and experiences. It felt voyeuristic and superficial because it lacked contextualizing personal perspectives of what it means to actually be a part of particular communities or hold sexual identities. Assuming everyone participating in the training is in a place to be able to learn effectively in this way, does not fully take into account cultural or religious background, neurodivergence, or past trauma.

Insights on Potential Damage from Erasure of Experience in Sex Education Training

Scotney: The erasure and othering of experiences that are not considered "mainstream" and the impact of that exclusion is harmful. As someone who is currently non-disabled, if I am not seeking and centering sex positive disabled voices, I miss out on ensuring my version of sex positivity is inclusive and affirming of disabled folks. We each have to do the work of finding out who is not a part of the conversation, uplifting those voices, and learning from each other.

Bianca: I felt gaslit throughout my education and training. Representation is powerful, but it is not power. When we don't even have representation embedded in the curricula, the power is only offered to one group and it is not shared. This erases the ways communities of the global majority have always already been collaborative and interdependent. It perpetuates a western settler colonial view of sexuality that is dangerous and upholds rape culture.

Cultural Responsivity: Learning from New or Different Communities and Populations

Bianca: I value "leadership by those most impacted" which I interpret as not thinking I have all the answers or I am the "expert" in the room. This is where sex positivity may show up as a new form of western colonization when we are not moving within a culturally relativistic way that recognizes how the U.S./or the West is perceived or understood by those who have been impacted by U.S.-supported wars, sanctions, bans, and blockades. Listening with our whole bodies is essential to these opportunities, as is building relationships which is a central part of an intersectional approach.

Scotney: I agree with Bianca and view my role as an "expert" as someone who is willing to find out what you want to know about sexual health education and make sure it is accurate information relevant to you. Sometimes that takes place through a survey, an information session, or a community assessment. I never provide sex education programming for a community I have not first engaged with and I never do this without bringing some sort of food. I think bringing culturally specific food is important because it shows you care about your participants as whole people. Hunger is not conducive to learning. Additionally, "breaking bread together" is a great way to demonstrate we educators are also a whole people who need sustenance.

Em: Living with the disabilities I have allows me to bring a unique and empathetic perspective to my work. For many of my LGBTQIA+ clients, I am the first professional to validate their identity. Many move outside of the insular sexual-shaming cultures, and abandon prejudicial perspectives about sex.

Studying mindfulness has taught me to perceive without prejudice – to enter conversations with openness, curiosity, deep listening, and less judgment. I teach these principles to help build awareness, reflectiveness, openness, and curiosity towards sexuality. I put incredible effort into speaking to a variety of backgrounds, experiences, and learning styles while creating community. I've never learned well with lectures or slides with lists of information. I benefit most from experiential learning, using all of my senses, practicing, and connecting with others. My approach is multimodal, combining movement, mindfulness, conversation, and creativity which helps reach a diverse audience, and participants leave having gained new information, embodied learning, and forged meaningful connections with others. Validation occurs in hearing from peers and sharing experiences of oppression and marginalization in conservative cultures. My strength is creating nurturing safe spaces to share experiences, and not be judged. When people feel understood and respected, they are much more likely to learn and to grow.

Laura: When I work in communities with different lived experiences than my own, I acknowledge this (to myself and the group) and I highlight that, because of our different experiences, I too will be learning in the space we create together. This includes presenting myself as a "facilitator," aiming to make it easier for people to learn, explore, shift, and tackle taboos around sexuality. I cannot assume the role of "teacher," because I do not have all the answers – and the pretense of having them would impose my lens on everyone else. Acknowledging this early creates a more equitable space and helps me connect with the community in an authentic and constructive way.

Sex-Positive Successes: Our Projects Promoting Diverse and Inclusive Sex Education

Scotney: One of my proudest achievements was creating You + Me = We: A Queer Sex Ed Program where we worked with LGBTQIA+ teens to create a queer sex education series. This was in direct response to Virginia state efforts to invalidate queer and trans youth. We intentionally created an inclusive, affirming curriculum that offered students critical frameworks to explore and understand diverse sexualities and genders in their own contexts. We've had many neurodivergent students over the last two years and we worked to make our content and teaching style accessible such as offering different options for activities, explaining metaphors or analogies, providing discussion questions or activities in advance to allow time for processing, and asking what else we can do to meet student needs. It's a constant learning process.

cherry: Disabled Parts is a website I created, in hopes of addressing the lack of sexuality education resources that feature and represent disability. In the tradition of Sins Invalid, Disabled Parts also uses storytelling such as poetry, creative nonfiction, and erotica, by queer and disabled community members, to illustrate and archive our experiences of sex, intimacy, and survival. Disabled Parts also has a growing library of resources, including videos, articles, and links, on disabled sexuality. Everyone is invited to submit resources to be featured. In partnership with several sex toy shops the site includes an initiative to consult and distribute free sex toys to disabled people who cannot afford them. Talking with individuals to understand what kind of toy can help change their sex life has been such a great learning and community building opportunity. I'm always humbled and affirmed in my work whenever people express gratitude for this space that they have never been offered.

Bianca: I've filled in gaps in an interdisciplinary way by reading and taking classes outside of sexuality focused offerings. I created my own offerings that merged sexuality and disability topics. I'm proud my offerings divest from a medical model of disability and embraces a justice model that welcomes us in without defining our disability, and our access needs can be met by divesting in surveillance common in education, such as turning cameras off, communicating in the chat, collaborating with live captioners or BSL (Black Sign Language) interpreters, and valuing disabled people showing up as they can with integrity.

Scotney: As someone who relocates to different countries and works with different immigrant communities often, one tool I have found to be invaluable is Drs. Sara Nasserzadeh and Pejman Azarmina's "Sexuality Education Wheel of Context" (2017). It provides questions for understanding the historical, socio-political, and cultural context of communities to encourage an approach that is culturally relevant and humble. Training that provides strategies to create more accessible and relevant programming for disabled and neurodivergent people has expanded my work.

Laura: In the Pleasure Project's Fellowship, I found a community of professionals who, like me, felt they were working in a field that hyper-medicalizes information and omits or barricades it behind a curtain of shame. Through the Pleasure Principles, I believe accessible, sex-positive, and pleasure-based sexual health information is possible. The Pleasure Project's 2021 systematic review in collaboration with the World Health Organization is a significant milestone to de-stigmatizing and normalizing culturally sensitive, pleasure-based conversations in a range of settings.

Promoting Positive Sexuality in Sexuality Education: Rewarding Moments!

Scotney: There are so many! Students staying after a workshop to ask me their more personal questions confirms the space created together established trust. I smile and get a warm fuzzy feeling reading anonymous evaluations saying how much they appreciated the content, materials, or my teaching style. I got an email from a parent whose student had gone home and said "Mom, I learned more in one of those classes than I have in 4 years of health classes at school!" These experiences remind me that comprehensive sexual health education matters when it is inclusive and relevant.

Em: I led an intergenerational workshop focusing on pleasure which had about 50 participants. Attendees represented an impressive range of cultures, belief systems, lifestyles, and perspectives. I used engaging, accessible resources, paintings of different vulvas, facilitated a mindfulness exercise, discussed the importance of pleasure, and used a large vulva-shaped pillow to teach sexological anatomy. The evaluations affirmed these approaches created a supportive and safe environment.

Laura: After a sexuality education session for adolescents that I co-facilitated in a favela in Brazil, we were approached by a woman who had witnessed part of the workshop. She shared her pleasure in knowing the youth had this space to receive crucial information openly while exploring different topics safely. She shared she would have benefitted from such spaces, and still would today, because she hadn't had her questions answered. She was pregnant with her sixth child, recently learned how to correctly use a condom, and proudly stated this would be her last pregnancy. This exchange was pivotal for my work – it was rewarding receiving local support, and her feedback demonstrated a further need. This conversation was fundamental for what would later become TabuTabu's largest community co-created initiative for women, Ana Autoestima.

cherry: I've been grateful to be on both the organizer and participant side of panels featuring people with disabilities talking about our experiences of sex and sexuality. Working with and learning from other disabled people has continued to be the single most important and enlightening part of my sexuality education. It's always affirming to hear from other disabled people because it illuminates our shared experience of undesirability. There is a universal disabled experience of feeling like we have less and different access to sex and dating because of ableism and misconceptions others and society put upon us. It's hard not to feel overwhelmed by frustration, envy, and inadequacy when trying to navigate sex and dating. It's always both grounding and difficult to hear from others about the importance of self-knowledge and finding the ways to be confident and assertive. It always highlights the need for us to lovingly remind ourselves and each other of our inherent worth. There's always a hopefulness I gain as well, hearing about the ways that others navigate sexuality, love, and romance. I rarely find places in popular media and mainstream sex ed discourse where my identities and experiences are reflected, so I'm grateful to hear from other disabled people directly, and it informs my desire to be a disabled for disabled sex educator.

Conclusion

The current need for expanding and implementing sex positivity in ways that honor individual and cultural experiences across the globe is being filled by emergent sexuality professionals who are committed to supporting their own learning and growth before serving community members. An improved awareness, incorporation, and honoring individuals' unique identities and social positionings into sexuality educator training continues to be needed at the macro level. Practicing interdependence offers a new movement for sex positivity especially in western areas where independence is the goal and isolation is normalized. The authors invite readers to consider where they, too, can learn more from those most impacted, strategically use their personal power to reduce oppression, and find joy in the relationships they intentionally create and nurture.

References

Dixon, R., Gilbert, T., Soto, M. Gathings, J., & DiPonio, S. (2021). Centering Racial Justice in Sex Education: Strategies for Engaging Professionals and Young People. Sex Education Collaborative White Paper. Available at www.sexeducationcollaborative.org

Nasserzadeh, S. and Azarmina, P. (2017). "Sexuality Education Wheel of Context: A Guide for Sexuality Educators, Advocates, and Researchers." CreateSpace Independent Publishing Platform.

The Pleasure Project (2021). *The Pleasure Principles: Pleasure-based sexual health.* https://thepleasureproject.org/the-pleasure-principles/

9

"DOES IT MEAN SOMEONE LOVES YOU IF THEY CALL YOU DADDY?"

Anonymous Sex Education Questions about Kink from 5th–12th Grade Students

Sam D. Hughes

Introduction

Comprehensive school-based sex education is a well-evidenced means by which a sizeable minority of students in industrialized countries get information and instruction about sexuality, often with the goal of promoting healthy relationships, sexual consent, avoiding unintended pregnancies, and reducing sexually transmitted infections (Goldfarb & Lieberman, 2021). In the U.S., for example, 38% of high schools include a program covering all 19 comprehensive sex education topics listed by the CDC (Dorri & Russell, 2024). These wide-ranging topics are typically covered with the intention of empowering students to make their own fully informed sexual choices and prepare students for the world of adult sexuality. More recently, many of these programs have also begun expanding their curricula to cover topics that go beyond heteronormative models of sexuality, such as including topics specifically focused on LGBTQ+ identities, experiences, and sexual health, though this expansion has

DOI: 10.4324/9781032631820-10

been regionally unequal (Garg & Volerman, 2021). Despite these admirable goals, the rising inclusion of sexual diversity in the curricula has largely only focused on LGBTQ+ people. To date, no comprehensive sex education curriculum used in schools of which I am aware intentionally includes content about kink, an umbrella term that refers to a wide variety of sexual, sensual, and intimate practices that fall outside of conventional social norms in the curriculum. Specifically, kink can involve activities like BDSM (Bondage, Discipline, Domination, Submission, Sadism, and Masochism), sexual role-playing, sexual fetishism (erotic attraction towards non-genital body parts, objects, materials, and situations that fall outside of social norms) power exchange, and sensation play (blindfolds, fireplay, ice, pain, tickling, etc.).

Typically conceptualized by the mainstream public as activities only practiced by adults, often under the framework of "spicing up things in the bedroom", kinky activities such as erotic choking have been reported as becoming more commonplace among minors (Herbenick et al., 2023). Moreover, as adults, kinky fantasies and desires are very common, with some studies even finding that the majority of people have fantasies involving some form of kink (Brown et al., 2020; Holvoet et al., 2017). Despite these increasing common practices, little is known about the psychology of minors who are exploring an interest in kink-oriented activities either in fantasy or behavior, as asking questions directly to youth involves ethical challenges to researchers and potential risks to youth if their involvement or interest is disclosed to disapproving parents or guardians.

This study sought to find a solution for these ethical challenges by eschewing directly asking youth questions about their sexual interests and desires, and instead taking advantage of an existing large dataset of anonymously submitted sex education questions from minors, collected by a non-profit organization that provides comprehensive sex education services, with the goal of answering the research question, "What are minors anonymously asking about kink in their sex education classes?" To explore this topic, I will first review the existing literature on the developmental timing of kink-oriented desires, then consider the implications of that timing for minority stress processes and mental health among sexual minority youth. I will then review the literature on topics typically included in school-based sex education curricula, and the more recent rise in inclusion of sexual diversity as a topic. Finally, to provide background and context on the specific method employed in this study, I will focus on the existing research on the role of anonymous question boxes in school-based sex education classes.

Developmental Timing of Kink-Oriented Desires

Early research around the birth of sexual science involved case studies of people with kink interests, many of whom reported childhood and adolescent experiences with clear antecedents to later adult kink interests, such as a fascination with shoes or excitement at being spanked (e.g., Binet, 1887; Krafft-Ebing, 1886/1965). Though conceptualized at the time through a highly pathologizing lens, contemporary research emphasizing a less clinical approach has replicated the same pattern: many kinky adults' narratives of their journey into discovering a kink identity feature proto-sexual experiences in childhood or adolescence that were often not understood as sexual at the time, such as volunteering to be tied up during childhood games (Breslow et al., 1986; Hughes & Hammack, 2022; Westlake & Mahan, 2023). However, these accounts consistently come from retrospective accounts of adults, so may run the risk of being selective reconstructions of memory ordered to help make meaning and narrative out of life events (McAdams et al., 2006). To date, no study to my knowledge, outside of a clinical or forensic context, has asked minors about their interests in kink while they are still minors.

Pointedly, adult retrospective accounts of kink identity development have also pointed to the ages of 11–14 as a time of particularly heightened turmoil and sensitivity around evaluating the meaning and moral acceptability of these interests (Aaron, 2018), with navigating and overcoming internalized stigma related to kink being an important task related to more positive mental health outcomes (Bezreh et al., 2012; Crane, 2022; Hughes & Hammack, 2019; Waldura et al., 2016). Given the conventional timing of this process as situated within the larger developmental task within adolescence of constructing and finding identity (Erikson, 1963), it is perhaps not surprising that adolescents from the ages of 11–14 may be deeply engaged in the process of coming to understand the meaning of their kink-oriented desires, and might come to ask questions about it anonymously in a comprehensive sex education course.

Minority Stress Theory

Decades of research focused on LGBTQ+ people has found that experiences of stigma (i.e., Goffman, 1986) in the social environment can come to be internalized, and prompt concealment of one's stigmatized identity to the detriment of one's physical and mental health (Eldahan et al., 2016; Flentje et al., 2020; Hatzenbuehler et al., 2013; Meyer, 2003). Termed *Minority Stress Theory*, this framework likely holds promise for understanding the experiences of kinky people regarding the health consequences of stigma. Optimistically, the model also posits that protective factors such as positive identity sentiment around the stigmatized identity, disclosure of one's identity, and social support from a community of similarly marginalized people helps play a protective role, and both qualitative and quantitative evidence has been found to support the validity of this framework for BDSM-oriented populations (Brown et al., 2022; Friedman, 2022; Hughes & Hammack, 2019). Keeping in mind that how stigma is managed and internalized or overcome carries critical implications for mental and physical health, how a sex education instructor (often seen as an authority figure in the classroom) handles a question about kink may carry a significant potential to either reinforce or challenge the potential risk of kink-related stigma.

Topics Typically Covered in Sex Education Curricula

Despite the importance of overcoming stigma for sexual minority students, many sex education programs have historically avoided content related to sexual diversity, instead adopting formats focused on heterosexuality, pregnancy prevention, and penetrative penile-vaginal sex, leading to frustration from lesbian and gay students for the irrelevance of such content to their lives (e.g., Hillier & Mitchell, 2008; Jarpe-Ratner, 2020; Naser et al., 2022). While some strides have been made in improving inclusivity for LGBTQ+ content in sex education classes (Brown & Quirk, 2019; Meadows, 2018), no program I am aware of intentionally plans to include kink-oriented *topics* as part of the formal curriculum. However, not planning a topic for explicit inclusion in the curriculum does not mean the topic won't come up in class. Specifically, the "anonymous question box" activity in which students anonymously write questions on index cards is a mainstay of comprehensive sex education (Angulo-Olaiz et al., 2014), and provides an inroad for students who have questions that might not be a part of the formally planned curriculum to come into the classroom.

Anonymous Questions in Sex Education Classes

Past analyses of these anonymously submitted questions has helped those developing curriculum and engaging in sex education instructor training gain insight into the information needs of youth of which instructors might be unaware (Allsop et al., 2023; Angulo-Olaiz et al., 2014; Stevens et al., 2013). However, these analyses have generally not gotten down to the level of specificity needed to identify questions about kink in particular, instead generating larger bucket categories like "sexual behavior" (e.g., Angulo-Olaiz et al., 2014), so the prevalence and content of questions specific to kink-oriented interests and activities is currently unknown.

The Present Study

This study sought to answer two research questions:

1) What do 4th–12th grade students want to know about kink in anonymous sex education question boxes?
2) How common are kink questions among all questions asked?

Given the generally unknown nature of the content and prevalence of these questions from past literature, this was an exploratory study that did not rely on hypotheses generated in advance, and instead primarily sought to describe these questions inductively.

Method

Participants

Participants were 4th–12th grade students at a variety of public and private schools in a Western U.S. state. I partnered with a non-profit organization that provides comprehensive sex education instruction to students, who had been systematically collecting a backlog of these anonymous questions submitted on paper by students to their sex education teachers. Because I was conducting a secondary analysis on this previously collected data from a nonprofit partner, no informed consent was included, and the study was determined to be exempt from IRB Review (University of California, Santa Cruz IRB Exemption#HS3185). Unfortunately, the questions were collected in such as way that students could anonymously submit multiple index cards, and other students might elect not to submit an index card, so we lack a precise number of students who were present in these classes, as well as lack demographic information on student gender and ethnic composition. However, a total of 49,735 questions were obtained from this backlog, of which a random sample of 25,541 was selected for analysis, estimated to be representing many thousands of students. Because a small number of the classes provided by the nonprofit organization were conducted in Spanish, 191 of these questions were in Spanish, while nearly all the rest were in English.

Design and Procedure

Translation

The 191 Spanish-language questions were translated and backtranslated (Brislin, 1970) by two bilingual high school summer interns working on the project as part of a Science Internship Program. Relying on Spanish-speaking high school students helped to ensure that the nuances of adolescent Spanish slang would not be lost in translation, nor would the meanings of words and phrases particular to youth.

Conventional Content Analysis

Following translation, a random sample of 1500 of the total set of 49,735 anonymously submitted questions (originally in English and Spanish translated into English) were analyzed by nine undergraduate coders to iteratively develop several hundred coding categories via a conventional content analysis (Hsieh & Shannon, 2005). Following the construction of an initial codebook and condensing of categories, six coders then worked in teams of three to code 500 randomly selected questions, establishing intercoder reliability (an unweighted Cohen's Kappa 95% confidence interval with a lower bound above .6) for approximately 1/3 of the codes after three rounds of coding, modifying the codebook to improve the clarity of definitions and examples in between each round. Disagreements were settled by bringing in additional coders or myself for additional advice. 25,541 questions were then randomly selected from the 49,735 total questions and split between nine coders (six coders from the reliability phase, plus three new coders, trained on at least 500 questions each before beginning coding.), in which each coder individually coded their sub-set of questions. Codes put into categories established as unreliable during the reliability phase were then consensus-coded by at least two other coders after this individual coding, ensuring that all three people unanimously agreed on every coding decision not initially established as reliable. Of the 25,541 questions coded, 317 (about 1 in 80) questions fell into at least one of the five content categories featuring content about kink, BDSM, and/or sexual fetishism: 1) Foot Fetishism, 2) "Daddy" in a Sexual Context, 3) Bestiality, 4) Rape Roleplay, 5) Generic Kink/BDSM/Fetishism (a catch-all category for references to "kink" in general). Notably, while engaging in an act of bestiality is not consensual, and therefore not considered to be a kink (which are consensual practices), many student questions about bestiality may have reflected fantasies about and interest in roleplaying as an alternative, which may still reasonably be considered kinky. Because of the difficulty of teasing out this nuance based on a single anonymous question, we elected to include all the questions about bestiality in the analysis.

Inductive Thematic Analysis

These 317 questions were then analyzed via an inductive thematic analysis (Braun & Clarke, 2006) collectively by the main author (who identifies as kinky) and an undergraduate research assistant (who does not identify as kinky). Having people with both of these positionalities in the coding team helped to ensure that both insider and outsider perspectives were represented in the analytic process. Data were approached via the lens of critical realism (Hanly & Fitzpatrick Hanly, 2001), assuming that there is actual meaning in the questions that it was the job of the researchers to discern, while also recognizing reflexively that one's identity and biases can impair our ability to access that meaning. Memoing and reflexive discussion was used to help both coders arrive at consensus on categories following an initial inductive coding round, and then both coders independently coded all 317 questions again using a codebook, and differences were settled via consensus.

Results

Developmental Timing

None of the questions about kink came from students in the 4th grade, and only 1.9% of the 317 questions came from students in the 5th grade, despite more than 20% of the total questions in the full dataset coming from students of this age. Instead, most of the questions (89.3%) came from students in the 6th, 7th, 8th, and 9th grades, around the same 11–14-year-old age range identified in past literature as when turmoil over kinky desires and identity become salient. Fewer questions came from students in the 10th, 11th, and 12th grades, but this was most likely the result of those grade levels consisting of a small percentage of the total dataset.

Thematic Analysis Results

We constructed six non-mutually exclusive themes identifying the kinds of questions about kink being asked by students. All 317 questions fell into at least one theme, with 266 questions involving just one theme, 35 involving two themes, and 16 falling into three themes. Quotations appearing in this sub-section have been edited for spelling and grammar to aid in readability. Each theme and example questions are described below, in order from most to least frequent:

Theme 1: Expressing a Need for Basic Definitions of Kink-Related Terms (36.0% of questions)

Questions submitted in this category had to do with asking for the meaning of a term related to kink. Some of these questions were phrased generally. For example, 18 separate students asked the identically worded question, "What is a fetish?" and another 12 asked, "What is BDSM?". However, some questions inquired about very specific kink practices like, "What is a chastity belt?", "What does ABDL/DL mean? I have heard this used in what sounded like a sexual situation?", "What is vore and what happens if I like it?", "Can someone get sexually aroused by a car?", and "What's a sex slave?". Questions from this category showed at least sufficient passing familiarity with language related to kink (potentially from the internet, peers, older siblings, etc.) to be able to ask for clarification regarding the meaning of those terms and were indicative of students who might be experiencing confusion around what these topics refer to.

Theme 2: Asking about the Mechanics of Kinky Practices (29.7% of questions)

Participants in this category had questions about how kinky practices were performed, or how a kink practice was mechanically possible. Some focused on technique, such as one student who asked, "How can you have sex with your feet?", and another who asked, "How do you give your homie a good toe suck?" Some inquired about cause-and-effect mechanisms around kinky practices, such as one student who asked, "If I shove a toothpick in my urethra, will I ejaculate harder?". Surprisingly, many questions in this category simply asked if it was possible to have sex with an animal, such as "Can you have sex with animals (Dog, cat, lion, elephant, shark, fish, cow, lizard, frog, etc.)", and "Can you have sex with a dog with a condom?". Relatedly, some students also had questions about how human/animal sex works in terms of pregnancy, such as one student who asked, "Can you get pregnant by a horse or gorilla?". This might reflect students who simply had a curiosity or may reflect students who have had fantasies or desires related to bestiality, that may need substantially more development of their understanding of sexual consent.

Theme 3: Clarifying Concepts of Consent and Legal Concerns regarding Kinky Practices (23.7% of questions)

Questions in this category focused directly on inquiring about legal issues related to kink and indicated a need to clarify concepts around legal and moral consent. For many questions in this category, participants showed a lack of language to describe rape roleplaying and consensual non-consent, often using variations on the idea of "rape but they want it" such as, "Is it rape if they say 'yes, you can rape me.'"?, "If the Girl wants to be raped does it still get the other person in trouble?", "If you want to get raped but you say no is it still rape if they rape you?". Others had more specific and articulate language, such as, "If someone roleplays kidnapping is it rape?", "Is it considered abuse if it turns you on for your partner to degrade you?", "What if 'abusive' contact is consensual (i.e. BDSM)", and "Where do kinks and BDSM sex fall into play with the law?"

Several asked for legal clarification regarding very specific kink practices, such as, "Is consensual spanking considered abuse?", "Would a 'sugar daddy' be considered sex trafficking?", "This is kind of a stupid question, but it is illegal to commit Necrophilia? If so, how does law enforcement find out?", and "If you have a foot fetish and you suck someone's toes and they're under 18, is it considered rape or sexual assault?". If part of the goal of comprehensive sex education is to provide students with an understanding of statutory rape, abusive relationships, and consent (topics which are covered in the curriculum of this and many other comprehensive sex education programs), then instructors may need to be ready to answer these specific legal questions about kink.

Theme 4: Conveying Apprehension, Concern, and Confusion over Stigmatization, Normality, Morality, and Pathologization of Kink (16.1% of questions)

Questions in this category generally came from students who were, at their core, asking the question of "is it okay to be kinky?", and may be those most at-risk for internalizing stigma around their kink interests.

Some students asked whether a practice was "normal" or "okay" such as, "Are BDSM relationships okay?", "Is it okay to call your boyfriend daddy or *papi*?", and "Are foot fetishes normal?", reflecting larger concerns over social rejection and abnormality.

Other student questions in this category seemed to indicate they already had internalized negative stigmatic messaging about kinks, such as, "If I have a fetish does that make me disgraceful?", "What if I'm straight but think dragon girls are hot? Send help I'm broken", "Is choking while have sex bad? What if you like it?" "Is it abnormal for me to be sexually aroused by memes?", and "I have a goat fetish . . . Am I turning into a terrorist?", though it is possible that last question might be an example of simply trolling rather than internalized stigma.

Some questions were a bit more ambiguous, such as one potential latex fetishist asking about wearing a condom without sex for pleasure, "2nd question can you wear a condom to school even though no sex just feel good [sic]". Occasionally some students asked more pointed questions about moral values like, "Should all kinks be accepted in our culture (for example, furry)?". Overall, this category reflected students who expressed sometimes significant concerns over morality and stigma surrounding kink topics, often heavily emotionally tinged.

Theme 5: Inquiring about the Causes, Motivations, and Origins of Kink-Oriented Desires (9.5% of questions)

Participants in this category often reflected an intellectual curiosity about the origins and causes of kink interests. Some of these questions were phrased generally, like "What are fetishes/kinks and why do people have them?" and "Are fetishes generated or set in stone?". Others were focused on specific fetish interests. For instance, "why do people like feet", "Why do people use sex dolls", "Why would people go all fifty shades of grey on their partner?", and "Why do some people like to be pooped/peed on during sex?". It is possible these questions might have come from someone who had these interests, using "why do people . . ." to not have to admit they themselves had those interests, or may have also represented people who did not have these interests looking to understand the antecedents of other people's desires that might seem strange to them.

Theme 6: Requesting Health and Safety
Information about Kink (6.3% of questions)

Participants in this category had more practical questions about health and safety related to kink. Some of these questions simply generally used the term "healthy", such as "Is it technically healthy if you like to be dominated?", and "How do BDSM relationships work & are they healthy?" Some indicated a need for clarity and information about safewords and safe signals in consensual BDSM, such as, "What if you were given consent to choke your sex partner during sex, but they kept telling you 'Tighter', then they die?"

Others focused on STI transmission related to non-consensual fetish interests, such as "What happens if a man has sex with a dead woman and then with an alive woman. What will happen to the alive woman?" and "Is it more healthy to have sex with an animal than a human? will you get rabies?" One question, worryingly, pointed to specific details that indicated the participant may be actively considering and/or has already engaged in sex with an animal: "Are there any bad side effects of having sex with your seven-year-old cat that you got when you were six?". Beyond the clear and present issues with consent, students in this category showed a clear need for clarity in terms of health and safety around these practices, which instructors need to be prepared to anticipate coming up in these question boxes.

Discussion

This study sought to understand the needs and interests of youth when it comes to their thinking about kink by examining 25,541 questions from anonymous question boxes submitted in comprehensive sex education classes. The results of this study revealed students had a wide variety of needs, especially from the ages of 11–14 related to applying concepts in consent education to kink, health and safety information, and potentially a need for validation and reassurance related to sexual diversity to avoid the harmful effects of internalized stigma.

Recommendations for Sex Educators

While it is extremely unlikely for kink-related content to ever be formally intended to be included in a sex education curriculum, as doing so would likely be politically fraught, sex educators should be trained to anticipate these questions coming up in 1 out of every 80 questions. Some students clearly have needs in terms of knowledge, safety, legality, and consent related to kink, and are willing to ask for that information anonymously, even though kink isn't part of the formally assigned curriculum. Training in how to handle those questions with sensitivity and age-appropriateness may be important for the prevention of harm and promoting the validation of sexual diversity beyond just LGBTQ+ identities. The sex education classroom is a key source to potentially provide age-appropriate information, or at least point to age-appropriate resources (e.g., *Scarleteen*, 2024) that would have relevant information for youth interested in kink.

This support may also be especially important for students who are neurodivergent, as students with autism are simultaneously more likely to have kink-oriented interests (Schöttle et al., 2017), and sometimes find BDSM and kink activities to be a more effective way to get their needs met (Boucher, 2018; Pliskin, 2022; Wignall et al., 2023), yet are less likely to get access to appropriate sex education (Brown-Lavoie et al., 2014; Hannah & Stagg, 2016; Stokes & Kaur, 2005).

Recommendations for Sex Researchers

The results of this study show that there are minors with a clear interest in kink, and adults' retrospective stories are unlikely to be merely misleading reconstructions. This study may be helpful to point to when trying to justify getting IRB approval to ask questions about these topics to youth, as is often done regarding LGBTQ+ topics. Relatedly, just as in LGBTQ+ youth research, in which IRBs are often willing to allow for an exception to the usual requirement of informed consent for parents, because of the potential harm to youth if their parents discover their participation, future researchers may be able to use this research to ask for a similar accommodation when researching kink-oriented youth.

Recommendations for School Counselors

Some youth in this study showed clear concerns in terms of trying to reconcile their sexual fantasies and desires with their own understanding of morality, which may have clinical mental health implications. Like with LGBTQ+ youth, having some preparation around the mental health needs of kinky minors may be important, especially given kinky adults reporting stigmatizing experiences from health professionals (Waldura et al., 2016).

Limitations and Future Directions

This was a single comprehensive sex education program, so we cannot compare with abstinence only or other comprehensive curricula. The study also lacks demographic information beyond grade level on the students, given that they are anonymous questions, so individual differences (such as which questions are asked by boys, girls, and nonbinary students) cannot be determined. Future researchers might want to take advantage of programs that split up students by gender to glean some of this information while retaining the anonymous nature of the questions or investigate how teachers respond behaviorally to these types of questions.

Conclusion

Like kinky adults, youth with an interest in kink must navigate a world in which their interests are often pathologized and pushed to the margins of sexuality. The sex education classroom, and particularly anonymous question-box activities within those classrooms, are a key site in which youth have an opportunity to ask for important information related to kink topics, and the results of this study show that many students are taking advantage of that opportunity. Sex education teachers, researchers, and school counselors should be prepared to take those needs seriously, as they speak to important issues related to consent, abuse, violence, internalized stigma, legal issues, mental health, and safety. Preparing students for the world of adult sexuality may entail preparing students for topics that are often conceptualized as taboo, especially if those topics end up being a central core of their adult sexuality. Even if there is no plan to include kink-related topics in the curriculum, professionals should be ready to "expect the unexpected" when supporting the intellectual and developmental needs of kink-oriented youth.

Conflict-of-Interest Statement

The author has no conflicts of interest to declare.

References

Aaron, M. (2018). Growing up kinky: Research shows how kink identity is formed. *Psychology Today*. Standard Deviations. https://www.psychology today.com/gb/blog/standard-deviations/201805/growing-up-kinky-research-shows-how-kink-identity-is-formed

Allsop, Y., Black, A., & Anderman, E. M. (2023). "Why do people do sex?" An analysis of middle school students' anonymous questions about sexual health. *Sex Education*, 24(4), 460–478. https://doi.org/10.1080/14681811.2023.2217760

Angulo-Olaiz, F., Goldfarb, E. S., & Constantine, N. A. (2014). Sexuality information needs of Latino and African American ninth graders: A content analysis of anonymous questions. *American Journal of Sexuality Education*, 9(1), 21–40. https://doi.org/10.1080/15546128.2014.883266

Bezreh, T., Weinberg, T. S., & Edgar, T. (2012). BDSM Disclosure and stigma management: Identifying opportunities for sex education. *American Journal of Sexuality Education*, 7(1), 37–61. https://doi.org/10.1080/15546128.2012.650984

Binet, A. (1887). *Le fétichisme dans l'amour*.

Boucher, N. R. (2018). *Relationships between characteristics of autism spectrum disorder and BDSM behaviors* [Undergraduate Honors Thesis, Ball State University]. http://cardinalscholar.bsu.edu/handle/123456789/201533

Braun, V., & Clarke, V. (2006). Using thematic analysis in psychology. *Qualitative Research in Psychology*, 3(2), 77–101. https://doi.org/10.1191/1478088706qp063oa

Breslow, N., Evans, L., & Langley, J. (1986). Comparisons among heterosexual, bisexual, and homosexual male sadomasochists. *Journal of Homosexuality*, 13(1), 83–107. https://doi.org/10.1300/J082v13n01_06

Brislin, R. W. (1970). Back-translation for cross-cultural research. *Journal of Cross-Cultural Psychology*, 1(3), 185–216. https://doi.org/10.1177/135910457000100301

Brown, A., Barker, E. D., & Rahman, Q. (2020). A systematic scoping review of the prevalence, etiological, psychological, and interpersonal factors associated with BDSM. *Journal of Sex Research*, 57(6), 781–811. https://doi. org/10.1080/00224499.2019.1665619

Brown, C., & Quirk, A. (2019). *Momentum is building to modernize sex education*. Center for American Progress. https://eric.ed.gov/?id=ED602827

Brown, S. L., Seymour, N. E., Mitchell, S. M., Moscardini, E. H., Roush, J. F., Tucker, R. P., & Cukrowicz, K. C. (2022). Interpersonal risk factors, sexual and gender minority status, and suicidal ideation: Is BDSM disclosure protective? *Archives of Sexual Behavior*, 51(2), 1091–1101. https://doi. org/10.1007/s10508-021-02186-3

Brown-Lavoie, S. M., Viecili, M. A., & Weiss, J. A. (2014). Sexual knowledge and victimization in adults with autism spectrum disorders. *Journal of Autism and Developmental Disorders*, 44(9), 2185–2196. https://doi. org/10.1007/s10803-014-2093-y

Crane, P. R. (2022). *Moderation effects of identity centrality and belongingness on internalized stigma and distress among BDSM practitioners* [Dissertation, Texas Tech University]. https://hdl.handle.net/2346/89223

Dorri, A. A., & Russell, S. T. (2024). Being out in high school: Positive implications for well-being in three U.S. cohorts of sexual minority adults. *Developmental Psychology*, 60(3), 1131–1144. https://doi.org/10.1037/devo 001736

Eldahan, A. I., Pachankis, J. E., Jonathon Rendina, H., Ventuneac, A., Grov, C., & Parsons, J. T. (2016). Daily minority stress and affect among gay and bisexual men: A 30-day diary study. *Journal of Affective Disorders*, 190, 828–835. https://doi.org/10.1016/j.jad.2015.10.066

Erikson, E. H. (1963). *Childhood and society*. Penguin Books.

Flentje, A., Heck, N. C., Brennan, J. M., & Meyer, I. H. (2020). The relationship between minority stress and biological outcomes: A systematic review. *Journal of Behavioral Medicine*, 43(5), 673–694. https://doi. org/10.1007/s10865-019-00120-6

Friedman, R. (2022). *Kink/BDSM Practice and kink/BDSM community connectedness as moderators of the relationship between stigma based stressors, childhood abuse, and mental health among plurisexual adults* [Dissertation, Palo Alto University]. https://www.proquest.com/open view/43ac2a64574a387a9a6998603b449b46/1?pq-origsite=gscholar&c bl=18750&diss=y

Garg, N., & Volerman, A. (2021). A national analysis of state policies on lesbian, gay, bisexual, transgender, and questioning/queer inclusive sex education. *Journal of School Health, 91*(2), 164–175. https://doi.org/10.1111/josh.12987

Goffman, E. (1986). *Stigma: Notes on the management of spoiled identity.* Simon & Schuster.

Goldfarb, E. S., & Lieberman, L. D. (2021). Three decades of research: The case for comprehensive sex education. *Journal of Adolescent Health, 68*(1), 13–27. https://doi.org/10.1016/j.jadohealth.2020.07.036

Hanly, C., & Fitzpatrick Hanly, M. A. (2001). Critical realism: Distinguishing the psychological subjectivity of the analyst from epistemological subjectivism. *Journal of the American Psychoanalytic Association, 49*(2), 515–532. https://doi.org/10.1177/00030651010490021001

Hannah, L. A., & Stagg, S. D. (2016). Experiences of sex education and sexual awareness in young adults with autism spectrum disorder. *Journal of Autism and Developmental Disorders, 46*(12), 3678–3687. https://doi.org/10.1007/s10803-016-2906-2

Hatzenbuehler, M. L., Phelan, J. C., & Link, B. G. (2013). Stigma as a fundamental cause of population health inequalities. *American Journal of Public Health, 103*(5), 813–821. https://doi.org/10.2105/AJPH.2012.301069

Herbenick, D., Patterson, C., Wright, P. J., Kawata, K., & Fu, T. (2023). Sexual choking/strangulation during sex: A review of the literature. *Current Sexual Health Reports, 15*(4), 253–260. https://doi.org/10.1007/s11930-023-00373-y

Hillier, L., & Mitchell, A. (2008). "It was as useful as a chocolate kettle": Sex education in the lives of same-sex-attracted young people in Australia. *Sex Education: Sexuality, Society and Learning, 8*(2), 211–224. https://doi.org/10.1080/14681810801981258

Holvoet, L., Huys, W., Coppens, V., Seeuws, J., Goethals, K., & Morrens, M. (2017). Fifty Shades of Belgian Gray: The prevalence of BDSM-related fantasies and activities in the general population. *The Journal of Sexual Medicine, 14*(9), 1152–1159. https://doi.org/10.1016/j.jsxm.2017.07.003

Hsieh, H.-F., & Shannon, S. E. (2005). Three approaches to qualitative content analysis. *Qualitative Health Research, 15*(9), 1277–1288. https://doi.org/10.1177/1049732305276687

Hughes, S. D., & Hammack, P. L. (2019). Affirmation, compartmentalization, and isolation: Narratives of identity sentiment among kinky people. *Psychology & Sexuality, 10*(2), 149–168. https://doi.org/10.1080/19419899.2019.1575896

Hughes, S. D., & Hammack, P. L. (2022). Narratives of the origins of kinky sexual desire held by users of a kink-oriented social networking website. *The Journal of Sex Research, 53*(3), 360–371. https://doi.org/10.1080/0022 4499.2020.1840495

Jarpe-Ratner, E. (2020). How can we make LGBTQ+-inclusive sex education programmes truly inclusive? A case study of Chicago Public Schools' policy and curriculum. *Sex Education, 20*(3), 283–299. https://doi.org/10.108 0/14681811.2019.1650335

Krafft-Ebing, R. von. (1886/1965). *Psychopathia sexualis; A medico-forensic study.* Putnam.

McAdams, D. P., Josselson, R., & Lieblich, A. (2006). *Identity and story: Creating self in narrative.* American Psychological Association.

Meadows, E. (2018). Sexual health equity in schools: Inclusive sexuality and relationship education for gender and sexual minority students. *American Journal of Sexuality Education, 13*(3), 297–309. https://doi.org/10.1080/155 46128.2018.1431988

Meyer, I. H. (2003). Prejudice, social stress, and mental health in lesbian, gay, and bisexual populations: Conceptual issues and research evidence. *Psychological Bulletin, 129*(5), 674–697. https://doi.org/10.1037/0033-2909. 129.5.674

Naser, S. C., Clonan-Roy, K., Fuller, K. A., Goncy, E. A., & Wolf, N. (2022). Exploring the experiences and responses of LGBTQ+ adolescents to school-based sexuality education. *Psychology in the Schools, 59*(1), 34–50. https://doi.org/10.1002/pits.22471

Pliskin, A. (2022). Autism, sexuality, and BDSM. *Ought: The Journal of Autistic Culture, 4*(1). https://doi.org/10.9707/2833-1508.1107

Scarleteen. (2024). https://www.scarleteen.com/

Schöttle, D., Briken, P., Tüscher, O., & Turner, D. (2017). Sexuality in autism: Hypersexual and paraphilic behavior in women and men with high-functioning autism spectrum disorder. *Dialogues in Clinical Neuroscience, 19*(4), 381–393.

Stevens, S., Thompson, E. M., Vinson, J., Greene, A., Powell, C., Licona, A. C., & Russell, S. (2013). Informing sexuality education through youth-generated anonymous questions. *Sex Education, 13*(sup1), S84–S98. https://doi.org/10.1080/14681811.2013.781020

Stokes, M. A., & Kaur, A. (2005). High-functioning autism and sexuality: A parental perspective. *Autism, 9*(3), 266–289. https://doi.org/10.1177/136236130 5053258

Waldura, J. F., Arora, I., Randall, A. M., Farala, J. P., & Sprott, R. A. (2016). Fifty shades of stigma: Exploring the health care experiences of kink-oriented patients. *The Journal of Sexual Medicine, 13*(12), 1918–1929. https://doi.org/10.1016/j.jsxm.2016.09.019

Westlake, B., & Mahan, I. (2023). An international survey of BDSM practitioner demographics: The evolution of purpose for, participation in, and engagement with, kink activities. *Journal of Sex Research*, 1–19. https://doi.org/10.1080/00224499.2023.2273266

Wignall, L., Moseley, R., & McCormack, M. (2023). Autistic traits of people who engage in pup play: Occurrence, characteristics and social connections. *Journal of Sex Research*, 1–11. https://doi.org/10.1080/00224499.2023.2239225

10

COMMUNICATING SEX IN DIGITAL SPACES

From Emojis to "What are You Into?"

Liam Wignall and Mark McCormack

Introduction

This chapter engages with the key dimension of "open and honest communication" within a positive sexuality framework. This dimension emphasises the value of discussions about sex beyond reproduction and biology, acknowledging sexual identities, behaviours, orientations, attractions, and pleasure, and how these are always situated in specific cultures and societies. Sexuality is not merely intrinsic, but also an integral part of many social identities. And these social identities are structured by norms, rituals, laws, and other social structures meaning that sexuality itself is always relational and dependent on the culture and society in which an individual is situated.

A positive sexuality framework stresses the importance of clear communication when it comes to sex. This communication occurs at many levels, such as: with ourselves and the ability to accept our sexuality (Hammack, 2018); with society and the ability to publicly express our

DOI: 10.4324/9781032631820-11

authentic sexualities (Anderson, 2013); and with our partners to discuss our sexual desires and needs (Willis et al., 2021). This ability to communicate sexually, however, is culturally contingent. For example, consider how parents discuss sexuality and relationships with their children, with huge differences – and resultant consequences – between Europe and America (Schalet, 2011).

On the surface, open and honest communication may seem one of the more straightforward aspects of the eight key dimensions of positive sexuality – it's simply talking about sex. However, sex can be a difficult topic of conversation, especially given its complicated history (Berkowitz, 2013). Across times and cultures, certain forms of sexuality have been stigmatised, pathologized, and criminalised – with some cultures still vilifying certain forms of sex and distinguishing between good and bad forms of sexuality (see Rubin, 1984). If you have a stigmatised sexual identity (Worthen, 2023), engage in stigmatised sexual practices (Hansen-Brown & Jefferson, 2022), or live within a culture that persecutes certain forms of sexuality (Amini & McCormack, 2019), there might be some aspects of sex that you cannot communicate freely about.

Within cultures that have more liberal attitudes towards sexuality, there can still be difficulties in talking about sex. Sex is framed as an intimate and private activity, and this often leads to sex simply not being discussed (Plummer, 2011). There are also often assumptions relating to sexuality, normally of heteronormativity, monogamy, and with a focus on penetrative orgasm (Anderson, 2012), particularly in sex education (Schalet, 2011); this was famously referred to as a 'missing discourse of desire' in sex education (Fine, 1988). This missing discourse can have significant negative consequences for people who fall outside these assumptions (Epps et al., 2023). When discussions about sexuality do not even recognize desire, obscuring the realities and passion of sex in many cases, it also makes it more difficult to discuss a vital component of sexuality – consent. And while the complexity of consent and desire are increasingly recognized in academic research (e.g., James-Hawkins & Ryan-Flood, 2023), they are still profoundly difficult to discuss in much of contemporary society.

While the content of sexual communication has been developing, how people communicate about sex has also undergone radical change. Much sexual communication, particularly for sexual minorities, now occurs online (Döring, 2009; Nixon & Düsterhöft, 2018; Wignall, 2022). With a cultural norm for communicating with others through digital platforms (Turkle, 2017), and changing physical spaces related to sex (Ghaziani, 2016, 2024), it makes sense that sexual communication now heavily includes a digital component.

This chapter explores how people discuss sex with (prospective) sexual partners, focusing on communicating sex in digital spaces. Mirroring research on sexual consent, we found implicit cues and phrases were used to indicate sexual interests and desires, rather than being explicit about sexual needs. It draws on two distinct research studies and examines two markedly different groups to examine these issues.

The first study examines how discussions of safe sex are navigated online by young adults, with a focus on the affordances provided by social media and digital communications, such as the use of emojis. Where formal sex education is limited, and there is growing concern around drug-resistant sexually transmitted infections, the ability of young people to talk about these issues online is particularly important.

The second study examines how gay and bisexual men navigate discussions of sex and kink on hook-up apps. In many kink cultures, consent is passionately recognized and discussed (Wignall, 2020), but broader discussions of sexual interest in kink are often limited (Simula et al., 2023). As such, our focus shifts from considering notions of consent and "safe sex" to how to raise questions of kinky sex with potentially non-kinky people on "vanilla" hook-up apps. Once the initial barrier of "sex talk" was overcome, participants used general and vague language to discuss their sexual interests, almost waiting for the other person to disclose their interests first; however, a minority were more forward with their sexual interests.

This chapter highlights that even for people chatting with the intention of meeting for sex, on platforms that help people find sex, there is still difficulty in communicating about sex. That this is true across different groups and topics – navigating kink in vanilla spaces, discussing condom use, and discussing consent – shows the importance of a more nuanced and multi-faceted understanding of the issues in order to foster positive sexuality.

A Brief Note on Methods

This chapter is based on two research studies that both used in-depth interviews to gain understanding of people's experiences and understandings of sexuality. Both studies used qualitative data, analysed using thematic analysis (Braun & Clarke, 2006).

Study 1: In-depth interviews were undertaken with 30 people aged 16–25 (mean age of 21.7) across England. Of the sample, 22 participants identified as heterosexual, and eight participants identified as gay or lesbian. Several participants recognized some level of fluidity in their desires. There were a diverse range of participants in terms of class and educational background, and an equal number of men and women were interviewed. The focus of this study was discussions of safe sex online, and the potential value of a condom emoji.

Study 2: In-depth interviews were undertaken with 30 cisgender men who engaged in kink, aged 21–62 (mean age of 27.6) across the UK. Of the sample, 27 participants identified as gay, two as bisexual, and one as mostly gay. Participants varied in terms of class and educational background. The focus of this study was the internet's impact on kink subcultures.

Study 1: Norms of Discussing Safe "Vanilla" Sex

Discussions of safe sex in many Western countries often start from a position of ignorance – with sex education having failed many young people and continuing to occur too late and focus on biological rather than social and relational aspects. Consideration of pleasure – and the possibility of the value of what has been called 'leisure sex' – are also absent (Maslowski et al., 2024).

Sex education was a marginal component of participants' discussion of safe sex. While this can stand as a critique of sex education as practised in UK schools, it is also evidence of the widespread discussion of sex in participants' social and sexual lives. Most positively, the majority of participants were able to discuss safe sex practices with their romantic partners. Approximately two thirds of those who had been in a long-term relationship reported having positive conversations with their partner about safe sex. As one participant said, "I feel more comfortable talking to a partner about anything that has to do with sex, and safe sex is absolutely part of that".

Two themes emerged in how participants discussed safe sex practices with hook-ups and new sexual partners. One group of participants were explicit in their discussion of safe sex. This would occur on mobile phones, over dating and hook-up apps or in person. While some participants found this "embarrassing" or "awkward", others felt it to be a "standard" part of hooking up. As one participant stated, "I just expect it. So, whether I ask them if they have condoms, or one of us buys them, we just know in advance that it will be safe". The second way participants dealt with safe sex on hook-ups was not to discuss the issue. Importantly, however, this was because they presumed condom usage would occur, or would be implied at some point in conversation.

However, there was concern that these unspoken rules might not be shared by others. This was supported by one male participant who tried to avoid using condoms on hook-ups, saying:

> If I bring a girl home, I only use a condom if she says, 'do you have a condom?' If she didn't say that, then I would raw dog it . . . With a partner, after a while of condoms, I'd bring up the topic of birth control. I don't hate condoms, but it ruins the flow of things.

Finally, a recurring worry related to hook-ups, particularly among the male participants, was the concern about having unsafe sex when drunk. One participant, aged 22, said:

> Feeling like not using a condom when you're feeling quite drunk is scary . . . Sometimes when you're out and you pull a girl and you think 'fuck it', I'm too drunk to stick it on. You're so drunk, you might think 'fuck it', and is she sober enough to ask?

Across the sample, there was a range of different expectations and beliefs related to discussing safe sex, which is problematic given the social contexts in which hook-ups occur, particularly related to drunkenness.

Using Emojis While Discussing Sex Online

Participants were asked how they discussed sex with potential partners and their friends online. Particular consideration was given to whether emojis would be useful as a way to discuss safe sex, with participants being asked about their thoughts on a hypothetical condom emoji as well. About three quarters of participants spoke freely about their sexual activity and desires, often in 'group chats' on various social networking apps. A female participant exemplified the type of discussion that occurred when she said:

> The group chat involves five girlfriends and one gay friend. Most of us have boyfriends now, but if any of us slept with someone we would text it to the group . . . There would be jokes about who we got with, jokes about who we slept with. It would be quite an open conversation about everything.

Few participants refrained from this conversation, either in person or on mobile phone app devices that enable group chat. Highlighting the fun and playful nature of much of the discussion around sex in friendship groups, participants used a range of emojis to refer to sex. These included creating penis shapes (e.g., 3====o), "the spray", the use of aubergine, banana, and peach emojis, "the classic finger poking through a hole", "the chicken, for cock, and loads of arrows pointing to holes and stuff" and "lots of wanking ones". This may be because emojis are a more playful way of discussing sexual activity, with emojis such as the peach, banana, and eggplant/aubergine commonly used as ways to flirt, joke or suggest sexual activity without being explicit.

However, there was less open discussion about their concerns about sex and healthy sexual practice. Slang terms were frequently used to refer to sex, both for humour and out of embarrassment. Highlighting this, participants often used smileys to imply sex was likely to occur. Here, smileys were used in both text and emoji form (e.g., :) and ☺) and participants reported that using these smileys made messages flirtier. One participant said, "If you put a winky face on the end of a sentence, it suddenly provides connotations that weren't there at all". As another participant said:

> If I put 'Netflix and chill' with the tonguey smiley, I want sex. It's code, right? We both know sex is on the cards, but we have to pretend we don't. Oh, and if I don't put that smiley, it means I actually want to watch Netflix.

However, this form of innuendo relied on shared norms between those talking. While many participants said this was true of their friendship groups, it is not necessarily the case for hook-ups. A male participant said "Everyone uses them in different ways. Some use them as a joke, others seriously and it's hard to tell which sometimes". As one female participant said, "This guy I hooked up with had apparently been flirting with me for ages before that. He kept on sending me the tonguey smileys, but I didn't realise he was flirting."

As part of the interview schedule, participants were asked what they thought of a condom emoji and whether they would use one if it existed. More than two thirds (24 out of 30) thought that a condom emoji would be a good idea, either for themselves or other people, and there were three key reasons for this.

The first use of a condom emoji would be to put on hook-up profiles (Tinder was frequently mentioned, as was Grindr) as a way of signalling that they used condoms. This was most common among gay male participants, but some straight participants said it too. One added, "You might not use it on your profile, but it would be an easy way of clarifying in a message. So, you're not too forward, but you can still say it in a nice, cartoony way."

The second use was to remind sexual partners to bring condoms. For example, a male student said, "Yeah, great. I'd be like 'I'll bring the 'condom emoji'. You send it without saying it, and it makes it less awkward." Another participant said, "Quick and easy. I normally say, 'play safe?' to clarify, but an emoji would be even simpler."

Thirdly, condom emojis were praised for their potential to make discussing safe sex easier and more fun. One participant liked the idea, saying, "It adds a bit of humour to a serious situation". Similarly, another participant said:

> I think I might find it more of a jokey thing, as emojis are more jokey than serious. But it might make people think about condoms more, as it's there and you have always got a picture of it. So yeah, it's a good idea.

Other participants thought that in addition to making it more fun, it would make it easier. One participant said, "It would be easier for shy people." Saying he wouldn't use it himself, he added "Condoms should be part of sex, so good to have one". Similarly, another participant commented, "Yeah, for shy people it might really help."

Those that rejected condom emojis did so because they did not see the value. Three participants thought they were "cringeworthy" and would not be used. Interestingly, the three other participants who thought the emoji "pointless", had poor sexual health practices themselves. Two had very little sex education, and the third spoke about regularly hooking up with different men without using condoms.

In this study, there were interesting dualities existing for participants in how they spoke about sex, and specifically safe sex. While participants were often comfortable discussing sex with their friendship groups, they were often coy about sex and referred to emojis to discuss the topic. Emojis were seen as a playful way of discussing sex but were also recognised as potentially childish and could often lead to misunderstandings about intentions. Participants saw the benefit of being more straightforward in their discussions of sex, and suggested the example of a condom emoji being potentially beneficial for communicating safe sex, yet also did not want to be overt with their sexual wants and needs.

Study 2: "Putting it out there": Signposting Kinky Sex in Online Vanilla Spaces

Open and honest communication is an important component of positive sexuality; however, it is often limited in a range of ways, particularly when sexual stigma and shame are present where sexual practices or desires are outside of sexual norms (Rubin, 1984). People guard against stigma, even when they understand such stigma to be the result of flawed social norms and social structures rather than individual defects (Goffman, 1963; Tyler, 2020). While most participants had very positive attitudes toward their own kink desires and practices, they still discussed how they mitigated potential stigma by not being purely explicit about their sexual desires on vanilla hook-up apps such as Grindr.[1] Summarising this approach, Robert said, "Unless the person I was chatting to had something kinky on their profile, I wouldn't bring it up until they did. I would maybe approach them though to find out what people are into – a draft conversation."

We have discussed elsewhere how these men negotiated consent online (Wignall & McCormack, 2023), and their kinky interests more generally

(Wignall, 2022), and in this chapter we focus on how they negotiated discussing sex and kink in "vanilla" (non-kinky) spaces.

Some participants were heavily engaged in kink communities, and this was part of their social identity. As such, they were often open about their interests in kink in a range of spaces and did not feel the need to hide their kink interests in vanilla spaces. Consequently, these participants would often include kink explicitly in their profiles on non kinky hook-up apps. For example, Cameron's Grindr profile featured pictures of him wearing kink gear, with his profile description reading: "Wruff!! Super kinky, but vanilla is still sweet" with the emoji of a pup (indicating pup play) and an emoji of a pig (indicating general kink play in the context of Grindr). When asked to expand on why he had these on his profile, he said, "I want people to know I'm into pup play [a form of kinky role play]. There's no point me flirting with a cute guy who then gets scared when the mask comes out." Similarly, Rory's Grindr profile picture was overtly kinky, with him wearing a rubber bodysuit with a rubber, full coverage hood on; some of his other pictures on the profile also showed his face, indicating that the hood was to demonstrate the sexual interests, rather than to preserve anonymity. He also used emojis on his profile to indicate his interests, specifically the "pig" and the "pup" emojis. Rory said, "I think most people nowadays know what having a pup and pig emoji in your profile means. That and my picture, I rarely get guys thinking I'm vanilla." Similarly, Justin didn't originally have kink on his vanilla hook-up app profiles, but updated it:

> I've been a lot more open on places like Grindr and other sites as well about what I'm into exactly that I wanted to explore it. I used to be more discreet, but I've started being more obvious and open because you get other people messaging saying 'I'm into that too.'

As with Study 1, the use of emojis was used by several participants who were open about their kink, preferring this to specific words. As such, participants' use of emojis on vanilla apps may be a way to still be overt about kink interests without being seen as too explicit. Rory supported this interpretation, saying he used them on his profile in place of words. He added, "People who know about this stuff are kinky and would be able to know I'm kinky by seeing [the pig emoji] on my profile. But at the same time, I'm not being massively explicit about what I'm into."

However, other participants were more covert about their kink interests, often signposting kink interest without directly stating it. As Peter said, "It's a way of putting it out there." Going into more detail, Dan said, "Putting the feet emoji on your profile . . . You don't know who is looking at your profile and it helps you to get interest from people who might be interested. I've had a few messages from people asking if I'm into feet." He added, "I guess some people see it, know what it means and move on, and then other people don't clock it or just think it is odd". In a similar way, Lee said:

> I only tended to discuss kink on Grindr because that's all I was looking for. I would respond if people asked about the things on my profile – I might have the pup or feet emoji, or the tagline 'far from normal.' I always gave a slight indication to what I like on my profile, but not overtly.

Asked about the importance of not being too overt or explicit, Scott said, "Kink is important to me, absolutely, but I also have a professional life. So, with emojis or hint on my profile, there's a level of deniability that's good." Ryan put this succinctly saying, "When I send nudes, I make sure my face isn't in them. Not having explicit kink words on profiles with my face is basically the same idea."

Discreet means of communication among kinky sexual subcultures is not a new phenomenon. The most obvious example of this historically is the hanky code, where (predominantly gay male) kinky individuals would wear different coloured handkerchiefs in the back pockets of their trousers to signal to others an interest in different kink activities; the side which this was worn would indicate a preference of being active/giving or passive/receiving with the kink. For example, a yellow handkerchief worn on the right back pocket would signal to others that they like to be pissed on by others.

Another pertinent example of discreet sexual communication for sexual subcultures is Polari, the slang language used by gay and lesbian communities across the UK during homophobic times to avoid being targeted by police officers, when same-sex sexual acts were criminalized (Baker, 2019). Like cockney rhyming slang, it indicated to others in the know that you were part of the "gay subculture," just as the handkerchief code was a form of displaying kink interests in the past. These codes are evidence of people recognizing that at least some in society may see these practices and desires as deviant.

"What are you into?" Pro-active Enquiries about Kink Online

The previous section examined how participants signalled kink interests on vanilla social media – in essence, a reactive way to showing kink interest that relied on the viewer initiating conversation upon seeing the code. In this section, we focus on how participants sought to initiate conversations about kink while still maintaining a level of covertness. This was done primarily through the question, "What are you into?".

Aiden did not include any hints in his profile about kink interests, but said he was proactive in asking others about theirs in a subtle way. He said: "When I'm looking for kinky meets on Grindr, I always ask 'what are you into'. If they say 'top' or 'bottom' or whatever, I move on. The correct answer is to list a kink or two, or three or four or five." When asked why he did this, he described a realization about the potency of the phrase:

> I'm not interested in anal, so whenever people asked me 'what's your position' or 'are you top?', I would say I wasn't interested, because I didn't want to fuck. But, it was such an immediate 'no' for me that I realized how that meant one thing, but 'what are you into' or even 'what are you after is something different'. That's why now on Grindr, if it's me who initiates the sex question, I always ask 'What are you into?'

Other participants also used the phrase. Ethan said, "Sometimes you move from chatting to flirting, and if I think there might be a power dynamic thing which could be hot, I ask, 'What are you into?', rather than anything more about position or role."

Some participants spoke about how they responded to the phrase "what are you into?", viewing it as an enquiry about kink. For example, Harry said:

> When talking about kink, the standard question [you get] is 'What are you into?' I just have a pre-set phrase on Grindr of the things I'm into. I just send the full list when people ask me what I'm into. Reactions vary. There is usually 'big list, that's full on, a lot there.' Then you gauge

the reaction and go from there. They're my likes, not musts. You don't have to do all the things with a person in one session.

He added, "But I don't have that on my profile. If someone asks me 'are you top', that means non-kink. If they ask me 'what are you into?', well, they get the list."

Rory used emojis on his profile to indicate kink, but also spoke about how those signs led to other subtle conversations. He said:

I don't know if it's my look that makes people assume I'm kinky. I've got tattoos and my septum pierced, so I guess that's why people speak to me about it . . . After the initial chat it goes onto 'What you into?' When they ask, I just tell them. I have a saved note of the list of things I am into, and I just send it to them. Ten out of ten people are fine with it, apart from one thing on the list, sounding [inserting metal tubes into the male urethra]. It's not a long list, but I've never had any negative reactions.

John initially explored kinks on vanilla hook-up apps, bringing it up in conversations:

I found people to do kink with mostly through Gaydar and Craigslist – they were the two sites I ended up using the most. I'd speak to people about kinks on there, but my profile wasn't kink orientated. It was a case that I wanted to meet like-minded gay people, but conversations normally turned round to 'what are you into?' in which case, I told people. You either got yes or no.

However, not all participants used this phrase, and some showed more concern about how they discussed kink. Josh said he cautiously engaged in discussions about kink on vanilla hook-up apps:

I generally keep things very vague. I don't want to say something I'm into in case they think that I won't meet for sex unless we do a particular activity. I'll say I'm versatile and I like topping – there is room for negotiation there. If they continue and say, what activities do I like, or what am I into I'll just say a bit of this, a bit of that. I don't think I ever say things like pissing on people, unless I get the impression that they're getting a bit bored or they're clearly open.

Conclusion

A positive sexuality approach is one that is based on core ideas of mutuality, respect, consent and respecting and accepting sexuality as a basic human right. For this chapter, the core focus has been on the component of positive sexuality around honest and open discussion of sexuality. This means not just being able to discuss sex, but to do so in ways that encourage the sharing of personal stories, and authentic acceptance of diversity and difference when it comes to sexuality. Yet, insufficient sex education in schools is a serious impediment to this, meaning that young people develop their own ways of discussing sex, safe sex and consent – with the internet and online communications adding significant complexity to these issues. We found that participants tended to discuss their sexual activity and desires in 'group chats' on various social networking apps, but there was less open discussion about safe sex. Emojis were a popular way to refer to sex, and a source of humour, yet participants highlighted difficulties in discussing safe sex more generally. Asked about the value of a condom emoji, more than three quarters of participants welcomed the idea, but had scepticism as to how effective it would be – given it is a literal representation of safe sex where emojis tend to be more suggestive.

We combined this study with one of how kinky individuals navigate discussions of kink in the online sphere. This is because another impediment to open communications related to positive sexuality is stigma, and many societal norms of sex still view kink as something violent or coming from trauma – and fail to recognize how it is an important component of some people's social identity (Wignall, 2022). In this study, we found that some participants avoided discussing their kink interests on "vanilla" apps, but others found subtle ways to subvert these norms. Some would use emojis – of feet, for example – to indicate a sexual interest, while others developed terms and questions to gauge potential interest in kink. Most common was the phrase "what are you into", which was seen as a subtle yet significant way of asking about sexual interests which could indicate kinky interests.

In discussing sex communication online, this chapter highlights the importance of emojis as a way of discussing sex. They were used as a way of making content sexual or flirting, used in place of sexual acts, or used to signal an interest in sexual activities. While emojis here were used in predominantly private or semi-private communication, it speaks to a broader trend where emojis are being used to refer to sexual acts on social media as a way of avoiding censorship. For example, the emoji for "corn" and the #corn is being used as a way of discussing porn and sexual content more broadly. This is a direct consequence of social media accounts being removed for overtly breaching guidelines for discussing sex. It may be that how sex is communicated publicly on social media may impact on private communication used. The use of emojis may speak to a broader impediment to positive sexuality frameworks – such as through censorship or stigma – even as they exist as important and fun methods of communicating sex.

Note

1 Some vanilla hook-up apps have explicit kink-related features, but these were not used by most participants. For example, Grindr has the option of 'tribes' where you indicate sexual preference, and one option is 'leather', but this was rarely used, with one participant highlighting the next nearest user with 'leather' ticked was "hundreds of miles away". Another example is the use of 'tags' on a profile to indicate specific sexual interests, but these also had limited use by participants, with one suggesting "putting WS as a tag on your profile is too explicit".

References

Amini, E., & McCormack, M. (2019, September). Medicalization, menopausal time and narratives of loss: Iranian Muslim women negotiating gender, sexuality and menopause in Tehran and Karaj. *Women's Studies International Forum*, 76, 102277. https://doi.org/10.1016/j.wsif.2019.102277

Anderson, E. (2012). *The monogamy gap: Men, love, and the reality of cheating*. Oxford University Press.

Anderson, R. M. (2013). Positive sexuality and its impact on overall well-being. *Bundesgesundheitsblatt-Gesundheitsforschung-Gesundheitsschutz*, 56(2), 208–214. https://doi.org/10.1007/s00103-012-1607-z

Baker, P. (2019). *Fabulosa! The story of Polari, Britain's secret gay language*. Reaktion Books.

Berkowitz, E. (2013). *Sex and punishment: Four thousand years of judging desire*. The Westbourne Press.

Braun, V., & Clarke, V. (2006). Using thematic analysis in psychology. *Qualitative Research in Psychology, 3*(2), 77–101. https://doi.org/10.1191/1478088706qp063oa

Döring, N. M. (2009). The Internet's impact on sexuality: A critical review of 15 years of research. *Computers in Human Behavior, 25*(5), 1089–1101. https://doi.org/10.1016/j.chb.2009.04.003

Epps, B., Markowski, M., & Cleaver, K. (2023). A rapid review and narrative synthesis of the consequences of non-inclusive sex education in UK schools on lesbian, gay, bisexual, transgender and questioning young people. *The Journal of School Nursing, 39*(1), 87–97. https://doi.org/10.1177/1059840521104339

Fine, M. (1988). Sexuality, schooling, and adolescent females: The missing discourse of desire. *Harvard Educational Review, 58*(1), 29–54.

Ghaziani, A. (2016). *There goes the gayborhood?* Princeton University Press.

Ghaziani, A. (2024). *Long live queer nightlife: How the closing of gay bars sparked a revolution*. Princeton University Press.

Goffman, E. (1963). *Stigma: Notes on the management of spoiled identity*. Simon & Schuster.

Hammack, P. L. (2018). Gay men's identity development in the twenty-first century: Continuity and change, normalization and resistance. *Human Development, 61*(2), 101–125. https://doi.org/10.1159/000486469

Hansen-Brown, A. A., & Jefferson, S. E. (2022). Perceptions of and stigma toward BDSM practitioners. *Current Psychology, 42*(23), 19721–19729. https://doi.org/10.1007/s12144-022-03112-z

James-Hawkins, L., & Ryan-Flood, R. (Eds.). (2023). *Consent: Gender, Power and Subjectivity*. Taylor & Francis.

Maslowski, K., Biswakarma, R., Reiss, M. J., & Harper, J. C. (2024). What have 16- to 18-year-olds in England learnt about reproductive health? A survey of school students. *Health Education Journal, 83*(2), 172–191. https://doi.org/10.1177/00178969241227314

Nixon, P. & Düsterhöft, I. (2018). *Sex in the digital age*. Routledge.

Plummer, K. (2011). *Intimate citizenship: Private decisions and public dialogues*. University of Washington Press.

Rubin, G. S. (1984). Thinking sex: Notes for a radical theory of the politics of sexuality. In C. S. Vance (Ed.), *Pleasure and danger: Exploring female sexuality* (pp. 267–319). Routledge.

Schalet, A. T. (2011). *Not under my roof: Parents, teens, and the culture of sex.* University of Chicago Press.

Simula, B. L., Bauer, R., & Wignall, L. (Eds.). (2023). *The power of BDSM: Play, communities, and consent in the 21st Century.* Oxford University Press.

Tyler, I. (2020). *Stigma: The machinery of inequality.* Bloomsbury Publishing.

Turkle, S. (2017). *Alone together: Why we expect more from technology and less from each other.* Basic Books.

Worthen, M. G. (2023). Queer identities in the 21st century: reclamation and stigma. *Current Opinion in Psychology, 49,* 101512. https://doi.org/10.1016/j.copsyc.2022.101512

Wignall, L. (2020). Beyond safe, sane, and consensual: Navigating risk and consent online for kinky gay and bisexual men. *Journal of Positive Sexuality,* 6(2), 66–74. https://doi.org/10.51681.1.622

Wignall, L. (2022). *Kinky in the digital age: gay men's subcultures and social identities.* Oxford University Press.

Wignall, L., & McCormack, M. (2023). Negotiating consent in online kinky spaces. In L. James-Hawkins, & R. Ryan-Flood (Eds.), *Consent: Gender, power and subjectivity* (pp. 210–220). Routledge.

Willis, M., Murray, K. N., & Jozkowski, K. N. (2021). Sexual consent in committed relationships: A dyadic study. *Journal of Sex & Marital Therapy,* 47(7), 669–686. https://doi.org/10.1080/0092623X.2021.1937417

EPILOGUE

Social/Environmental Challenges and Positive
Sexuality: The Immediate and Beyond . . .

D J Williams and Emily E. Prior

While the chapters in this volume have tackled a number of key contemporary issues moving us toward a much more sex-positive world, we also
anticipate that new issues and challenges will emerge and become particularly significant down the road as positive sexuality builds momentum.
Below are some issues that we think social scientists, practitioners, policymakers, and educators will need to continue to address and prepare for.

Information Proliferation and the Widespread
Lack of Critical Assessment Skills

While anti-intellectualism has long been an issue in American society, it
appears to be more problematic now than ever before (Nichols, 2017).
In an age of technology where consumers are constantly bombarded with
information, it becomes increasingly crucial that citizens develop skills
to critically assess such information. From a positive sexuality perspective, while there are multiple legitimate ways of knowing, the value of

DOI: 10.4324/9781032631820-12

knowledge depends on the keen ability of consumers to assess and utilize knowledge in a manner that is consistent with its underlying assumptions. In other words, while subjective and objective ways of knowing both have value, it is a mistake to think that both are equal in addressing *any* issue. Some ways of knowing are better suited for addressing particular matters, while other forms are better for other issues. Bergstrom and West (2021) remind us that in a hyper-capitalist society, we are constantly being pressured to buy products, click on websites, support various causes – thus bullshit information is deployed to get us to act accordingly. Indeed, the explosion in information production and accessibility has far exceeded efforts to help consumers critically evaluate specific information and anticipate its potential beneficial and/or harmful effects. Finding effective ways to help people improve their skills at critically evaluating information, then, is the huge task before us.

Misinformation and disinformation are especially prevalent when it comes to sexual knowledge, since many people have rather strong attitudes and beliefs about these topics, which are commonly shaped by sex-negative assumptions. The lack of high-quality knowledge concerning sexuality, specifically, and lack of critical skills, more generally, across the general public emphasize the importance of positive sexuality moving into the future. Indeed, moral panics around sexuality often sweep across both the political left and the right (Kahn, 2022), which can lead to proponents of positive sexuality being targeted. As an extreme example, several sexuality scholars, including ourselves, occasionally receive hate mail apparently based on not only their research findings, but sometimes simply the topics themselves. Positive sexuality researchers, educators, and practitioners should build strong support networks, apply rigor to their work, focus on common societal values, and prioritize self-care (Williams, 2021).

Mass Consumption and Future Harms

Positive sexuality prioritizes multiple ways of knowing, humanization, and peacemaking. The beautiful planet on which we, and all other forms of life, live must be respected and cared for. We are all connected, and our various efforts should be cognizant of the potential subsequent impacts to all. From such a context, it becomes necessary to scrutinize many of our current "normal" ways of living and the fallout that consumer capitalism has on both our natural and social environments. Regarding sexuality, specifically, this has led to some individuals adopting a form of *ecosexuality*, a recent concept that focuses on nature, the earth, and natural elements as partners in sustained ecology as well as potentially intimate partners (Content Engine, 2023). While ecosexuality approaches are now emerging, we see the potential for such approaches to both strengthen and diversify in future generations.

Unfortunately, there are substantial personal, social, and environmental harms, such as climate change, personal debt, and mental health issues, that result from contemporary lifestyle norms within a global-capitalist society (Raymen & Smith, 2019; Smith & Raymen, 2018). Our view is consistent with that of DeValve (2023) in that successfully addressing such matters – thus transforming suffering into insight, wisdom, and healing – requires coordinated efforts from all peoples, disciplines, discourses, and perspectives. Moving further into the future, positive sexuality, then, becomes increasingly more than sexuality, but also a connection with our natural environment and its needs.

Specific Needs across Diverse Locations

We also must recognize that in many respects, positive sexuality is not currently a universal concept and in fact notions of multifaceted and unique sexualities is often viewed as "Western," and thus "liberal," outside of the U.S. In 2020, diplomats from 50 countries called for an end to LGBTQ+ discrimination in an open letter to Poland's government. President Duda has been quoted as stating that "the LGBT movement is 'more destructive' than communism," thus supporting laws that do not allow same-sex marriage, civil unions, or the right for LGBTQ+ people to adopt children (BBC, 2020).

In 2022, the OneLove campaign, supported by many western European countries, attempted to show solidarity at the World Cup held in Qatar (BBC, 2022). Various players from these countries pledged to wear the OneLove armband during the games to promote this initiative. However, this action was banned by the Federation Internationale de Football Association (FIFA), stating that homosexuality is illegal in Qatar and that participants in the World Cup must abide by the laws of the host country (Reuters, 2022).

Similarly, in Ghana, the legitimate existence of homosexual identities and relationships continues to be denied (Ako, 2023). This denial goes so far as to outlaw any such identities or relationships, making it illegal and potentially deadly for those who are not visibly heteronormative and/or cisgender.

This lack of recognition of diverse sexual identities and relationships, as well as the belief that to do so would mean potentially giving into a Western mindset, creates a chasm that positive sexuality may find difficult to breech. We may have to consider using or creating other terminology, as well as working to be more culturally competent, in striving to find new ways to promote safe conversations where positive sexuality components may be realized.

Technology and Artificial Intelligence

Technological advances, including artificial intelligence (AI), is rapidly increasing within the sphere of sexuality. Although a variety of sex toys, sex dolls, and sex robots are now openly marketed on the Internet, these items have not yet received significant attention from researchers (see Döring & Pöschi, 2018). However, this is beginning to change. As the usage (or at least awareness) of technology for sexual purposes increases – which it inevitably will as we move further into the future – then sexuality researchers, practitioners, and educators will be obligated to become more proficient in directly dealing with these matters.

At present, some aspects of sexual technology appear to be better received by the general public than others, though like sexuality more broadly, such acceptance is largely dictated by cultural norms. Of course, there is a wide range of technological possibilities associated with sexuality, and the amount of current controversy varies. For example, research in the UK has found some support for AI chatbot involvement in providing basic sexual advice in clinical contexts (Nadarzynski et al., 2021). At the other end of the spectrum, are AI powered sex robots that are becoming increasingly human-like. Although highly controversial, humanoid sex robots appear to have potential therapeutic benefits for human use, such as for individuals who may be lonely, recovering from sexual trauma, or living with specific disabilities (see Di Nucci, 2017; McArthur, 2017). At present, scholars are debating the ethical implications associated with sexual technology and AI, and these issues will become more prominent further into the future (see Danaher, 2020; Nyholm, 2022). Positive sexuality should be valuable in helping to navigate such controversies and challenges.

Toward A Post-Human World?

So, what does the future hold? Just in the past few years we have seen an increase in the use of social media, live distance communication software (e.g., Zoom), generative artificial intelligence (GenAI), and other technologies that allow us to communicate in various ways and across distances. Although the 2020 pandemic brought many of these technologies to the forefront, they are still used frequently in education, the workplace, media, and between friends and relatives.

One such technology, Metaverse, combines human interaction in the real world as well as a virtually constructed universe (Liu & Siau, 2023). Although not the first of its kind, this more interactive platform is being used not only for entertainment and socializing, but also in education, therapy, and other contexts. As Metaverse attempts to better humanize the experience, it may become increasingly difficult for users to know if they are chatting with another actual person or a chatbot with really good language recognition.

We can also expect an exponential increase in global population, with a current estimate of 10.4 billion people by 2080 (a mere 55 years from the date of this publication!) (The Lancet, 2022). It is expected that this increase in population will continue to see inequalities in health and access to essential resources in much of the world. Although global life expectancy is expected to increase, the least developed countries will continue to see a lower life expectancy than their counterparts. Also, based on current worldwide leanings toward conservative politics, it is estimated that advancement in sexual rights and healthcare, especially for women and girls, will not be addressed in time to help future generations progress significantly toward equity.

Based on discussions of an extinction crisis (Dirzo et al., 2022), GenAI technologies, and predictions of global overpopulation and lack of resources; the future doesn't look particularly positive. In fact, can we be certain that humans, as we know ourselves, will actually be around centuries from now? Will we need to redefine what it means to be human? Will we find ourselves searching for a model that better encompasses a new reality? Possibly. These are questions that continually need to be addressed. Indeed, we expect that the future of positive sexuality research, education, and practice will continually evolve.

References

Ako, E. Y. (2023). Same-sex relationships and recriminalization of homosexuality in Ghana: A historical analysis. *Sociolinguistic Studies, 17*, 45–65.

BBC (2020, September 27). *Poland LGBT: Diplomats from 50 countries call for end of discrimination.* https://www.bbc.com/news/world-europe-54317902

BBC (2022, September 21). *World Cup 2022: England captain Harry Kane to wear anti-discrimination armband.* https://www.bbc.com/sport/football/62982043

Bergstrom, C. T., & West, J. D. (2021). *Calling bullshit: The art of skepticism in a data-driven world.* Random House.

Content Engine (2023). Ecosexuality: What is it and why is it on the rise? In *CE Noticias Financieras* (English ed.). Content Engine.

Danaher, J. (2020). Sexuality. In M. D. Dubber, F. Pasquale, & S. Das (Eds.), *The Oxford handbook of ethics of AI* (pp. 403–417). Oxford University Press.

DeValve, M. J. (2023). A theory of suffering and healing: Toward a loving justice. *Critical Criminology, 31*, 35–60.

Di Nucci, E. (2017). Sex robots and the rights of the disabled. In J. Danaher & N. McArthur (Eds.), *Robot sex: Social and ethical implications* (pp. 73–88). Massachusetts Institute of Technology Press.

Dirzo, R., Ceballos, G., & Ehrlich, P. (2022). Circling the drain: The extinction crisis and the future of humanity. *Philosophical Transactions of the Royal Society B, 377*.

Döring, N., & Pöschi, S. (2018). Sex toys, sex dolls, sex robots: Our under-researched bedfellows. *Sexologies, 27*(3), e51–e55.

Kahn, U. (2022). Fifty shades of a moral panic. In A. R. Clifford-Napoleone (Ed.), *Binding and unbinding kink* (pp. 133–156). Springer Nature.

Liu, Y. & Siau, K.L. (2024). Generative artificial intelligence and Metaverse: Future of work, future of society, and future of humanity. In Zhao, F., Miao, D. (eds) *AI-generated content. AIGC 2023. Communications in Computer and Information Science, vol. 1946.* Springer.e

McArthur, N. (2017). The case for sex robots. In J. Danaher & N. McArthur (Eds.), *Robot sex: Social and ethical implications* (pp. 31–46). Massachusetts Institute of Technology Press.

Nadarzynski, T. Puentes, V., Pawlak, I., Mendes, T., Montgomery, I., Bayley, J., & Ridge, D. (2021). Barriers and facilitators to engagement with artificial intelligence (AI)-based chatbots for sexual and reproductive health advice: A qualitative analysis. *Sexual Health, 18*, 385–393.

Nichols, T. (2017). *The death of expertise: The campaign against established knowledge and why it matters.* Oxford University Press.

Nyholm, S. (2022). The ethics of humanoid sex robots. In B. D. Earp, C. Chambers, & L. Watson (Eds.), *The Routledge handbook of philosophy of sex and sexuality* (pp. 574–585). Routledge.

Raymen, T., & Smith, O. (2019). Deviant leisure: A critical criminological perspective for the twenty-first century. *Critical Criminology, 27*, 115–130.

Reuters (2022, November 29). *World Cup 2022: What is the OneLove armband and why did FIFA ban it?* https://www.reuters.com/lifestyle/sports/world-cup-2022-what-is-onelove-armband-why-did-fifa-ban-it-2022-11-24/

Smith, O., & Raymen, T. (2018). Deviant leisure: A criminological perspective. *Theoretical Criminology, 22*, 63–82.

The Lancet (2022). Editorial: Measuring the future of humanity for health. *The Lancet (British Edition), 400*(10347), 137.

Williams, D J (2021). Negotiating opposition to positive sexuality research, practice, and education: Insights from personal reflection. *Journal of Positive Sexuality, 7*, 4–10.

LIST OF CONTRIBUTORS

Priscilla "Lilly" Allen is the Sister Michael Sibille Professor of Aging and Geriatrics at the Louisiana State University School of Social Work. She also currently serves as a Board Member of the Louisiana Enhancing Aging through Dignity, Empowerment and Respect (LEADER) coalition.

Arutyun Ambartsumyan earned his master's in social work from California State University, Northridge. He then specialized in crisis intervention, suicide prevention, and LGBTQ+ support while working at the Los Angeles County Department of Mental Health. He is currently pursuing a jurisprudence doctorate at Abraham Lincoln University where he aims to advocate for justice reform in marginalized communities affected by the legal system.

Moshoula Capous-Desyllas is a Professor of Sociology at California State University, Northridge. Her research interests and passions involve the use of arts-based methodologies as a form of activism for social justice, and as a way to highlight the voices of marginalized individuals, groups and communities.

Eric Chambers (he/him) teaches linguistics at the State University of New York at New Paltz, and is the current Director of Research for the Center for Positive Sexuality. His research focuses on the intersection between language and sexuality, with an emphasis on Critical Discourse Analysis and Positive Discourse Analysis.

Marcos Chavez received a double Bachelors in Sociology: Social Welfare and Social Justice and Chicanx Studies from California State University, Northridge and is working towards obtaining his master's in social work. Marcos is a published poet and artist with a discreet and sensitive side that evokes the world around him with a painter's brush and the heart of a beautiful warrior. Marcos is a gentle, old soul with an activist's passion and vision for equality.

Sam D. Hughes is an Assistant Professor of Psychology at Emporia State University, Kansas. His research work focuses on the psychology of LGBTQ+ people, as well as kink, BDSM, and sexual fetishism with a focus on identity, stigma, institutions, intersectionality, and social context. Relying on both qualitative and quantitative methods, his work has appeared in peer-reviewed academic research journals, and has also been covered in *Vice*, *Psychology Today*, *Insider*, *Cosmopolitan*, and Dan Savage's *Savage Lovecast*.

carrie "cherry" kaufman is a queer, multiply disabled, white, Jewish artist, organizer, sex educator, certified death doula, and kitchen witch. She is the creator of DisabledParts.com, a website featuring stories about disabled sexuality.

Kathy Labriola is a nurse, counselor, and hypnotherapist in Berkeley, California, providing affordable mental health services to alternative communities for over 30 years. Kathy is author of four books on consensual nonmonogamy. She has been a card-carrying bisexual and polyamorist for 50 years, and is extra crunchy, rides a bike, lives in a housing cooperative, grows organic vegetables, and raises chickens.

Bianca I. Laureano is a queer, fat, LatiNegra, disabled, gender expansive femme sexuality educator, curriculum writer, sexologist, and AASECT CSE and CSES (certified sexuality educator supervisor). She is the foundress of the virtual freedom school ANTE UP!

Ari Lewis earned his Master of Applied Positive Psychology (M.A.P.P.) at the University of Pennsylvania with his focus on positive sexuality. At Columbia University, he earned an MA in Psychological Counseling, a EdM in Mental Health Counseling, and an advanced certificate in Sexuality, Women and Gender focused on providing therapy to clients in CNM relationships. Ari teaches at Touro University's Graduate School of Social Work and provides psychotherapy, working with clients with compulsive sexual behavior at the Sexuality, Attachment, and Trauma (SAT) Project and at Ari Lewis Therapy.

Victoria L. Loy received her M.A. in Sociology from California State University, Northridge and is actively committed to social justice work in nonprofit organizations that empower and uplift marginalized communities. Her passions include the use of arts-based methodologies as a powerful tool for social change and activism.

Professor Mark McCormack is Deputy Dean of Research and Enterprise at Aston University, Birmingham. His research examines social trends related to gender and sexuality and how they map onto everyday experiences of individuals including work on drag cultures, consumption of porn, and the interface of sexuality with illicit drug use.

Vanessa R. Panfil is an Associate Professor in the Department of Sociology and Criminal Justice at Old Dominion University, Norfolk, Virginia. She is also the author of *The Gang's All Queer: The Lives of Gay Gang Members* (2017).

Emily E. Prior (she/her) is a Sociology and Psychology Professor and researcher in Los Angeles, as well as the founder and Executive Director of the Center for Positive Sexuality. Her work primarily focuses on the intersection of marginalized identities and social norms.

Laura Ramos Tomás is an AASECT certified sexuality educator of European origin, working in non-formal education spaces in Latin America through her organization TabuTabu. She co-creates programs on sexual wellbeing and justice with communities of the global majority who usually haven't had access to affirming and pleasure-based sexuality education.

Anna Randall (she/her/hers) is the Co-Founder & Executive Director of TASHRA – The Alternative Sexualities Health Research Alliance. She speaks nationally and internationally on the sexual health of unrecognized and stigmatized sexual minorities. In addition to leading research and clinical provider training teams with TASHRA, she is in private practice as a sex therapist and clinical social worker, focusing on diverse individuals and relationships.

Elisabeth "Eli" Sheff is a researcher, expert witness, coach, speaker, and educational consultant. With a PhD in Sociology and certification as a Sexuality Educator from AASECT, she specializes in gender and sexual minority families, consensual non-monogamy (CNM), and kink/BDSM. She has served as faculty at seven universities and currently chairs the CNM Legal Issues Team for the American Psychological Association, Division 44 Committee on CNM.

Richard Sprott received his Ph.D. in Developmental Psychology from the University of California, Berkeley in 1994. He is currently the Research Director of TASHRA — The Alternative Sexualities Health Research Alliance.

Em Thev was an AASECT certified sexuality, relationship, and mindfulness educator living with invisible disabilities, and is a purity culture survivor. Through her organization, Honey Rose Haven, she helped thousands of people worldwide overcome sexual shame and cultivate healthy, passionate relationships through one-to-one educational sessions and workshops.

Liam Wignall is a senior lecturer in Psychology at the University of Brighton, Sussex. He specializes in research on kink/BDSM, looking at the impact of the internet and community engagement on identity formation, and has published on this in *Kinky in the Digital Age*.

D J Williams is a Professor of Sociology, Social Work, and Criminology at Idaho State University. He is also a current Executive Board Member and former Director of Research at the Center for Positive Sexuality in Los Angeles.

Aimee Wodda is an Assistant Professor of Criminal Justice, Law and Society at Pacific University, Oregon. Her research focuses on the intersection between institutionalized forms of harm and gender, sexuality, and the law.

Scotney Young is a Black American and Chicana AASECT certified sexuality educator committed to offering practical tools and information to help people better understand and enjoy their bodies and relationships. As an ANTE UP! certified sexuality professional, her work is rooted in community collaboration and justice with a special focus on elevating youth voices and experiences.

INDEX

For Product Safety Concerns and Information please contact our EU
representative GPSR@taylorandfrancis.com
Taylor & Francis Verlag GmbH, Kaufingerstraße 24, 80331 München, Germany

9 781032 631325